Advertising

FOR

DUMMIES®

2ND EDITION

Advertising FOR DUMMIES®

2ND EDITION

by Gary Dahl

1807
WILEY
2007

Wiley Publishing, Inc.

Advertising For Dummies®, 2nd Edition

Published by
Wiley Publishing, Inc.
111 River St.
Hoboken, NJ 07030-5774
www.wiley.com

For general information on our other products and services, please contact our Customer Care Department within the U.S. at 800-762-2974, outside the U.S. at 317-572-3993, or fax 317-572-4002.

For technical support, please visit www.wiley.com/techsupport.

Wiley also publishes its books in a variety of electronic formats. Some content that appears in print may not be available in electronic books.

Library of Congress Control Number: 2006936762

ISBN-13: 978-0-470-04583-1
ISBN-10: 0-470-04583-3

Manufactured in the United States of America

10 9 8 7 6 5 4 3 2 1

2B/RT/RS/QW/IN

About the Author

Gary Dahl is an award-winning copywriter, creative director, and advertising agency owner. His career spans 40 years, during which he has handled all facets of advertising for hundreds of clients. His agency, Gary Dahl Creative Services, in Campbell, California, specializes in electronic advertising. Dahl's ability to creatively capture the essence of a client's business in 30 or 60 seconds of clear, concise broadcast copy is a result of having written and produced hundreds of television commercials and thousands of radio commercials for a wide variety of businesses, including financial, automotive, wireless, education, retail, high-tech, and dot-coms.

Gary Dahl has a unique understanding of what it takes to successfully convey a client's message to potential customers. As the creator of the retail phenomenon, the Pet Rock — which still ranks as the fastest selling and most publicized novelty gift product in retail history — Dahl has proven the extraordinary power of a creative idea combined with an effective, well-planned marketing strategy. He has been featured in *Time, Newsweek, People, Playboy,* and other major magazines; has appeared on numerous network TV shows; and has been interviewed by countless radio networks worldwide, including NPR, the BBC, and the Australian Broadcasting Company.

An accomplished public speaker, Dahl has made advertising/marketing presentations to numerous university advertising and marketing communications classes, advertising and civic organizations, and business and professional clubs throughout the country. He and his wife, Marguerite, live in the hills above Los Gatos, California.

Ruth Mills is an editor and writer with more than 20 years of experience in book publishing. She has edited and published books on a wide range of topics, including business, finance, biography, general-interest non-fiction, and fiction. She has worked with authors who were CEOs of major corporations (including Continental Airlines and Sears) and journalists from such major publications as *BusinessWeek, Forbes, Fortune,* and *The Wall Street Journal.* She also developed several series of books with *Entrepreneur, Adweek,* and *Black Enterprise* magazines. Finally, she has ghost-written seven books on business topics, including advertising, real estate investing, personal finance, and the success story of a well-known business entrepreneur.

Dedication

To Marguerite, my soul mate and the love of my life.

Publisher's Acknowledgments

We're proud of this book; please send us your comments through our Dummies online registration form located at www.dummies.com/register/.

Some of the people who helped bring this book to market include the following:

Acquisitions, Editorial, and Media Development

Project Editor: Natalie Faye Harris

(Previous Edition: Elizabeth Netedu Kuball)

Acquisitions Editor: Stacy Kennedy

(Previous Edition: Holly McGuire)

Copy Editor: Sarah Westfall

Technical Editor: Tom Hirons

Editorial Manager: Christine Beck

Media Development Manager: Laura VanWinkle

Editorial Assistants: Erin Calligan, Joe Niesen, David Lutton, Leeann Harney

Cartoons: Rich Tennant (www.the5thwave.com)

Composition Services

Project Coordinator: Patrick Redmond

Layout and Graphics: Carl Byers, Lavonne Cook, Joyce Haughey, Stephanie D. Jumper, Shelley Norris, Barry Offringa, Laura Pence

Anniversary Logo Design: Richard Pacifico

Proofreaders: Dwight Ramsey, Techbooks

Indexer: Techbooks

Publishing and Editorial for Consumer Dummies

    Diane Graves Steele, Vice President and Publisher, Consumer Dummies

    Joyce Pepple, Acquisitions Director, Consumer Dummies

    Kristin A. Cocks, Product Development Director, Consumer Dummies

    Michael Spring, Vice President and Publisher, Travel

    Kelly Regan, Editorial Director, Travel

Publishing for Technology Dummies

    Andy Cummings, Vice President and Publisher, Dummies Technology/General User

Composition Services

    Gerry Fahey, Vice President of Production Services

    Debbie Stailey, Director of Composition Services

Contents at a Glance

Table of Contents

Introduction

・・

*A*dvertising, despite whatever impressions you have or information you've heard, isn't complicated — or rather, it's only as complicated as you want it to be. Sure, a lot is involved with advertising. Print, broadcast, outdoor, direct mail, collateral materials, Internet — each media has its own positives and negatives, its own mysterious production language, and its own unique rates. How does a novice decipher this stuff? How do you know what to buy and what to ignore?

Yes, advertising can seem complicated, even intimidating, but the good news is that it ain't rocket science. You just need a few tricks of the trade that help you design, write, and implement a creative, hard-hitting, memorable ad campaign for your business. The purpose of this book is to show you those tricks.

About This Book

You can read this book front to back, or you can simply refer to it as you would any reference book, dipping into the chapters you need right away. Whichever way you read it, you may discover some shortcuts, insights, techniques, and money-saving facts that can get you the most bang for the buck while taking some of the mystery out of this all-important element of your business.

Think of *Advertising For Dummies,* 2nd Edition, as a guidebook to map your way through the back alleys, side streets, and secret pathways leading to effective advertising. Advertising can be a very intimidating subject — it has its own language; it comes in a huge array of media choices; it requires, when done right, creativity, clarity, and solid production values to cut through its own clutter; and it costs a lot of money. But advertising is also essential to the success of your business. Use this travel guide to chart your course down the hidden boulevards of advertising, and you may discover that, indeed, the streets are paved with gold.

Conventions Used in This Book

When this book was printed, some Web addresses may have needed to break across two lines of text. If that happened, rest assured that I haven't put in any extra characters (such as hyphens) to indicate the break. So, when using one of these Web addresses, just type in exactly what you see in this book, pretending as though the line break doesn't exist.

What You're Not to Read

You don't have to read any text preceded by a Technical Stuff icon in order to understand the chapter subject (though I urge you to read it if you're feeling the need for some surplus advertising brainpower). Some information also appears in gray boxes known as sidebars. These sidebars are asides and not critical to the text, so you don't have to read them — though you may miss out on some interesting information or anecdote if you skip them entirely!

Foolish Assumptions

This book is not for the CEO of a major corporation with virtually unlimited funds for slick, glossy production, and mind-boggling amounts of cash for media buys. Instead, this book is for entrepreneurs, owners of small to mid-size businesses, and professionals selling important services — in other words, anyone who's trying to drum up business and create a successful company with the help of advertising. This book is for the rest of us — the people for whom an advertising budget represents an important percentage of gross income and, therefore, a drain on the old take-home pay that must be considered very seriously.

Over the years, I have helped numerous clients project clear, concise, creative messages within limited budget parameters. I used to dream of boundless production budgets with which to produce award-winning ads for both print and broadcast. I always wondered what it would be like to take a complete crew — cameramen, sound and lighting technicians, stunt drivers, fashion models, actors, makeup people, hairstylists, even caterers — to some exotic locale where I would have a one-month deadline within which to shoot a 30-second, $2 million spot. It never happened. My guess is that less than 1 percent of all professional advertising people actually work on the major national accounts, creating the ads you see each night during prime time — the ads produced with unrestricted budgets, which, sadly, still seem to miss the mark more often than not. The other 99 percent of advertising profession-als are guys like me.

How This Book Is Organized

This book is divided into five easily digestible parts, and each part is divided into chapters. Here's the scoop on what each part covers:

Part I: Advertising 101

From the moment you get out of bed in the morning, to late at night when you turn off the television and turn out the lights, you're bombarded with thou-sands of advertising messages. Advertising is here, there, everywhere. And into this clutter you now insert your own advertising. What you discover in this part are the fundamentals of effective advertising. I also help you identify your target market, set your sales goals, narrow your focus, and develop an advertising plan that works. I delve into the complicated world of co-op adver-tising reimbursement, in which your ad dollars are augmented by others.

I think you may be pleasantly surprised at the quality of media you can afford, even on the smallest budgets. Mass media may, at first glance, appear to be unaffordable. But regardless of the expense, when you consider how many people you can reach with mass media, it's the smartest way you can spend your money. What you *can't* afford to do is fritter away a limited ad budget on questionable media that's better suited to wrapping fish than it is to attracting new customers to your business. So in this part, I help you plan an advertising strategy that actually brings customers through your door.

Part II: Creating Great Ads for Every Medium

This part of the book is the longest, because the depth of your media choices is simply mind-boggling (and new forms of media, both good and bad, are introduced nearly every day). In this part, I stick to the mass media choices of online ads and your own Web site, as well as newspaper, magazine, radio, television, collateral, and outdoor advertising. I walk you through the steps of writing broadcast and print ads that motivate and sell. I show you what goes into producing radio and TV commercials, as well as print ads and brochures, and I queue you in on what you need to know to build a Web site and advertise on the Internet. I also show you why *continuity,* delivering the same message across all media, is the all-important key to a successful ad campaign.

Part III: Buying the Different Media

This part gets down to the nitty-gritty — the actual spending of your hard-earned advertising budget. Here I take a hard look at investing in Internet advertising, negotiating with print media to get the best possible page position at the lowest possible price, and why buying television time isn't nearly as complicated as putting a man on the moon.

Here's the best part of these chapters: I give you the inside scoop on getting all kinds of free stuff (even vacations) as part of your media expenditures. The chapters in this part give you the information you need in order to maximize your ad budget by spending it wisely. Finally, if you've considered hiring an ad agency, this part is where I tell you who the players are and the pros and cons of going this route.

Part IV: Beyond the Basics: Creating Buzz and Using Publicity

In this part, I show you how to generate word-of-mouth and buzz about your products or services. And I explain the difference between publicity and public relations, help you write a good press release, and show you how to get it published (hey, it's free advertising). Finally, I walk you through the unique nature of advertising specialties and premiums while showing you how to increase their effectiveness, and I reveal how to become involved in sponsored promotions and events. I even demonstrate how to invent successful promotions of your own.

Part V: The Part of Tens

What, you may be asking, is a Part of Tens? It's the part of every *For Dummies* book that cuts right to the chase. If you don't have time to read anything else in this book, read these short lists of do's and don'ts. In these lists of ten, I instruct you on writing effective, creative, clear copy for all media and help you decide whether or not your business could use the services of an advertising agency. (If you're too busy to even read that chapter, hire an agency right away.)

Icons Used in This Book

Icons are those little pictures you find in the margins of this book. I use them to grab your attention and steer you toward key bits of information. Here's a list of the icons I use in this book and what they mean:

Some of the points I make in this book are so important that you want to commit them to memory. If you file these tidbits in your memory bank, you will have gathered some very important details about the advertising business.

This icon marks insider tips I've gathered over the years. They can help you avoid some of the mistakes I've figured out the hard way and give you a leg up as you navigate the various elements leading to effective advertising.

As I lead you through the hidden back streets of advertising, I don't want you to stumble and fall. So I've marked some of the larger potholes and cracks in the sidewalk with this Warning icon.

Whenever I wax nostalgic and feel the need to share stories of my past experiences or interesting examples from others in the ad biz, you see this icon.

The advertising trade brings with it a ton of technical stuff, and I've marked these areas with this icon. The good news is that you can safely skip over any paragraph marked with this icon. But if you read it, you may discover information that you can use to wow (if not confuse and dismay) the sales reps and other ad people you deal with, not to mention your neighbors down the street.

Where to Go from Here

You're holding this book because you felt a need to discover the ins and outs of the ad game. Think of this as a traveler's guide that contains the charts and maps you need in order to find your way through the weird and wonderful world of advertising. You can begin your journey in the beginning, or you can dive right into the middle — whichever works best for you.

Part I
Advertising 101

In this part . . .

Advertising: It's here, it's there, it's everywhere! Everyone is assailed with advertising messages every waking moment. The obvious media — television, radio, newspapers, magazines, billboards, and direct mail — are just the tip of the advertising iceberg. Your cereal boxes, milk cartons, clothing, bedding, fashion accessories, and even your automobiles are covered in advertising. Into this cauldron of advertising vehicles has been thrown the Internet, grocery carts, the reverse side of cash register tapes, ATM screens, even displays in some public restrooms — and all of this hype contributes to advertising clutter.

If you want to advertise your business (and you most certainly should), you have to enter this world, jumping in with both feet. Daunting? You bet. Impossible? No way. In this part, I share the fundamentals of advertising, help you develop (and stick to!) a budget for your advertising needs, and show you how to boost that budget by partnering with others via co-op advertising. I also offer guidelines on defining and positioning your message and aid you in developing an ad campaign that can be effective for your business.

Chapter 1

Advertising: Mastering the Art of Promotion

In This Chapter

▶ Being aware of the advertising around you (as if you could avoid it)

▶ Putting the fundamentals of good advertising to work for you

▶ Taking a few lessons from the pros

Advertising is a $300 billion industry in the United States alone. Plunkett Research, Ltd. (the company that provided this figure) points out that the large numbers don't stop there. In the United States, advertisers flood the following mediums in droves:

- 1,749 broadcast TV stations (and that's not including cable and satellite TV outlets)
- 13,599 radio stations
- 2,250 daily and Sunday newspapers

And those figures don't even take into consideration the thousands of magazines, direct mail, Web sites, blogs, outdoor advertising (billboards, bus shelters, and so on), or specialty or alternative advertising, which includes everything from airplane banners at the beach to tchotchkes, small items like tote bags, pens, and t-shirts that merchants and businesses give away to remind consumers to do business with them.

With all these choices of how to get your message out there, how do you decide what's the best medium to reach the customers you're looking for? And how can you develop an ad campaign that won't get lost in the morass? You don't have to hire an ad agency (though you can: Chapter 16 offers guidance on how best to do this, and Chapter 20 gives you ten ways to know whether you need outside help). But you can also do it yourself, and this book tells how.

In this chapter, I fill you in on the basics of advertising — what's effective and what isn't. Then I give you a short course on all your advertising options — radio, TV (network and cable), magazines and newspapers, direct mail, outdoor, the Web, and more — and I show how you can put them to work for you. Finally, I end with stories about two legends of advertising as well as brief introductions of more recent ad giants, because if you focus on the best and figure out what they've done well, you can try to incorporate some of their genius into your own advertising — and come out ahead of the competition.

Making Advertising Work

Effective advertising sells a product or a service that fulfills all the promises made about it. On the other hand, effective advertising also sells inferior products or services, but only once!

So what makes advertising effective? Effective advertising is:

- ✔ **Creative:** It delivers the advertising message in a fresh, new way.
- ✔ **Hard-hitting:** Its headline, copy, or graphic element stops readers or listeners dead in their tracks.
- ✔ **Memorable:** It ensures that the audience will remember *your* business when they think about the products and services you're selling.
- ✔ **Clear:** It presents its message in a concise, uncomplicated, easy-to-grasp manner.
- ✔ **Informative:** It enlightens the audience about your business and products, while giving them important reasons to buy from you.
- ✔ **Distinctive:** It is unique and immediately recognizable as yours.

The well-established brands that most people use every day — brands like Coca-Cola and Pepsi, McDonald's and Burger King, Budweiser and Miller, Bayer and Advil, Ford and Chevy, Tide and Cheer — live up to the promises made in their advertising. In fact, the products live up to the promise in such a dramatic fashion that those products have become a part of the everyday lives of millions of people. These products have been *branded,* which simply means that when you think of soft drinks, fast food, beer, pain relievers, cars, or laundry detergents, these brands come to mind. As surely as the cowboys of the Old West branded the haunches of their cattle, these products have been branded into your psyche — and the psyches of millions of other consumers.

When you begin to create advertising for your product or service, keep these suggestions in mind:

- ✔ **Don't make promises you can't live up to.** Although your ad may draw more people to your product initially, you can't retain these people as loyal customers in the long run if you make promises you can't keep.

- ✔ **Identify the best features of whatever it is you're selling and develop your advertising around these features.** Think about how your product stands out from the competition, what sets it apart, and then focus on those attributes.

- ✔ **Try to create a memorable advertising message for your product.** You want people to think of your store, your product, or your professional service whenever they're in the market for such a thing.

If your message is creative, clear, and concise, if your product or service is something that can truly benefit people and live up to its hype, then you're on the road to producing effective advertising.

If your advertising makes bold promises about your product, you may convince a lot of people to try it. But if those people buy your product and give it a try, and the product turns out to be less than you advertised it to be, you will most certainly never see those consumers again. Think about it: How many times have you responded to an advertising message for a new, improved, astounding product, only to be disappointed with the item after you tried it? You probably even felt like you'd been ripped off. If your advertising message leaves consumers with the same feeling, you simply won't get anywhere.

Getting to Know Your Media Options

Advertising comes in all shapes and sizes. And a big part of developing your ad plans and campaign is to decide which mediums are best suited to advertising your particular business. Following is a brief overview of your options, with details from Plunkett Research, Ltd. to give you a ballpark idea on how many billions of dollars are spent annually in each medium in the United States.

Regarding radio

Radio advertising is a $20 billion business — and it has expanded both because listeners can now tune in on the Internet and because of the development of satellite radio (Sirius and XM subscriber-based programming). But it's also competing with MP3 devices, which means there may be fewer listeners to any given radio station or program.

But if your business appeals to consumers who're likely to subscribe to this type of programming, or if you can reach them on broadcast radio during drive time or particular radio programs (especially those with celebrity hosts), then you should consider this medium. Chapter 8 provides guidance on developing memorable radio spots, and Chapter 14 offers information on buying radio time to maximize your reach — and your budget.

Rating TV

TV is a $68 billion business — and that includes the almost 2,000 broadcast stations plus the many cable and satellite TV stations. The growth in the number of stations has actually made it easier for advertisers, because TV programming is so much more targeted. For example, the audience for The History Channel is probably very different from, say, Lifetime or Oxygen or WE, the Women's Entertainment channel.

Still, TV advertising is the most expensive medium (even with the tips offered in Chapter 9 on how to create TV commercials and keep down the costs!), so you should consider TV commercials only if you can afford them. TV is still a mass medium, even with the more-focused channels mentioned, and your ad budget may be better spent on a more narrowly focused media. But if you decide TV is for you, see Chapter 15 for guidance on how to find the right station and negotiate the best deal for your ad and your business.

Contemplating print

Print advertising encompasses both newspapers (daily and Sunday papers), which is a $49 billion business, and magazines, which is a $21 billion business. Newspapers are obviously a good choice if your business is regional and you're targeting a broad consumer base; magazines are more-specifically tailored to different readers — for example, a subscriber to *Glamour* probably isn't also subscribing to, say, *Maxim,* though the media kits of each provide the details on the number and demographics of the subscriber base. Chapter 7 offers insight on how to write and design eye-catching print ads, and Chapter 13 offers ideas for how to choose the right publication and negotiate a good rate for your ad.

Keep in mind, though, that many people who used to get information from newspapers and magazines now have the additional option of online subscriptions — to either those same publications or to alternatives that have never been printed on paper but are available only on the Internet. Chapters 6 and 12 cover how to create and buy ad space in this new media.

Imitation: The sincerest form of flattery

Every now and then I see or hear an image advertisement that is so creative, so wonderfully conceived, and so (relatively) inexpensively produced that I wish I had written it myself. It has been said that no original ideas are out there, but occasionally a fresh, new approach to delivering the same old message comes along. And I file it away in my memory as something that, someday, I may want to imitate. If the ad is especially impressive, I even find out which agency is responsible for it and write it a congratulatory note.

One such ad was a radio spot for Berkeley Farms, a major Northern California dairy. Instead of creating a straight, consumer-directed ad extolling the virtues of its milk, the company created a recruitment ad for "new employees." Instead of just telling its audience what superior milk they can take home when they buy the Berkeley Farms brand, a warm, motherly, female voice opens the spot with the wonderful line, "If you're a cow, I want to tell you about Berkeley Farms — it's a great place to work." She goes on to tell any cows who may be listening that they can expect to be fed only the finest hays and grains, which a full-time vet

is always on call in case they get sick, that their stalls are always kept clean and tidy, and that they are foolish cows indeed if they chose to work anywhere else.

This spot is a memorable one because it uses a creative twist — talking to the cows, not the consumers — to a great advantage. Hey, if this dairy is good enough for the cows, then it must be good enough for you! And this spot can undoubtedly inspire me to think of a fresh point-of-view for some retail commercial I write in the future.

When you sit down to write advertising for your business, using ideas and techniques from other advertising to help you find your own "creative hook" is perfectly okay. No, I am *not* giving you permission to lift someone else's copy verbatim or to steal a concept out of hand. But good advertising done by others can be a great source of creative inspiration. Even the big boys do it. One advertising agency comes out with a fresh, new look in its ads, something that hasn't been seen before, and everyone else jumps all over it. It happens all the time. Just be sure you know the difference between imitating and plagiarizing, and stick to the former.

Musing upon direct mail

Direct mail is a $45 billion business, and it's alive and well even with the growth of e-mail and other Internet advertising. Charitable organizations still send pitches for funds to continue their good works (like The Red Cross, The American Cancer Society, and Doctors Without Borders). Similarly, cultural institutions use direct mail to solicit donor support, which they need to supplement ticket prices from their audiences (think of your local theater company, public radio station, and even PBS). And direct mail includes the myriad catalogs that fill all of our mailboxes — from Land's End to L.L. Bean to Victoria's Secret, to J.Crew (to name just a few). Chapter 10 focuses on developing strong direct-mail messages that can stand out among the abundance in the mailbox.

Scrutinizing outdoor advertising

Outdoor advertising includes everything from billboards on highways to ads on bus kiosks, in subway cars, on taxis, or even on benches and other signage. As a $6 billion industry, it's a small part of overall annual ad expenditures, but if you think it's right for your business, Chapter 11 tells how to choose the type of outdoor ad that can work best for you and how to design memorable advertising in this medium.

Ogling online ads

Last, but by no means least, is the newest ad medium — online — even though the Internet hardly seems "new"; still, it's only been since the mid-'90s that companies have used the Web to advertise products, services, and businesses. Chapter 6 offers the pros and cons of online advertising on various Web sites (as well as how to develop your own), and it tells how to create various types of online ad formats, do e-mail advertising, and create your own blog. Chapter 12 picks up where Chapter 6 leaves off and helps you with the financial side of online ads: hiring someone to help you create ads or your Web site and buying space on other sites.

Poring over publicity

Technically, publicity isn't really part of advertising, but good publicity can serve to advertise your business. Publicity is really about getting someone *else* to advertise your business. Basically, you're calling attention to what you're doing in a way that your newspaper may want to report on it, or a magazine may want to write a feature article about your business, or a TV show host or radio host may be so intrigued by something you've done that they talk about you on their shows. The two chapters in Part IV offer lots of great ideas and success stories on how some businesses have done this successfully.

Where your advertising appears is every bit as important as what message it contains — maybe even more so. Advertising is a numbers game: You want to spend as little money as possible, as effectively as possible, to reach as many people as possible, in order to make your phone and your cash register ring.

Consider your many media options very carefully. You can waste your advertising dollars very easily by using the wrong media for your advertising goals. Mass media advertising *is* affordable (turn to the chapters in Part III for more information on costs). But so-called "affordable" advertising in the wrong

ANECDOTE

A spectacularly ineffective advertising vehicle

One of the other tenants in our office building — a small insurance company specializing in assigned-risk auto coverage (for customers whose driving records aren't exactly stellar) — recently unveiled its latest, breakthrough advertising vehicle. And I do mean *vehicle*.

I came to work one morning and couldn't miss it, parked out on the curb in all its glory. The company had pounded out the dents on a 1960s Volkswagen bus, spent $50 to have it freshly painted a sparkling bathtub white, and bolted a 4-by-8-foot, double-faced billboard to the roof to advertise its business. Because the old wreck needed brakes, our business neighbors quit driving it around town and parked the thing conspicuously in the parking lot in front of our

building, much to the chagrin of the other tenants. The sign that sat atop this moveable beast, purportedly to tell the world about the company's insurance business, included no less than 32 words (including *sure thing* and *no driver refused*) and an 11-digit phone number, all arranged helter-skelter in 6 different fonts and painted in 3 different colors.

The bus was a gigantic waste of advertising dollars. But the business owner probably thought, like so many small to mid-sized retailers and service businesses do, that he couldn't afford "real" advertising. So he tried the VW bus routine instead. I don't think I have to tell you to avoid this kind of mistake at all costs.

---

media is a gigantic waste of your dollars and your time. No matter how affordable the media is, if it doesn't bring customers through your door, you aren't really saving money. On the contrary, you're draining your limited budget without being the least-bit effective.

Lessons from the Legends: Figuring Out Your Advertising Needs

REMEMBER

Although your advertising may not come close to the greatest ads created by the top ad agencies (after all, that's not your intent in the first place), you can still gather greatness from the best. The creative legends of the advertising business have a perceptive understanding of consumers (and how to motivate them). Because they understood consumers, they were able to produce advertising that was so effective that it remained memorable decades after the campaign's end.

In the following sections, I describe some of the gurus of advertising whose work has taught me much of what I know — and can do the same for you.

David Ogilvy

The first book I ever read about the advertising business was *Confessions of an Advertising Man,* by David Ogilvy (recently reissued in paperback by Southbank Publishing). Ogilvy was an inspiration to me — and to thousands of other advertising professionals. He died in 1999 at the age of 88, yet he's a true legend in the advertising world, even though the ads he made famous were created decades ago.

Ogilvy is also famous for succinct statements about how to create compelling, memorable ads. Here are just a few that I try to live by when writing ads for my clients:

- ✔ "On the average, five times as many people read the headline as read the body copy. When you have written your headline, you have spent 80 cents out of your dollar."
- ✔ "Never write an advertisement you wouldn't want your own family to read. You wouldn't tell lies to your own wife. Don't tell lies to mine."
- ✔ "Every word in the copy must count."
- ✔ "We sell or else."
- ✔ "Advertise what is unique."

Born in England, David Ogilvy didn't even get into the advertising business until he was 39 years old. He had tried everything from selling stoves door-to-door, to a brief tenure as a chef in Paris. He was even a member of the British Secret Service. Financially broke at the age of 39, he cofounded an advertising agency — Hewitt, Ogilvy, Benson & Mather. And he made a list of five clients he wanted to land: General Foods, Bristol-Myers, Campbell's Soup, Lever Brothers, and Shell Oil. Eleven years later, he had them all.

Ogilvy preached the virtues of sales-driven copy. He also expected advertising copy to be expressed with clarity, relevance, and grace. He knew that the real purpose of advertising is to sell. His ads may have been gorgeous, but they were filled with unique product difference and sell — albeit with an emotional edge. He invented eccentric personalities to capture the reader's attention, based on the idea that memorable faces help make memorable brands.

Ogilvy also said, when talking about creative types who worked for (or wanted to work for) his agency, "Every copywriter should start his career by spending two years in direct response." What he meant is that the primary purpose of advertising is to sell.

Dot-coms to dot-bombs in one easy lesson

Whenever I think of Bill Bernbach's very insightful quote, "Dullness won't sell your product, but neither will irrelevant brilliance," I'm reminded of the super-expensive commercials for various fledgling dot-com businesses that ran during the Super Bowl broadcast in January 2000. Clearly, most of these businesses had never bothered to read Bill Bernbach, because their commercials simply reeked of "irrelevant brilliance."

And most of the dot-com spots, purchased for as much as $1.5 million per 30 seconds, were so contrived, so devoid of a selling message (let alone a call to action), and so downright confusing that they wasted most, if not all, of their millions of ad bucks. This misuse of funds is also true of companies in other industries that choose to gamble the entire year's ad budget on the Super Bowl commercials, but the 2000 dot-com debacle was the worst. The majority of these companies didn't survive more than six months after their spots appeared — other than Pets.com, whose adorable sock-puppet spokesman starred in several Super Bowl commercials (before the company eventually went kaput).

Why weren't these flashy ads successful? Because they not only forgot Bernbach's rule, but they also ignored one of Ogilvy's — namely, "We sell or else." Their spots were so clever that they forgot to include a selling message that actually motivates someone to buy. Sadly, many even forgot to mention what service or product it was that they were selling. And, most important, they forgot to tell viewers why anyone should buy it.

These companies and their agencies got so lost in having a creative, good time on unlimited production budgets that they forgot why they were buying the incredibly expensive time on the most-watched show on television in the first place — they simply forgot to sell us something.

Bill Bernbach

Bill Bernbach was the Creative Director for Doyle, Dane, Bernbach during its heyday. Working with Helmut Krone as Art Director, Bernbach invented a new way to project a message to consumers, by introducing wonderful creativity and a kinder, gentler approach to advertising. The agency led the way with its fanciful Volkswagen ads from the 1960s, which supplied both entertainment and product information. Do you remember "Think small"? It was a huge shift in advertising communication and became the industry standard that lives to this day.

So memorable and trend-setting was that original Volkswagen advertising that when the New Beetle was introduced in the 1990s, the agency for Volkswagen of America, Arnold Communications of Boston, chose not to create a completely new campaign from the ground up, but rather to emulate the original concept. For example, the campaign for the New Beetle featured lots of *white space* (a Krone innovation that means just what it says — the ad wasn't filled with color and copy from edge to edge), a small photo of the VW New Beetle in profile, and brief copy that read, "Zero to 60? Yes." This kind of advertising is great stuff, and a compliment to the original ads created by Doyle, Dane, Bernbach over 40 years ago. In fact, Arnold Communications, when submitting its work for awards, still lists Krone and Bernbach as creative contributors.

Bill Bernbach, like David Ogilvy, was good for a pithy quote now and then, including the following: "Dullness won't sell your product, but neither will irrelevant brilliance."

Wieden and Kennedy

Dan Wieden and David Kennedy took advertising out of its traditional centers of the ad world (Madison Avenue in New York City., Chicago, and to some extent, Los Angeles) by setting up shop in Portland, Oregon. They're listed on the top 100 people in advertising (for the last century, no less!). They've done great work for Microsoft, ESPN, and many other clients, but they're still probably best known for revolutionizing the sneaker industry — or at least the advertising of it — by creating Nike's "Just do it" campaign.

Chapter 2

Setting and Working within Your Advertising Budget

. . . .

In This Chapter

▶ Figuring out how much you can — and should — spend on advertising

▶ Buying ads where your potential customers look for them

▶ Making the most of your budget

. . . .

Companies like Procter & Gamble, General Motors, and McDonald's spend more on advertising each year than the average small to mid-size business could ever hope to gross in a lifetime. No one knows (and the companies aren't telling) what their advertising budget to gross income ratios actually are, but you can bet they're high. These companies have spent a king's ransom to successfully position their products to be top-of-mind with the entire buying public — and it costs them a yearly fortune to maintain this *branding* of their products. (For more on branding, check out *Branding For Dummies* by Bill Chiaravalle and Barbara Schenck [Wiley].) If one of these big company's products begins to slip in overall sales, it throws $25 million in extra advertising funds at the problem without a second thought. The total amounts of their ad funds are simply astounding — for example, Coca-Cola spent $2.5 billion on advertising worldwide in 2005.

You, on the other hand, very likely look upon your advertising dollars as a seriously important personal investment — an investment that (shudder!) comes right off the bottom line and, therefore, is never a part of your hard-earned take-home pay. For this reason, you need to do some careful planning as you decide what percentage of your gross sales you can realistically afford to spend for advertising. You don't want to overdo it, but you can't skimp too much either. As with many things in life, balance is what it's all about.

In this chapter, you discover what some companies spend on their advertising so you can decide what you want to spend. You also take a look at how and where your competitors are advertising and why it's crucial to know exactly who your target market is and how your business can appeal to it (if you don't already!). I also give you tips on how you can get the most bang for your advertising buck by weighing the pros and cons of advertising in major or local newspapers; in national, regional, or specialized magazines; on radio; on broadcast or cable TV; and on the Internet.

Determining How Much You Can Afford to Spend

So, what dollar amount, or percentage of gross sales, should you invest in your advertising budget? The question is a very tough one. And although I can give you some guidelines, only you are able to answer it when it's all said and done. After all, *it's your money.*

A good place to start when you're setting a budget is in examining your goals. If you want to become the Big Dog — that is, if your driving ambition is to elevate your business into an industry-leadership position and blow your competition away — then of course you need to spend a lot more money than if you're satisfied with just getting by. In this book, I make the assumption that you want to do much better than just getting by — you wouldn't be advertising at all if you didn't want your business to grow and prosper. But in order to see the kind of success you're after, you need an ad budget.

Over half of new businesses fail within their first two years. This depressing statistic is probably due to a number of factors, but a lack of working capital (cash) is usually at the top of the list. Most businesses start out with great hopes and limited cash, and it's the hand-to-mouth reality of a start-up that kills most of them. When people open new businesses, they often forget to set aside enough money for a large enough ad budget to get their name out there. You can invent a better mousetrap, but not having enough working capital to afford to tell the world about it is like trying to tow a boat with a rope.

To get an idea of what typical businesses spend on advertising, I asked several of my agency's clients what percentage of gross sales they spend. Not a single one of them could give me a straight answer to my question. They had each used a different formula to arrive at their budget number, and they each planned their advertising expenditures, using different criteria.

Our agency has one retail client who spends as much as 10 percent of gross sales on advertising. Although this percentage may seem high, some businesses *must* spend that amount in order to compete, and I've worked for clients who spent even more. On the other hand, I've seen businesses spend 2 percent or less on advertising — and in the case of very small companies, some don't spend even that much on a sustained basis. Most small businesses spend between 2 and 7 percent of their gross sales on advertising, though some allocate as much as 10 percent.

Percent of gross is a very helpful budgeting tool, but it can leave a start-up business with inadequate exposure. Start-ups often must budget a percentage of projected gross, overspending in the introduction of your business to build business to a profitable level.

You can use these figures as general guidelines to help you set your own advertising budget, but keep in mind that each business is unique. What works for one company may not work for another. When in doubt, follow this simple rule: Spend as much money on advertising as it takes to make and sustain an impact in the marketplace, but don't spend so much that you run the risk of putting your business into financial jeopardy.

You can begin the process of setting a budget by trying to come up with some answers to the following questions:

- How big is your business?
- How much yearly income does your business generate?
- What do you want to accomplish with your advertising, and how much will that cost?
- What is your competition spending?

If you're in a highly competitive business, such as cell phones, restaurants, clothing boutiques, or car sales and repairs, you need to step up to the plate with some serious bucks in order to hit a homerun in your marketplace. Your competition is spending their brains out, and you have to do the same. On the other hand, if your business enjoys a unique status in your market, if you provide merchandise or a service that people can't find elsewhere, then you can get away with much lower spending.

If your budget is too limited to make an impact in the market on a daily or weekly basis, stash your cash until you're having some special event or sale and then attack the media full-force. In advertising, you're better off having a big voice once in a while than a weak voice every day.

Developing an Advertising Strategy and a Tactical Plan

You probably went into business to succeed — and that means you'll do whatever it takes to reach this lofty goal . . . as long as it's legal and within fiscal reason. But in order to succeed with your advertising — or with anything in life, actually — you need a plan of action. In this section, I help you come up with a plan that works for *you*.

Researching and evaluating your competition

A good step to consider when devising your advertising plan, and planning the extent of your budget, is to analyze what your competition is doing. In Part III, I give some guidelines and relative costs for all media, but you can pin it down even further with a few well-placed phone calls in your own area. Here are some guidelines:

- ✔ **Do you see ads for your competitors in the newspaper on a regular basis?** If so, call the paper and ask for its retail display-ad rate in order to figure out how much the competition is spending to advertise there.

- ✔ **Do you hear competitors' radio commercials often?** Call the station's sales department and ask about its rates. A salesperson will likely tell you *precisely* what your competition is spending so she can talk you into doing the same thing.

- ✔ **Does your weekly mail bring coupons or brochures from your competition?** Again, contact the vendor of the mail pack that sends these coupons and find out what those ads cost.

Why should you want to know what your competition is spending? Because this information gives you some basis for planning your own budget. Forewarned is forearmed, which in this case means that gathering information about the other guys helps you make a quantified judgment as to how much you need to spend in order to compete with them. If you own a mom-and-pop hardware store, you may have a tough time generating a budget that can compete with the monster-size warehouse stores — but don't panic. Simply outspending the other guy (or even trying to keep up with him) isn't the whole answer.

You may be relieved to know that you can spend a lot less than your competition and still make more of an impact by being more creative with both your message and your media buying. You *can* make up for a lack of money with an abundance of creativity and careful — no, make that *diligent* — media negotiation and spending. You can also make your available advertising budget stretch if you don't waste any of it on irrelevant media that brings you little or no business.

Regardless of the limits of your ad budget, and whether you're trying to reach a broad audience, accept this as a given: You *can* afford mass media. You can afford to buy radio commercials, ads in a mass-circulation daily newspaper, spots on broadcast television and cable stations, ads in the regional editions of major magazines, and a variety of Internet advertising, including your own Web site. This media may, at first, appear to be unaffordable. But, regardless of the expense (which may be less than you think), when you consider how many people you can reach, it's the smartest way you can spend your money.

What you *can't* afford to do is fritter away a limited ad budget on questionable media, like the dozens of ads you find in your mailbox every day, that are better suited for wrapping fish than they are for attracting new customers to your business. The old saw "You get what you pay for" is never truer.

Identifying your target market

By identifying your primary target market, you can do a better job of narrowing your media buys, which leads you to a bottom-line budget figure that makes sense. This information also helps you when the time comes to design and write your ads. Teenagers, as you know, speak an entirely different language than adults, so not only must you buy the media they're attracted to, but you also want to write and design your ads to attract their attention in the first place.

For example, if you own a skateboard store, then you're going to target teens rather than senior citizens, right? And those teens aren't reading the newspaper or looking at direct mail pieces; instead, they're online at their favorite Web sites, listening to very narrowly programmed radio stations, and watching certain TV shows. If, on the other hand, you're selling luxury cars that are purchased primarily by affluent adults over 55, you can do well by placing ads in the business section of your paper and buying spots on radio stations programmed with news, talk, oldies, or classical music. In other words, just a little bit of thought into who your target market is and what forms of media it pays attention to can save you lots of money and tons of grief.

Knowing your product's appeal

What you're selling helps you determine what media you should be buying. Are you selling tires? Then make print your primary media, because you need to list all those different brands, sizes, and prices in those long columns of itsy-bitsy type. You may also call attention to your print ads with some radio spots. And, if you want to show how clean and beautiful your shop is, consider some TV. Direct mail, if it's a stand-alone piece for you and you alone, can be somewhat effective as well.

On the other hand, are you selling a professional service such as accounting, financial management, or consulting? Then you want to look at news, talk, or another radio format listened to by business people. If print is in your ad plan, then the local business journal or the business section or main news section of your newspapers are good bets.

If you're selling beauty products or run a hair or nail salon, you need to reach your target market by buying on radio stations that can prove to you their audience composition includes mostly women. Women also read the newspaper's business page in great numbers, as well as the entertainment, society, style, home, and main news sections. And dozens of television shows, even entire cable stations, are targeted toward women — for example, the Lifetime network, WE (Women's Entertainment), Oxygen, and many others.

What I'm getting at here is that you must narrow your focus in order to get a handle on the amount you need to invest in advertising, by identifying your primary market segment. There's no sense in taking the shotgun approach when a well-aimed rifle shot can find more of who you're looking for — and for a lot less money. If you're selling a female-oriented product, you don't want to waste too much of your ad budget advertising to men, and vice versa. Sure, you'll get some spillover, and you can't do anything about that. But targeting your media buys as narrowly as possible saves you money in a big way.

Maximizing Your Budget

You need to spend enough money on advertising to make an impact in the marketplace. You need to make some noise — be heard above the din of other advertising messages. But you don't want to spend more on advertising than you can comfortably afford. Making the most of the money you have can be a difficult tightrope act.

One of my clients, whose advertising budget remains steady from month to month regardless of ups and downs in sales, preaches *consistency* as the number one rule in his advertising plans. His philosophy is simple: In order to compete, you must be heard. You want consumers to think of your business when they're in the market for the products you sell, so you should at least have *some* advertising presence at all times. His thinking is, over the year, it all averages out.

On the other hand, not everyone can afford to have an advertising presence year-round. You may not even need to be out there every day. By virtue of your unique product or service, you may be able to do a fine job by only advertising special events or sales on an as-needed basis. This kind of advertising requires a bit more planning and creative-media buying in order to get the job done, but it's a workable option for many businesses.

Finally, many businesses simply don't have enough money to do much more than advertise when they absolutely have to, such as at Christmas or back-to-school times.

No matter what group you fall into, keep in mind that you can save big bucks in many different ways, several of which I outline for you in the following sections.

Getting the most out of your creative and production

Creative and production are areas that, with just a bit of good writing and skillful execution, are perfect places to save money without sacrificing effectiveness. Your ads can look and sound like champagne, even though your budget can only afford beer. You don't need to spend a small fortune producing a television commercial to sell something that could easily be explained in a well-written and cleverly produced radio spot. Nor do you need to buy a full-page, four-color newspaper ad when a small-space, black-and-white ad with a killer headline and graphic will likely attract as much or more attention. And you needn't waste money on a so-called celebrity spokesperson to pitch your business on radio if you can hire an actor who simply has a great voice.

You can save money on advertising production if you begin with a clever concept and good writing that take cost-effective production into consideration from the very beginning. In other words, don't write a TV spot that must be filmed beneath the Eiffel Tower if you can't afford to send a film crew to France. Putting together a radio spot by using French music, European traffic sound effects, and an actor with a believable French accent may be a bit more cost-effective. If you do it right, the listener will add the mental image of the Eiffel Tower for you, free of charge.

Okay, so you're not planning to do a full-blown commercial shoot in Paris, but you may be tempted to write and produce a TV spot because you feel your product is so darned *visual* that the consumer simply must see it to appreciate it. Here are two truths to ponder before you bite off more than you can chew:

- ✔ Television production costs more than radio production.
- ✔ Radio *can* conjure visual images in the mind of the listener if you use it correctly.

Armed with this information, why not write a radio commercial that's filled with visual imagery and costs only a pittance to produce as compared to a TV spot? These mental images (the *theater of the mind,* as I call it) can be more effective than showing the actual product. For example, a chain of furniture stores my agency handles hasn't done television in years because we proved to them that radio can effectively paint mental pictures of the various furniture pieces they're selling. With the same amount of dollars they were spending on one or two broadcast or cable TV stations, they're now buying time on a half-dozen radio stations — and their business has never been better.

Begin by planning a creative concept that can, at the same time, be produced inexpensively and is clever enough to be heard above the roar. Easier said than done, you say? Perhaps. But it's not impossible, and it can be quite a bit of fun. Besides, why would you want to do boring advertising? Consumers don't want to see or hear any more boring advertising — they're already saturated with it. They'd much rather see or hear clever, funny, memorable ads that, more often than not, will jolt them into responding. This type of advertising is what you should be shooting for.

Want a voice for your radio spot or TV commercial? Call your ad agency, or look in the Yellow Pages under "Talent Agencies & Casting Directors."

Using media you can afford

I get into the meaty parts of media negotiation, planning, and buying in Part III. But for now, I help you consider a few of your options as you formulate your budget strategy. This section may give you some pleasant surprises, or at least dispel some of your beliefs about media affordability.

Online

One way to advertise your business is, of course, on the Internet. You can build your own Web site, or you can hire someone to do it for you — and the Internet itself provides guidelines. Just type "creating a Web site" into a search engine and you can find loads of resources to either walk you through the process or to find people who can create a Web site for you. Most companies — even small businesses — have found this format is an inexpensive way to make their presence known to potential customers. A well-designed Web site increases your credibility, makes it easier for potential customers to discover the products and services you offer, and allows you to sell directly on the Internet.

You can also advertise your business on other companies' Web sites in a variety of ways that match your needs and budget — for example:

- **Banner ads:** The rectangular ads that appear on a Web page inviting viewers to click on the banner, which then takes them to your Web site.

- **E-mail lists and newsletters:** Send a quick e-mail to customers who have expressed interest in receiving information from your business. Be careful not to send an e-mail to just anyone: You don't want your business to be viewed as spam or junk e-mail!

- **Links to your Web site:** When consumers are searching the Web for information on a particular topic, they find links to other Web sites promoting products or services related to that topic — such as books, magazines, and other publications, as well as associations and organizations of users of that product, service, and so on. These links are called *sponsored links.*

- **Interstitial ads:** This fancy name is for something you now see all the time on the Web — the pages or pop-up boxes that appear mysteriously after you click on a link but before you get to the place you clicked to get to. An interstitial page may open and close automatically, and they can be highly effective if done well. If these ads are interesting, consumers may allow them to remain on screen for far longer than the usual banner ad, so the CPM (cost per thousand) should be quite high.

  Pop-up ads have a drawback. As you probably know from your own experiences surfing the Web, pop-up ads can also be quite annoying, so if yours *isn't* interesting or relevant to what the consumer was originally looking for, many consumers will shut it down immediately.

- **Rich-media ads:** These ads include drop-down boxes, moving images, sound, or music that starts when consumers move their mouses over the ads, small games, and other forms of multimedia advertising. In general, both customers and the Web sites that offer rich-media ads like them because consumers don't have to actually leave the site to interact with the banner, and *clickthrough* (which is when a consumer actually clicks on an ad to visit the Web site being advertised, instead of just viewing the ad but not going further) can be quite high.

✔ **Keyword advertising:** This Internet form is where you pay a search engine, directory, or some other Web site to have your ad or the link to your site pop up first when someone does a search on the keywords you buy. For example, if a consumer is searching for information on knitting, she may type "knitting" into an Internet search engine. Because your business is designer knitwear or knitting instruction (and you've paid that search engine for keyword advertising), your ad is among the first to appear to the customer.

✔ **Word-of-mouth advertising:** The Internet is also the perfect place to take advantage of this form of online advertising via message boards, online clubs, blogs, chat rooms, and the list goes on — and most of it is *free.*

These types of online advertising are just a few you should consider for your business. Spend some time surfing the Web to see what type of ads are being run by other companies that offer the same type of product or service as your business, and decide what works best for you (and your budget — don't forget the budget!). Don't be hesitant to think outside the box to see what other businesses that *don't* compete with yours are doing, because you may also want to borrow some of their approaches to Internet advertising! Flip to Chapters 6 and 12 for more information on advertising on the Internet.

Newspaper

In the area of print, you don't need to buy large ads in order to be noticed. Take a look at your daily paper and you can see that, in most cases, the smaller ads are placed at the top of each page — they sit atop the large space ads. The newspaper's layout department just does it this way, for some reason. Now, while I can't deny that the eye may be first drawn to the largest ads on a page, it stands to reason that if your message is clear enough, presented in a clever way, and positioned near the top of the page with a good headline and an eye-catching graphic element, you can get as good a response as the guy whose big, fat ad is sitting beneath yours and contains none of the above. See Chapters 7 and 13 for more information on advertising in print.

Radio

Advertising your business on the radio varies widely in price, depending on the time of day you want. For example, WXTU 92.5 country music in Philadelphia charges $425 for a mid-day ad but only $75 to $100 for an evening ad. So think carefully about when your target audience is most likely listening and what works best for your budget. Want to find out more? Check out Chapter 8.

One of the top-rated news- and talk-radio stations in the Bay Area sells prime-time ads (during the morning and evening commute) for prices in the $1,000- to $1,500-per-spot range, but its late night (midnight to 6:00 a.m.) ads can be had for as low as $100 a spot. I actually know of one local business that buys the late-night time slot on this station and pays for the commercials with $100 bills. The beleaguered station sales rep has to schlep over to his office to collect the money this guy pays in advance for whatever number of spots he can afford on any given week. This strategy may sound a bit hokey, but advertising on this station during the late-night time slots really works for this guy. He has a presence on a major station, which gives his business an aura of prestige, and he gets it on a surprisingly low budget. So, what is the moral of this little story? On radio, you don't need major ad bucks in order to sound like you do.

Another affordable way to buy radio is by taking advantage of the *package deal,* which includes a certain number of prime spots, a few mid-days, a few overnights, and a few *rotators* (spots that the station may run anywhere it likes). Radio stations usually tell you that they'll sell these packages to you for only "$50 a spot!" or whatever the amount — referred to as an *average spot cost.* And that's true if you look at the average cost of the ads when grouped together. But because you reach a lot more people during the morning commute than you can hope to reach at 3:00 a.m., an average spot cost isn't the best way to analyze the cost effectiveness of package deals. You're better off asking the station rep how many *gross impressions* the spots in the package will generate — that number tells you how many people will actually *hear* the ads, which in turn helps you decide whether the package is all that it's cracked up to be.

Cable TV

Cable television is an affordable media, but if you use it, you need to be diligent about a few details. Here are some questions you need to ask before you buy:

- ✔ On which of the cable channels will my spots run?
- ✔ At what times will the spots run on those channels?
- ✔ In which zones will my spots run?

Sound confusing? I can tell you how confusing it really is: Cable TV has been known to reduce a professional media buyer to tears. And a seasoned ad agency's accounts payable manager once said that he'd rather schedule a root canal than try to decipher a cable station's invoice. Here's why: Every cable company is selling ads on a hundred or more different channels; each channel is programmed to reach a separate and unique market segment and is broadcast into various zones within the overall coverage area. So, although eminently affordable, particularly at a paltry two bucks a spot in some cases, make sure you know precisely what you're buying. Chapters 9 and 15 explore cable TV in more detail.

Broadcast TV

TV advertising prices vary widely depending on the time of day. For example, at the time of this writing, Channel 6 (ABC/WPVI) in Philadelphia charges the following prices at different times of day:

- $1,000 for a 30-second commercial that runs during its weekday local news at 5 a.m.

- $1,400 for a 30-second commercial that runs during weekday local news at 12 noon

- $3,300 for a 30-second commercial that runs during weekday local news at 5 p.m.

- $5,000 for a 30-second commercial that runs during weekday local news at 6 p.m.

Of course, these prices vary from week to week and season to season. The total range of prices is anywhere from $500 to $50,000 — the high end being the price for a 30-second commercial during, say, the finale of a popular TV drama or national sporting event.

But broadcast television can be affordable in certain time slots. One chain of auto-repair shops for which I have done work buys one or two 30-second commercials daily on the early morning news show (6:00 a.m.) and the early fringe news program (5:00 p.m.) on the local ABC-TV station. Because he's on these local news shows every day, and because these shows are very reasonably priced, he has a substantial television presence (at least with the people who watch those shows) for less than $5,000 a month.

Late night, early morning, and even midday time slots may offer just the kind of programming that your target market views. And these time slots are priced within the budgets of most local advertisers (so *that's* why you see all those car dealer ads at those times).

National magazines

Yes, unbelievably, you can afford to buy ads in big-time magazines like *Time, Newsweek, Sports Illustrated,* and the like by buying advertising in what's called their *regional editions.* You can place your ad in one of these publications, or a predetermined group of publications that is sold as a package, for relatively small amounts because all the big magazines break down their circulation (and actual printing) into zones or regions. For instance, you can buy an ad for the circulation of the entire Bay Area, or break it down to just your city. Some magazines will also sell you a *cover wrap,* sort of like a book's dust jacket, which can be a fairly prestigious way to get the word out there!

Bottom line: Go bargain hunting

You want an advertising presence in media that gives you your best chance of attracting large numbers of customers. The various media options listed in this chapter are only a few of the many ways you can save money and still buy media that does you the most good. In Part III, I provide even more information on the various forms of media and how to buy them.

Concentrate your available dollars in good, solid media — even though you may not be able to afford to buy prime-time TV commercials or full-page magazine ads. Don't toss away your money on cockamamie "deals" offered to you by off-the-wall media that no one will pay attention to. In other words, don't buy a rotten egg when you can afford a lovely omelet.

Go bargain hunting. Your local media, even some of the national media, have some great deals.

Although magazine advertising is a rather dramatic vehicle for a local business to use, it doesn't cost nearly as much as you think. When you can buy a big-time publication that allows you to pay only for the area from which you can reasonably expect to attract business, you can afford to at least look like a major player. So, if you want to impress the neighbors and keep up with the Joneses, pop a full-page ad into *Time* magazine. That ought to get their attention! For more on national magazine ads, turn to Chapter 7.

Chapter 3

Boosting Your Budget with Co-Op Programs

In This Chapter

▶ Clearing up what co-op advertising funds are

▶ Finding suppliers who have funds you can use

▶ Being aware of the supplier's restrictions

▶ Applying for, and receiving, co-op money

Many suppliers, manufacturers, and distributors of various major products and goods have advertising money set aside for use by their retailers. These funds are called *cooperative advertising* (*co-op* for short). The term *cooperative* means just what it says: If you spend some money, the manufacturer will also spend some money — the two of you cooperate to get the advertising job done.

Although co-op advertising is sometimes very complicated, frustrating, confusing, and time-consuming, it's well worth the effort. Co-op funds are wonderful when you can add these extra dollars to your own advertising budget and use them to make a much bigger splash in your market. In this chapter, I give you the information you need to put co-op funds to work for you, demystifying this often-confusing part of the advertising arena.

Knowing Who Uses Co-Op Funds

Each week, you probably receive one or more multi-page, color brochures from your local supermarkets. These brochures are filled with this week's bombastic specials on everything from soft drinks to bathroom tissue, dog food to deodorant — and they usually contain coupons you can use when you shop at their stores. These newsprint brochures are almost entirely paid for with co-op funds provided to your local grocer by the companies that produce the dozens of items listed inside. Each of the manufacturers, suppliers, or distributors pays for the percentage of advertising space it receives in each brochure.

For instance, if the toilet paper company is getting one full page of a 20-page flyer, it tosses 5 percent of the total cost of the brochure into the pot. By advertising only those products that provide co-op funds, your grocer can, in theory, produce and distribute these weekly brochures without spending a dime of his own money.

Virtually any small business you can think of sells products for which co-op ad funds are available. If you're a store owner, look around *your* store, and you may be able to identify products from big-name manufacturers who, in all likelihood, have co-op or vendor dollars set aside to aid you in selling these items.

Many small businesses either don't know co-op money is available, or they find the thought of collecting the funds too daunting. For this reason, a lot of available cash is left on the table because small businesses often think they have better things to do than fill out forms and adhere to certain rules in order to collect a few extra bucks to throw at advertising. You can work this situation to your favor, however, by taking advantage of the money your competitors aren't seizing for themselves. Yes, it's work. But when you receive a nice check from one of your manufacturers, or some free goods, or a big discount off your next purchase, the extra work is well worth your time and trouble.

Supply and demand are *very* important things to remember when you're considering co-op funds. Here's an example for you to mull over: The manufacturers and distributors that supply the grocer provide a certain amount of co-op money based on the total amount of their products the grocer purchases. If the grocer buys 1,000 cases of creamed corn for a special price and then advertises "dramatic savings" on that merchandise in his weekly mailer, he may get $1,000 in extra co-op funds as part of his deal with the creamed corn supplier. And you can bet that the grocer won't buy 1,000 cases of any particular brand of creamed corn unless he also gets a boost of co-op money from the supplier to help him peddle it.

When you add up all the items advertised in these flyers, you can be sure that someone in the grocer's advertising department spent a heck of a lot of time finding and figuring out what money was available from which suppliers, and how to collect and spend it. A local chain of supermarkets for which I have done advertising work has a full-time employee who does nothing but handle co-op funds.

The grocery business is just one example of who takes advantage of co-op funds and what they must do to collect them. Many other businesses offer co-op funds. For example, when you walk into a bookstore and see certain books displayed prominently at the front of the store or on end-caps (the face-out display of books at the end of an aisle), you probably know those store owners or managers didn't feature those particular books simply because they enjoyed reading them. Instead, the publishers of the books on display *cooperated* with the store owners by spending money to advertise those books. And those promotions typically tie in to some theme or holiday, such as books by African-American authors during Black History Month (February), coffee-table books at the December holidays, or golf and other stereotypically "manly" pastimes around Father's Day.

And, of course, it's not just bookstores that do this: Hardware and home-improvement stores partner with the manufacturers of the tools and raw materials they sell, and even service businesses may be able to find companies that offer co-op funds available to them, if the service includes products available from other vendors. In other words, co-op opportunities are as diverse as the companies that offer it. But you can always find a catch — there's no such thing as a free lunch (free creamed corn, perhaps, but no free lunch). The retailer or small business (that's *you*) must adhere to certain rules and make certain purchases in order to qualify for and collect co-op money. But don't be dismayed — it's worth it! (For more on these qualifiers, check out the section "Understanding the Rules, Regulations, and Restrictions.")

Another form of cooperative funding is called *vendor money.* Vendor money is *in addition to* any of the manufacturer's co-op funds you may be entitled to. It's usually passed along to the squeakiest wheel — the clever retailer who knows it exists and has the cheek to go after it. Vendor money has no strings attached; you receive it either in the form of cash or as a discount on future purchases.

Finding Out Which of Your Suppliers Have Co-Op Funds Available

The suppliers of many of the products that you sell most likely have available advertising funds that they're happy to provide you — if you follow their sometimes convoluted rules and go to the trouble to ask for it.

For example, I have one client who told me that, in his first ten years in business, he never applied for co-op advertising funds because he didn't know they existed. Not a single manufacturer from whom he was buying merchandise had bothered to tell him they had co-op funds available to augment his very limited ad budget. So what's the moral to this story? If you want co-op funds, *you have to ask!*

Look at all the brands you're selling, read every factory invoice, calculate what you're spending with each of your suppliers, and go after them for ad bucks. Chances are, at least *some* of the companies who supply you with inventory have co-op or vendor dollars available. This section helps you get the co-op ball rolling.

Knowing who to talk to

Each of the vendors who sell to your store has assigned a sales representative to work with you. These people visit you on a regular basis — of course they do, they want to sell you stuff! These sales reps are a great place to start the process of finding co-op funds. Even though they may not be inclined to offer you information on co-op funds on their own (because of some bonus arrangement they may have with their employers), they can definitely tell you about them if you ask.

If you get a positive response from one or more of these sales reps, get the lowdown on how you can go about collecting some of this money. Ask what you need to do to qualify for funds, and what, if you do qualify, they require you to do in order to receive a check. If the manufacturer's rep tells you that no co-op funds are available to you, press the issue and ask whether vendor dollars are an option (which have no strings attached other than a few initial qualifiers).

You may also want to talk to the marketing and/or advertising managers of these suppliers. These people control the advertising funds (including co-op money), which means you can get your answer straight from the horse's mouth. If the marketing or advertising manager says that the company doesn't offer co-op funds, show how smart you are by asking for vendor dollars. This question definitely gets a marketing or advertising manager's attention because, chances are, he's never mentioned these available dollars to anyone.

If you're working with an ad agency, ask your agent what her experience is with businesses similar to yours, and where these other businesses may have found co-op money. Agency people know where the bodies are buried, as they say in the ad biz. I even know of one group of radio stations in my area that has a co-op department for the express purpose of helping its direct advertisers find money they may not otherwise have known was available to them. (Of course, the radio stations benefit from this found money, too, because the companies spend that money advertising on their radio stations.)

One way or another, ask as many people as you can think of within the various companies you deal with about co-op funds. Unless you're selling something obscure like arts and crafts made by individuals, you're likely to find some hidden money somewhere.

You've found your funds, now how do you get the dough?

After you've located the funds you need, you must run an obstacle course on your way to collecting them, providing all the proof the vendor requires that you actually ran the ads (see the section "Understanding the Rules, Regulations, and Restrictions" in this chapter). Then, and only then, will you receive your co-op funds in some form or another.

Suppliers can pay co-op funds in strange and unusual ways, including, but not limited to:

- ✔ Cash reimbursement
- ✔ Additional merchandise
- ✔ Discounts off future merchandise purchases

No matter what form of co-op payment you receive from any given supplier, always keep one thing in mind: It's found money — money you wouldn't otherwise have if you hadn't gone to the trouble to ask for and earn it.

Understanding the Rules, Regulations, and Restrictions

Each of your suppliers has a unique set of rules to which you must adhere in order to collect even a dime of co-op funds from them. The rules and restrictions set up within co-op programs can be so complicated that you may wonder whether these suppliers want anyone to even *try* to collect. But even though the restrictions can be a bit off-putting, if you follow the rules to the letter, your suppliers will reward you with either some extra cash to invest in advertising or some additional merchandise with which you can make a big, fat profit. All in all, the pain is worth the gain.

If you work with an ad agency, it may be able to help you navigate the rules and regulations. For example, my agency deals with several clients who count on co-op advertising funds to either augment or completely provide their advertising budgets. Because these accounts have hired my agency, we do all the work of collecting the funds for them. It's one of the services we provide, and we do it month after month for multiple accounts (each with different rules of collection). Collecting co-op funds can be time-consuming, but if you know the rules and follow them, you can do it without much trouble.

When you're working on your own, without an agency, you need to do the legwork yourself. In the following sections, I walk you through the process of using co-op funds — and collecting your money.

Co-op funds may be earned (and accrued) over a specific period of time and carry with them a deadline for use. This deadline is known as "Use it or lose it." Make sure you find out about any deadlines imposed by manufacturers on the use of their available co-op advertising funds, and be sure to spend the money before it disappears.

Getting your ads preapproved

Manufacturers don't just hand out co-op money as if it were candy. You can contact a manufacturer about a potential co-op ad campaign, or a manufacturer may contact you and suggest one. But before you can begin to spend any co-op money (no matter whose idea it was), you must get your ads preapproved by the manufacturer you're working with.

Suppose you own a paint store. One of your major manufacturers has told you that it will co-op an advertising campaign to sell 1,000 gallons of Putrid Peach paint it has lying around. Your supplier tells you that, if you contribute some of your ad bucks (you pick the amount you think you'll need to dispose of this paint within a reasonable amount of time), it'll match you 100 percent up to $5,000. Your total ad budget could, therefore, be $10,000 — more than enough to buy some local radio time and a couple of big ads in the newspaper.

Your next step is to get your ads preapproved by the manufacturer. In most cases, your supplier requires you to have all your advertising preapproved by the factory to make sure it adheres to the manufacturer's co-op guidelines. Your supplier may have an approval form for you to fill out. Along with this completed form, you must submit copies of radio scripts, a CD or MP3 file of the final produced commercial(s), and at least a rough layout (plus a copy of the final, finished copy) for your newspaper ads. (Be sure to ask what your manufacturer requires for various mediums.) Then the manufacturer's advertising or marketing department either sends you a stamped approval as is or advises you to make certain changes. The department may also simply advise you of the required changes and stamp and sign the approval "Approved with changes." Be sure to follow the manufacturer's co-op rules and guidelines carefully, making whatever changes they request.

Never run co-op advertising without first obtaining signed preapproval from the supplier.

Obtaining proof of performance

After you've made the manufacturer's requested changes to your ads (if there were any), you need to make sure to get what's called *proof of performance* from the media, which is really just verification that you ran the ads as you said you would.

To return to the paint store example from the preceding section, when you buy your ads from the radio station, advise them that you're using co-op funds (they usually know precisely what information you need). Make sure you receive the following verifications and co-op information with the station's invoices:

- ✔ **A notarized copy of your finished script listing the number of spots run and the total dollar amount those spots represented in your total media buy.** If you're using more than one script, each script needs to be notarized with the above information.

- ✔ **A notarized or certified invoice listing the run times of each spot, the title of the script for each spot, and the total dollar amount of the buy.**

Advise the newspaper how many *tear sheets* you need to provide for the manufacturer (tear sheets are copies of the actual printed page on which your ad appeared — the manufacturer lets you know how many you need to provide as proof of performance). The newspaper provides those tear sheets along with its notarized total invoice. (For more on newspaper ads, check out Chapter 7.)

The media you're working with should know what your manufacturer needs as proof, but if not, be sure to ask the manufacturer. The proof of performance looks different for every medium.

Advertising cooperatives: Not the same as co-op funds

Advertising cooperatives are a different beast altogether. Unlike co-op funds, advertising cooperatives *cost* you money. But it may be the best money you ever spend, because you enjoy high-quality production and your fair share of the clout of a substantial combined media budget.

Advertising cooperatives (also known as *dealer ad groups*) are common in the franchising business and the automotive business. The franchise business discovered a long time ago that it can do a much better job at advertising if it asked each of its franchisees to pony up a percentage of gross sales, which then goes into a "war chest" where it accumulates until enough cash is available to do a large-scale media buy

for all the franchises together. An individual store can't hope to do advertising on a scale to match the combined budgets of many stores. Strength in numbers is the name of the game.

The advertising cooperative also uses its money to employ the services of an ad agency that produces top-quality TV, radio, and print advertising, as well as in-store, point-of-purchase display materials, and, in the case of food franchises, menus, banners, bags, and so on. If you're in a business that can take advantage of the media buying power and quality production provided by an advertising cooperative, be sure to get involved. Your business will most likely benefit.

Submitting your co-op claims package

After your ads have run and your campaign is attracting customers in droves, all you need to do is submit your co-op claims package. Your package includes your preapproval form, your proofs of performance, and a written request for reimbursement of the promised percentage of the campaign.

Continuing with the paint store example from the beginning of this section, imagine that you've made the requested changes, the ads run, the campaign is a success, and hundreds of people with questionable color sense fight their way through your doors. The Putrid Peach paint is history. Now you just submit the entire package — the signed preapproval form, the notarized media invoices, the notarized radio scripts, the CD or MP3 file of the finished radio spots, and the newspaper tear sheets — to your supplier along with your written request for reimbursement.

There. Wasn't that simple? Now all you need to do is wait for the co-op check to arrive in the mail. And, what's the bonus to all of this hoopla? You got rid of that disgusting paint color!

Chapter 4

Defining and Positioning Your Message

In This Chapter

▶ Knowing what customers want in your business, product, or service — and providing it

▶ Pinpointing what you want to say

▶ Devising a campaign that knocks their socks off

*W*ith a limited advertising budget, your product, service, or company name isn't on the tip of the national tongue, nor are people from New York to Los Angeles whistling your jingle. But you can define your strengths and position your advertising message in such a way that you give yourself the best possible chance for success. And with 50 percent of all new businesses going under within the first two years, you want to do everything you can to improve these rather daunting odds for your business.

When you first opened your business, you probably felt confident in doing so because you were convinced you could provide better service, a more unique line of products, and more creative solutions to consumers' problems than they could find anywhere else. You found an attractive, convenient location; stocked up on really cool merchandise or offered a really distinctive service; expanded your business hours for better customer convenience; and have been enjoying at least the first blush of the success that usually follows a well-thought-out business plan. To paraphrase mass-production genius Henry Kaiser (whose ship-building division, during World War II, built one new Liberty Ship every day), "You found a need and filled it." But now you need to take it one step further with an advertising campaign that brings in more customers, adds more dollars to your bottom line, and validates all the reasons you went into business in the first place.

In this chapter, I fill you in on a few of the key factors that customers use when they choose one business over another — factors you want to keep in mind when you come up with ways to advertise your business's strengths. Then I walk you through the process of positioning your message, where you let your customers know exactly why they should buy from you. Finally, I end the chapter by outlining the basics of coming up with an effective ad campaign, using a real-life example from my own business as a guide.

Understanding Why People Choose One Product or Service over Another

As you devise your positioning strategy and, ultimately, your advertising message, you need to keep in mind why people choose one product or service over another. That way, you can help to ensure that they choose *your* product or service over your competition's. In the following sections, I cover some of the main reasons people choose one product (or service or company or store) over another.

Image is everything

People drive or walk long distances past one fast-food restaurant, service station, doughnut store, or hair salon in order to patronize another because the image of the store they seek out is more in tune with their own tastes and desires. Image, as they say, is everything.

When it comes to image, peer pressure (or what you think the rest of the world is doing) also comes into play. People want to project the right image, and often, they do that by choosing the product, service, or store that they think helps them do so. For example, if dozens of people are working out at one particular gym in town, their friends may also try that gym because "everyone else is doing it." Price, quality, convenience, and many other factors come into play, but if that gym's image is the one that the customers can best identify with, then it most certainly gets the most business.

Your business's good reputation for customer service, fair value, good prices, and after-sale concern and care also goes a long way toward ensuring your success. If you can honestly say that you provide the very best of any of these virtues, broadcast it widely.

You've got personality!

Customers often choose one business over another based on the personality of the business. And that, of course, begins with you and the people who work for you. For example, I've become a regular at a very good Italian restaurant in my hometown for the simple reason that the personality of the place (and of the people who work there) suits me to a T. It has just the right combination of location, ambience, menu choices, and friendly, caring management and staff to have won my undying loyalty.

A half-dozen outstanding Italian restaurants are all within a six-block walk of the one I frequent, and my wife and I have tried them all. But we visit the same one quite often because, from the moment we walk through the door until we waddle out a few hours later, each employee treats us like visiting royalty, whose continued satisfaction and patronage is a very high priority. Everyone, from the bartender to the waiter to the busboy, makes us feel not only welcome, but at home.

So if you own a restaurant and want to advertise your establishment's unique personality, you can use a headline such as, "Like having dinner at Mama's, but without all the kids." If you're a car dealer and want to tell your customers that they can find something unusual during their service appointment, you can say, "Put your feet up, have a cup of gourmet coffee, catch up on the soaps, and relax in our customer lounge." In other words, if you truly believe that your business has a sparkling personality and offers certain benefits that customers can't find elsewhere, then find a creative way to use these strengths in your advertising. Then be sure you deliver on the promise after the customers arrive. Don't call attention to something that isn't really there, something that you don't — or can't — really offer.

Convenience: More than location

The top three factors in getting rich on real estate are: location, location, location. The same may be true of your store or business. Convenience can be a huge incentive to customers. But when I say *convenience,* I'm not just talking about location. Convenience may be ample free parking within a few feet of your door, or easy freeway access, or a well-thought-out store design so your customers can get in and out quickly, or a store policy of always helping customers load merchandise into their cars, or a service policy of always delivering on time.

If you do have a convenient, available location with great parking and a bright and cheerful ambience, easy access, an easy store layout, or any number of conveniences that customers find attractive, include this information in your advertising message. Convenience is also a very simple and effective way to differentiate your store from other, less-convenient, less-attractive stores.

For example, when I need hardware items, I patronize a small local store, instead of one of those big discount warehouses, because of the convenience factor. The store is small (it would fit into one corner of one of the large chain stores, and you'd never even know it was there) so I can quickly find what I need and be on my way. It also has a large parking lot right outside its back door. I know I could save a lot of money if I went to the chain stores, but I'm willing to pay for the convenience of the mom-and-pop.

If I were the owner of this small hardware store, I'd advertise with messages such as, "Park within 20 feet of our door. You may pay a few pennies more for nails, but think of the money you'll save on shoe leather!" Or, "Is saving a nickel on nails worth getting hammered in a parking lot?" Or, "Drive for miles, search three acres for a parking place, get lost in a huge labyrinth, save 50 cents. Can we talk?"

Similarly, if I owned a service business, such as a car and limo service, I'd advertise with a message such as, "Don't stress about getting to the airport on time — call us instead! We'll pick you up on time and get you to where you're going, in the comfort of one of our luxury cars, driven by our safe and professional drivers."

Don't sacrifice service!

Service, in my estimation, is the most overused and under-delivered promise made in advertising today. Just about every business claims to deliver the very best in "service," or "customer service," or "customer care," but in reality, hardly any business actually does provide great service. Most market research shows that what customers want *most* from their bank, supermarket, dry cleaner, car dealer, shoe repair shop, accountant, or whatever, is good, old-fashioned service. All businesses know this, but most businesses seem totally incapable of delivering it.

My agency handles a local Audi dealer that lives and dies by the results of factory-sponsored telephone surveys it does following every new car sale and every service appointment. The results of these customer satisfaction surveys go a long way in determining this car dealer's relationship with the factory and with how many cars it allots him each month. He ranks very highly in his survey results, and we advertise the fact that his dealership is top-rated in customer service. And this advertising focus on service (as well as fair pricing and a wide choice of inventory) is obviously working — this dealer, located in San Jose, California, sells so many new Audi cars that he's now number two in the nation.

If you use service as a reason for customers to try you out, then you'd better deliver the goods. If you can't service your customers in an efficient, courteous, timely manner, or deliver, replace, or repair what you promised when you promised it, then don't tell customers you can. *Don't make any promises you can't keep,* because people will soon see through you and your promises like a piece of cellophane.

Let 'em know your uniqueness

A certain way to attract customers (more certain than anything else I know) is to offer something they can't get anywhere else. If you've stocked your store with creative, hard-to-find items that other stores simply don't carry, then you are way ahead of the game. If your doughnut store can state for certain that your doughnut holes are smaller (and, therefore, your doughnuts are more substantial) than a doughnut junkie can hope to find elsewhere, then *that* is your message. If you carry truly unique greeting cards in your stationery store, cards that aren't available anywhere except at your location, then people looking for such an item are sure to respond.

Of course, if you're selling the idea that your business is unique, you need to work overtime to assure that it remains so. Do you remember when Starbucks was the only place where you could get gourmet coffees? It didn't take long for hundreds of imitators to come along and make the same claim. If you're successful in positioning yourself as totally unique, you can be sure that others will copy you — and you'll have to continually reinvent yourself to stay ahead of the competition.

The price is right

In some (but not all) cases, advertising the *manufacturer's suggested retail price* (that's the MSRP you hear about on car commercials all the time) is helpful. In the automobile example, where a dealer typically sells cars for *less* than the MSRP, the dealer looks very good. But in the case of a candy bar, for example, where the MSRP is 50 cents, but the big chain stores sell it for 40 cents, and the airport gift shop sells it for a dollar, you find customers scratching their heads and wondering what the heck the *real* price is on this candy.

Be very careful when using price or terms as reasons for customers to visit your store. When you advertise price, you run the risk of getting caught in what I call the *price trap*. If you're only selling price, you have to continue to lower that price — or come up with even better terms — on an ongoing basis in order to continue to attract new customers.

For example, the cell phone business has fallen into the price trap. When you look in the newspaper, you may have a tough time choosing a wireless phone company or deciphering the best available bargain because you have to sift through the various stores' offers of free minutes, free phones, free long-distance, free mobile-to-mobile calling, and any number of price and terms offers. And all of these stores have to continually create new and better offers in order to compete.

You can't be all things to all people

As you define and position your advertising message, be careful not to over-promise. Promising a level of service you can't deliver, or a convenient location that isn't, or low prices when yours aren't really all that low, can be a deadly mistake. Be honest with yourself about what is really unique and desirable about your store or business, and then be honest when you start making claims about it.

On the other hand, don't panic because you can't deliver the very best of *everything*. Maybe your prices really aren't any cheaper than those of your competition, but your business is located so conveniently, or has such a great ambience and personality, or carries such a unique inventory, that you're confident people only have to try you once in order to become loyal, happy regulars. If that's the case, then when you're designing your ads, don't make up false benefits based on price — position your message to exploit your strengths, namely that perfect location with all that free parking and all the friendly, cheerful faces waiting inside. *Remember:* One good promise on which you can truly deliver is better than trying to be all things to all people.

Researching and Assessing Your Competition: What Sets Your Product Apart?

Creating an ad campaign is a big step that can cost you some serious money, so it deserves some very careful planning. Before you get into the actual process of designing your advertising campaign, however, you need to identify and promote the specifics that make your product or service unique, known in the ad world as your *unique selling proposition* (USP).

Your advertising should never speak in generalities. Including just your business's name, location, and all the wonderful things you're selling isn't enough. You need to give the consumer a very good reason — or better yet, *several* good reasons — to visit you. You do this by first identifying your distinctive strengths and then calling attention to those strengths in your ads. This process is called *positioning your message.*

Determining the key reasons why consumers drive (or surf, if you're online) right on past other stores, that may sell the same merchandise as you do, in order to seek out *your* store is the first step in identifying your USP and positioning your message. You need to convince consumers that your store or business is the smartest, best, most-logical place that they can ever hope to buy that merchandise or service. After you identify these keys, focus in on them as the basis for your creative advertising message — in other words, promote and publicize your strengths.

A unique selling proposition successfully exploited

One of my agency's clients owns a chain of furniture stores. These stores aren't your everyday, garden-variety furniture stores featuring living room, bedroom, and family room items. Oh no, they are some of the only stores in the entire San Francisco Bay Area that carry a huge inventory of hard-to-find dinette sets and bar stools. Although most furniture stores carry *some* of these items (usually hidden way back in the corner of the showroom), this guy has hundreds of styles of dinettes and a huge inventory of hard-to-find bar stools and home bars. His showrooms are cavernous, and when he has a floor sample clearance sale (which he runs twice yearly), customers beat down his doors. His repeat business percentage is astounding, thanks to his complete dedication to customer service.

His advertising hits hard at what he calls *casual dining furniture,* which he has available in more styles than a customer could possibly find at any other store, and in price ranges to suit any budget. In fact, casual dining furniture is all he does. And he originally opened his stores with this limited, but unique inventory in mind. So he uses this unique selling proposition in his advertising with great success. This guy truly does have something unique to sell, which makes writing his ads all the easier.

A good way to start the process of advertising your strengths is to let your mind wander backward to recapture all the reasons you were convinced that your business would succeed in first place. Ask yourself the following questions:

- ✔ What makes your company special?
- ✔ What is unique about your inventory (if your business is a store or you're selling products)?
- ✔ What service do you provide that clients can't find elsewhere?
- ✔ Are your business hours more expanded than the competition's?
- ✔ Is your location easier to find? More convenient? With better parking? Or, do you pick up and deliver directly to your customers?

If you can remember what it was that originally motivated you to start your business, you're halfway home in identifying what motivates customers to seek you out. The same reasons you were enthusiastic enough about your business plan to take the entrepreneurial plunge translate nicely into a creative concept and motivational copy that drives customers to your business (turn to Part II for more information on how to do this in each ad medium).

Don't confuse your potential customers with too much information — inform them with a well-conceived, creatively executed, and carefully positioned message. Don't try to sell everything you have in the store (or every service you offer) in a single ad. Doing so only causes sensory overload. Zero in on one or two important, relevant items so your customers have a prayer of understanding your message.

You want to position your message keeping in mind not only your business's strengths, but also your primary market (in other words, the people who are most likely to buy your product). When you take both of these important factors into consideration, you not only position the resulting message, but you also target it — like a bull's-eye, so you can then take your best shot.

Developing a Strategy for Your Advertising Campaign

After you've identified the many good reasons people would be foolish *not* to shop at your store, or to utilize the unique services you provide, and assuming you know your market and to whom you want to sell, you're ready to move forward with planning your ad campaign. You know why you're selling what you're selling, you know whom you're selling to, and you're now armed with the information you need to create wonderful and memorable ads. This is the fun part.

Of course, it's fantastic if you can run a sustained radio and TV campaign; buy flashy, full-page print ads; slap your message up on dozens of billboards and buses; and do a major-league mailing to every zip code within a mile of your store, all at the same time. But that kind of ad campaign — one that covers all the bases — is very costly. Assuming you *don't* have unlimited advertising funds, you need to get a bit more creative with your message and your spending. And that process begins with two questions:

- ✔ What can you afford?
- ✔ What media best targets your primary market segment?

Regardless of how much you spend or where you spend it, you need to make sure *your* ads cut through the clutter of advertising messages that bombard your customers every day. Focus your message in a clear and creative way so that your ads attract the attention of, and motivate the largest possible number of, your primary market.

For example, if your business is a boutique selling women's clothes, cosmetics, or jewelry, and you're targeting women between the ages of 25 and 54, you want to write and design your ads using words, phrases, and graphics that appeal mostly to them — for example:

✔ Use words like *savings, sale,* and *free.*

✔ Include phrases like "New fall colors and styles," "Free gift with every purchase," "Buy one, get one free," and "Hurry in today for best selection."

✔ Add graphics to print ads and mailers to illustrate in a clean, uncluttered fashion what you're selling.

You also want to place your ads with media that give you the best chance at reaching these women in quantity. For example, if you're buying radio time, select those stations that can prove to you that its audience composition is heavy on your primary demo (women between the ages of 25 and 54). Obviously, running your spots on a teeny-bopper station that plays only teen-pop icons isn't wise (regardless of what the radio time salesperson tells you about the station's audience composition). For print, place your ads in the newspaper's main news, local news, entertainment, gardening, and society sections. You may not want to place your print ads for this market in the sports section of the paper. (Yes, women read the sports pages, but not in the numbers that men do.)

Above all, no matter who your audience is, you want to include in your ads enough creativity and content so your ads are not only heard and seen, but also understood and remembered. And *where* you place your ads is every bit as important as *what you say* in them.

Case Study: Advertising a Chain of Women's Plus-Size Clothing Stores

Using the target demo of women in the 25 to 54 age bracket (from the previous section) as an example, here's how I went about designing and executing an ad campaign for a northern California chain of women's stores. My client's product was plus-size clothing, which, of course, is very visual — a customer needs to see it in order to get interested in it. And stylish, attractive clothing in plus-sizes is often hard to find. So I leaned toward TV as the primary media to buy right away. I also figured that, when the stores had specific sales, I would add newspaper ads, but primarily to advertise price. The television ads would establish the store name in the minds of the store's target audience, and the newspaper ads — when they had really great markdowns and discounts to advertise — would serve them well in augmenting the TV spots.

Although this client did have a dozen stores throughout the area, he didn't have a budget substantial enough to be on the air or in the paper every day. So, when designing the campaign, I had to consider that each of the spots would need to include all the relevant information a customer needs about the stores. In other words, he couldn't do what the major clothing chains do — namely, use a spot showing all the hot new fashions and end the spot with just a logo and company slogan, assuming that everyone already knows his stores and where they are. I had to pretty much start from scratch and do the whole sales pitch within each commercial. Each commercial needed to stand on its own.

What my agency did to sell women's specialty fashions on a budget is what you need to do — sit down and plan your work, and then work your plan. It's a step-by-step process that, when done right, usually produces excellent results. I cover the steps of this approach and how we followed them in the following sections.

Identifying the USP: The unique selling proposition

We began with the product (women's specialty clothing) and the primary target market (plus-size women between the ages of 25 and 54). This type of clothing is sometimes difficult to find in the latest colors, patterns, and styles, but our client's stores offered an enormous inventory of flattering, complimentary, up-to-date fashions in all varieties and in special sizes — that's its USP. After all, plenty of stores sell specialty clothing for women in smaller sizes and, well, ordinary clothing in plus sizes, but not many stores sell specialty clothing in plus sizes. This factor is what was unique about this store, and we wanted to emphasize that in the ad campaign.

Moreover, the market for these fashions is substantial; it was really just a matter of reaching the primary audience in sizeable numbers with a message that was relevant, informative, and creatively presented. These stores truly had what plus-size women were looking for; our job was simply to get the news out there.

Knowing the budget — and staying within its limits

After we had identified the unique selling proposition, we added into the equation the advertising budget, which, when compared to major clothing chains, was extremely limited. However, knowing that these fashions didn't necessarily change with every season, we came up with some very visual, relatively inexpensive, TV spots that we could then run in *flights* (time segments) over a period of several years. Our *production costs* (the actual cost of filming and editing the commercials) were modest in comparison to the quality of the final product, because we were willing to travel a few hundred miles in order to employ the services of a not-so-big-time, but extremely talented, film company. And we also hired a wonderful group of plus-size models who worked on a *buy-out basis* (with no residual payments, just a one-time fee). It was a successful example of what you can do with just a bit of planning and a dab of creativity.

Shooting the ads

For this campaign, I wrote several TV spots with an eye toward relatively inexpensive production, hired some professional models, employed the services of a truly remarkable film company in Sacramento, California, scouted some locations, and headed to the state capitol to shoot some spots.

My agency produced three 30-second spots for under $20,000 (although this figure may sound expensive, the client ran these same three spots for several years, so they ended up being rather cheap). Then we put them on various TV stations in *flights*. (*Flighting* is an ad-biz term that means, for instance, buying advertising for two weeks at a time, then going off the air for two weeks, then back on the air, and so forth.) The spots showed the models wearing various dresses and separates and wandering around beautiful locations such as the mall, the zoo, and the park. We shot everything outside on location (as opposed to in a studio) with 35-millimeter film, and the footage was simply gorgeous.

The clothing this chain sold was very stylish and very unique, and the commercials showed the merchandise beautifully. Because this clothing was hard-to-find, and because the commercials did such an excellent job of simply showing a wide variety of styles, the campaign was a very successful one that we brought back, as though it were brand-new, about twice a year. And I enjoyed a good relationship with the store owner until he finally decided to retire.

Selecting the right media

We had created some wonderful television commercials showing our beautiful fashions, and we needed to place those spots into TV programming that would not only reach our primary demographic, but also would be affordable within a limited media budget. Notice I said, *TV programming*, not *stations*.

How many times do you grab the remote and click to other stations while you're watching TV? You bounce all over the dial looking for programming that appeals to you, don't you? You don't stay with one channel all day and night out of loyalty (as you may do with radio). With that in mind, remember this: When you're buying television advertising time, don't buy the channel, buy the *programming*.

We placed our ads on programs — affordable programs — that attracted women in large numbers: soaps, afternoon talk shows, early-morning and afternoon news, game shows, and so on. Local and regional advertisers can usually afford to buy advertising on these shows, whereas the prime-time stuff is often out of reach of most small business's budgets (although some highly successful and well-watched game shows are affordable when combined with a broader schedule that includes less desirable programming).

Applying these ideas to your ad campaign

These same rules (listed in the previous sections) apply to any and all products or services. So, whether you're selling hardware or fast food, cars or doughnuts, ceiling fans or fashions, or whether you're providing tax-preparation services, home-improvement help, or computer troubleshooting, follow these guidelines as you begin to design your advertising.

Look hard at what it is you're selling and to whom you're trying to sell it. Identify and hammer home what makes your product or service unique, different from all your competition. Then, in the most creative, hard-hitting way you can devise, create your ads to focus attention on your unique product difference. Then you only need to place those ads in media that can bring you the greatest return on your investment, media that reaches large numbers of your primary target demographic. It sounds simple, right? And it is. This ain't rocket science . . . it's advertising, and you can do it just like anybody else.

Chapter 5

Forming an Effective Ad Campaign

. . . .

In This Chapter

▶ Zeroing in on your target market

▶ Observing the work of your competition

▶ Learning from ads that you respond to most

▶ Developing a creative hook to seize your market

▶ Molding your campaign around your message

. . . .

*W*hether your advertising budget is a million dollars a month or only a thousand dollars a year, you'll waste that money if your ads aren't effective. What makes ads effective? A combination of content and creativity. Your ads need to give the consumer a good reason to act (the content), and they have to be unique enough in their design and copy to attract the consumer's attention in the first place (the creativity). Countless forms of media expose consumers to so much advertising on a daily basis — some of it so subtle that consumers don't even know they're absorbing it — that generating advertising for your business is a real challenge. However, your task isn't impossible — it just takes some serious thought. More serious than, say, clear soda or Internet pop-ups.

Consumers constantly see and hear bad advertising that's unclear in its message, confusing in its content, and just plain aggravating in its production. On the other hand, many forms of media expose them to some truly great advertising that includes memorable graphics, killer copy delivered in a clear, concise manner, and fresh, new creative hooks.

The good news is that you don't need a huge ad budget in order to create effective ads. Truly superior advertising is created every day, and much of it on a budget. Sadly, in many cases, the people doing the bad advertising are spending the most money.

You don't have to create the next great advertising slogan — "Just do it" or "With a name like Smucker's, it has to be good"— to get people to buy your product, use your service, or come to your store. You just have to display a bit more creativity than the other guys and devise a compelling message so people choose you over your competition.

No matter your budget, audience, or vision, you can do good advertising, and in this chapter, I show you how. I explain how you should hone in on and find out as much as possible about your *target audience* — that's marketing-speak for the people you most want to attract as customers. I also advise getting to know your competition — especially their advertising — so you can differentiate yours from theirs. Finally, I describe what a creative hook is and how to develop that creative hook in all your advertising, whether you're doing TV commercials, radio spots, Internet banners, outdoor ads, or newspaper or magazine ads.

Identifying and Targeting Your Audience

To begin the creative process of finding your one-of-a-kind message, ask yourself a few simple questions:

✔ **What are you selling, and what makes it so unique?**

For example, if you need to sell kids toys, what makes your merchandise different from what people can buy from other big retail chains? Are the toys handmade, imported from other countries, or vintage?

✔ **To whom do you want to sell it?**

In other words, who exactly are you targeting as your ideal consumer? Parents, of course, but what type of parent? Do you want to target wealthy, upscale parents, who are most interested in educational games that will help their kids learn, for example? You may also think about marketing to aunts, uncles, and grandparents, who often want to spend more on their nieces, nephews, and grandchildren than the parents do.

✔ **Why should people buy the product or service from you?**

Are you open very late at night so that parents who work long hours can drop by your store? Do you offer free delivery of large items so that walk-in customers don't have to lug your product home? Are you (and your staff) especially knowledgeable and approachable about suggesting great toys for different age groups?

These questions prove useful whether you're selling toys or computer repair. (Flip to the section "Concocting a Creative Hook to Get Your Audience's Attention" for a detailed example of the process of identifying and targeting your audience.) When you have the answers to these questions, you should do two things: Focus on your primary market and do your research.

Focus on your primary market

Many business owners fall into the trap of believing that their products or services are "for everyone"— that is, anyone would be interested in or need the products. After all, if you have kids, you need toys and kids' clothes, right? If you have a car, you need workers to service it. And if you don't want to prepare your own tax return, you need a tax whiz to do it for you. So, why do the businesses that sell these products or services need to identify primary markets?

The answer is that, even if your business appeals to a broad market of diverse consumers, you need to identify who your *ideal* consumer is. If you're selling expensive toys, for example, your primary market is wealthy parents (even though, theoretically, any parent can save up to buy a special gift). If you're in the car repair business, you want to focus not only on what you do *best,* but also on what segment of the market needs your business *most* (not to mention what may be the most lucrative). For example, if you're the only business in town that knows how to repair foreign sports cars, and you happen to live in a city or neighborhood that houses plenty of these, your primary market should be foreign car owners. That's not to say that you'll turn away the driver of the Volkswagen if he needs a new transmission; the Jaguar owner just needs your expertise more.

After you've identified your primary market, your advertising should match that focus (see the section "Concocting a Creative Hook to Get Your Audience's Attention").

Research your market

Knowing your target audience is critical: Your ads won't work if they don't appeal to what your potential customers want or need. Research and find out as much as possible about the people you want to sell to. For example, if you run an independent bookstore (remember those?), it's easier to sell books, magazines, and newspapers to people who already read voraciously, so you need to find those folks and figure out as much as you can about their reading habits and preferences. If you're selling running shoes, find out who the avid athletes are in your community and how old they are, how often they run, where they work out, who they listen to for advice on running gear, and what they're not getting from competing shoe stores.

Your market research can take many forms. If you oversee the advertising for a new business (or you want to go after a new type of consumer for your business), you can start by checking out some basic demographic information. The best research comes from primary sources — in other words, you should call around for information. For example, if your business is foreign-car repair, you should find out how many foreign cars are in your city or community. The simplest way to find out is to check the Yellow Pages for dealerships that *sell* foreign cars. Call those dealers and ask for information. Let them know that you're not interested in competing with them; you just want to offer a service. They may be more than willing to give you the information you want and to refer business to you.

Of course, you should first make sure that companies you call don't offer similar services, because then you would be competing with them!

You may also be able to find information in publications, which may track demographics, sales information, trends in your industry, and other useful consumer information. For example, an auto publication may track the number of Jaguars sold in the United States and in specific regions or cities.

Finally, you can get some useful information from your potential customers, especially those in your primary target market — that is, the people you most want to buy from you. Conduct an informal poll by asking potential customers what they're looking for that other businesses don't provide. In the foreign-car example, you would contact people you know who own Jaguars or Mercedes and ask them what type of service and price they're interested in. Similarly, if you're opening a toy store, ask parents where they shop and why, and find out what products, services, or price levels they *wish* they could find at the stores they shop. You want to differentiate your business from your competition (in a good way) by targeting customer needs and attracting business! (See the following section for more on separating your business from the competition.)

Checking Out Your Competition's Ads so You Can Differentiate Yours

Before you develop your own ad campaign (you start the tangible process in the section "Concocting a Creative Hook to Get Your Audience's Attention"), you should look at what your competition is already doing. You can learn so much about your business and the market from your competition. Your goal isn't to be an Ad Thief; you want to determine how your business is different and what you can offer and advertise to compete effectively with other players in your business.

For example, suppose your business is a garden center. You're probably not the first garden center to open in your community, so you should check out how the other centers are advertising what they do best. (If you're the first center, you should start with the research I outline in the previous section.)

You may find that one of your competitors advertises "Colorful Garden Ideas" and that its garden center is "The place to shop for all your gardening needs!" (See Part II for different ways to get your message out.) Those ad headlines tell you that the business is focusing on a broad selection of products, which is fine; many gardeners will certainly be looking for a broad selection.

But maybe the strongest selling point of your business is that "You provide helpful, friendly advice from knowledgeable, experienced gardeners!" Your pitch will certainly appeal to many customers who have bought beautiful plants or seedlings in the past, only to see them wither and die. In analyzing how you differ from the competition, you've identified your primary market (see the section "Focus on your primary market"): people who want to have a garden but don't know how to buy what's best for their locations, light sources, and the soil on their property. The helpful, friendly advice from knowledgeable, experienced gardeners is really what you're selling; it separates your business from your competition.

To figure out how to transfer your knowledge of your target market into a successful ad campaign, check out the section "Concocting a Creative Hook to Get Your Audience's Attention."

Focusing on Ads That You Respond to Most

After you've researched your target market, analyzed your competition, and found out how your business differs (from preceding section), you should also review ads from other businesses (not in your industry) that appeal to you. Looking at other businesses' ads can help get your creative juices flowing, so you can start developing ads for your business that will hopefully appeal to your prospective customers.

Great advertising ideas are all around you, from the funny to the heart warming. Even though a magazine ad, newspaper ad, Internet ad, or radio or television commercial features a product, service, or business that's nothing like yours (see Part II for discussions on advertising within these forms of media), you can still get creative ideas from what you respond to.

I have the strongest response to ads that use humor. The humor appeals to me, so I pay attention to what products the companies are advertising. And if I'm in the market for such products, I'll be more likely to remember the ads because of the humor.

Hooking customers with humor

Here are some of my favorite recent ads from the world of television. I remember these products because of the humor involved, which is the goal of all funny ads:

✔ Nextel's commercial that shows two corporate guys in suits dancing to funky music on a tape player. A colleague interrupts them angrily, demanding to know the status of the company's shipments; the guys stop dancing, get the info via their technology, and resume dancing as soon as they've placated their colleague.

✔ The sock puppet for Pets.com. The sock puppet was the most popular purchase from this ill-fated Web site, which went out of business quickly because consumers weren't interested in buying pet food and supplies over the Internet. (The makers of the site obviously didn't research their market; see the section "Research your market" for more info.)

✔ The talking sheep from Serta. The mattress company wants to advertise the fact that its mattresses are so comfortable that people no longer need to count sheep. This is a great creative hook to peak the interest of consumers (see the section on creative hooks). The company also decided to sell sheep merchandise in addition to its mattresses because consumers responded favorably to the adorable "mascots."

✔ The Swiffer ad featuring a woman dancing around her neighbor's home, cleaning everything in sight, to the tune of "Whip it," a punk hit from the early 1980s.

But you (and your primary market) may respond best to other types of ads. For example, you may respond to straightforward descriptions of what the product or service does — especially if humor isn't appropriate in your business (if you run a funeral home, for instance). In the same vein, you may respond best to a simple picture, which can be worth more than a 1,000 words, as in the following examples:

✔ If you run an exercise center or a weight-loss service, or a hair salon that specializes in highlights, you can use before-and-after photos to great effect.

✔ If your business is food related (either a specialty store or a catering service), you can feature pictures of truly mouth-watering, appetizing food.

✔ If you focus on anything creative — you design and make clothing or knitwear, photo albums or picture frames, or furniture or cabinetry, for example — you should consider showing pictures of your work.

✔ If you run an automotive body shop, you may want to show sequential photos of how you brought it back to life — a prolonged before-and-after, so to speak.

You should be your first resource when it comes to what advertising is appealing . . . but don't stop there. Ask your family, friends, neighbors, and colleagues what appeals to *them*. This informal research is easy to do (and free!).

You have one more resource that can help you develop a new ad campaign: your old ad campaigns! In addition to checking out your direct competitors' ads and looking at other business's ads that appeal to you, review what you've done in the past to see what worked and what didn't (if you have that information). If you find something that worked really well, you don't need to reinvent the wheel. On the other hand, if you need a fresh approach, at least you'll know what not to do!

Concocting a Creative Hook to Get Your Audience's Attention

Because you want your advertising to stand head and shoulders above your competition, you need to work hard at finding — or, if you prefer, inventing — something that will grab the potential customers in your primary market (not necessarily by the neck) and drag them into your store or motivate them to call your business. A *creative hook* is an emotional trigger that attracts buyers; it appeals to their self-image and affirms that you provide what they're looking for. A creative hook is what every good ad needs in order to cut through the advertising clutter. The hook may be a slogan, a phrase, a jingle, a single line of copy, or a unique look that appears in all your ads. But whatever you choose, it must be yours and yours alone, because you'll use it across all media to differentiate your business from all the others. The bottom line: You need to put a new spin on the same old message by coming up with a memorable creative hook.

For example, the Energizer Bunny is a creative hook — it just keeps going and going and going — and it appears in television, print, and in-store ads promoting how long-lasting the Energizer batteries are. McDonald's creative hook, at one time, was its jingle, "You deserve a break today," which was permanently burned into the consumer memory. The minute you heard this jingle, you instantly knew what the product was. And AAMCO Transmission used a horn in its radio and TV spots as a creative hook; the horn even taught you how to spell the company's unusual name ("Double A, honk-honk, M-C-O").

Creativity can take the form of copy content, the actors you use in television commercials, the graphics you choose for print ads, an unusual musical background for radio spots, humor, or any number of things. Even though being creative is often a strenuous task, finding a new twist that you can inject into your ads is worth the extra effort. Just remember: Each ad must contain *all* the information consumers need in order to make a thoughtful decision as to whether they will act.

How a creative hook became an advertising phenomenon

When I first came up with the idea for the Pet Rock, I envisioned it as a spoof of a dog-training manual. But in researching book publishers, and then distributors, and then retailers, I soon realized that trying to sell this highly unusual concept as a book would be an uphill climb. Plus, according to my research, the average shelf life of the average book (at least one not written by a big-name author) is just a matter of weeks — if you can get it printed and onto the shelves in the first place. That was unacceptable as far as I was concerned. Maybe, I thought, Andre Gide was right when he said, "If a young writer can refrain from writing, he shouldn't hesitate to do so."

So, back to the old drawing board. I knew that what I needed to find was a creative hook. And my answer was that, instead of writing a book, I'd create a product. I devised a way to package

The Official Pet Rock Training Manual, along with an actual rock lying on a bed of excelsior inside a miniature pet carrying case, complete with air holes. This way, I could skip the bookstores entirely and put the whole enchilada into department stores and gift and stationery stores. It was simply a better, more creative way to sell the book.

When this innovation came to me and the packaging was designed, the Pet Rock — the novelty gift product that quickly became an instant sensation — was born. The creative hook that took the Pet Rock from paperback book to upscale gift item was so subtle that it seemed to go over the heads of many marketing experts, who still think I had a lot of nerve selling rocks for five bucks. I wasn't selling *rocks* for five bucks apiece (who in his right mind would pay to buy a rock?); I was selling *books*.

No matter the hook you choose, make sure it's memorable and unique. You can make the task of creating the hook easier with the help of colleagues and peers. In the following pages, I show you the brainstorming ropes and include an example of a marketing campaign that uses creativity and style to lure students to a community college.

Creative brainstorming

So, how do you get creative? What secrets can you uncover that will transform you from businessperson to creative genius? Unfortunately, I can't offer you a magic potion. But I can tell you that you can jump-start your creativity by gathering a few friends, family members, or employees around and doing what the professionals do: Hold a creative brainstorming session.

Advertising agencies often hold *creative sessions,* or *brainstorming sessions,* when they're designing new campaigns (or redesigning old ones). In my mind, these meetings are the most fun an ad person can have — at least while at work. (See Chapter 2 for more on ad agencies.)

You can always find a more creative, memorable, unique way with which to get your message across. Your idea doesn't need to be earth-shattering in its creativity — just different, clever, and memorable enough to grab the eye or ear of the consumers and motivate them to at least consider giving you a shot. The trick, of course, is to find what that hook is for your business or product.

Involving everyone in the brainstorming process

In a creative session, all the people who will be working on a particular account — owners, creative directors, copywriters, artists, even the account service people — gather in one room. You trade as much information as possible about the account, the product, and the primary market, and then you begin tossing out ideas. The initial ideas beget more and more ideas, which will, eventually, result in the perfect creative answer to the problem at hand.

The only rule in a brainstorming meeting is that no idea will be laughed at or discarded out of hand. The session should be a stream-of-consciousness type of gathering, and no idea is far-fetched or stupid. Every idea gets tossed onto the table and considered.

Recording your brainstorming ideas

In creative sessions, when someone throws out an idea, a scribe should write it in marker along with other ideas onto large sheets of paper (a cheap and easy way to record your ideas; plus, you can keep the sheets for reference, which you can't do if you write on a blackboard or whiteboard). As the sheets of paper fill up, your scribe should tape them to the walls. Before long, the room will be festooned with ideas — good and bad — from wall to wall. The entire group should study the ideas, and then refine, change, and resubmit them. Eventually, the creative hook — your new advertising message — begins to take shape. And when everyone in attendance agrees that a certain concept is the best answer to the problem, the group focuses on that superlative idea and begins to massage it into the final product.

Creativity is hard work. Ideas don't just jump up and bite you (although the bad ones have some pretty gnarly teeth). You need to search for them very diligently . . . but they *will* happen. I've gone into creative sessions with no clue as to what we could come up with for a particular account, and I've walked out armed with great, new ideas that we could ride for months to come. The creative session is the two-heads-are-better-than-one approach — a tried-and-true method of generating dozens of fresh, new ideas.

Creative example: Developing a campaign for a community college

My advertising agency handles student-recruitment advertising for two Bay Area community colleges in California. In order to devise a fresh, new creative approach for this account, we went through the following process (of which I go into more detail in the sections to follow):

1. **We reviewed all the old advertising, from our campaigns and from the competition's campaigns.**

2. **We thought about** *what* **we were selling and what made these colleges unique.**

3. **We figured out** *to whom* **we wanted to sell these college programs, and why our target market should be interested in these particular colleges — in other words, why our targeted students should "buy" from the "product" these colleges were offering.**

4. **We came up with a creative hook for our new ad campaign.**

5. **We morphed our idea into a tangible campaign compatible for radio and other media.**

6. **We reviewed the process and the results of our efforts.**

Reviewing previous ad campaigns and the competitions' ads

Our first step was to go back through all the colleges' previous advertising campaigns to see if we could identify any glaring flaws. We found the ads to be . . . well . . . kind of boring. The ads just listed a bunch of facts and figures (for example, which classes the colleges offered during certain enrollment periods and how much those classes cost). They threw out their statistics in the form of print and broadcast advertising and hoped for the best.

Unfortunately, the ads didn't differentiate the colleges from the many other junior colleges doing equally boring advertising (which we had checked out as part of our research before creating a new campaign). As a result, our client colleges' advertising wasn't getting very dramatic results, which is why they came to us looking for something that would actually work.

Identifying the target market

To pinpoint your target market, you should apply the list of questions I present in the section "Identifying and Targeting Your Audience." In the following list, I walk you through the various steps we took as an agency to produce some new ads for the colleges — ads that have increased student enrollment each and every time they've run:

First question: What are you selling, and what makes it so unique?

Answer: We're selling a quality education delivered by highly qualified instructors in a beautiful campus environment.

Second question: To whom do you want to sell it?

Answer: To kids fresh out of high school and to adults who want to upgrade their current job skills or to return to the job market after an absence.

Final question: Why should people buy it from you?

Final answer: Because, unlike so-called trade private technology schools (which can be quite expensive) or four-year colleges (which can be downright unaffordable), our community colleges deliver a first-rate education, providing day, night, weekend, or Internet classes, for just $7 per credit hour to California residents.

Finding a creative hook for the new ad campaign

After answering the questions from the previous section about our target market, my agency developed a radio soap opera with the authentic sound and feel of the old-time radio soap operas that were all the rage before television came along.

We used our creative hook to challenge listeners to bettering themselves by becoming more educated, and we did it in a fun, nonthreatening way. But wait, you say. What do teenagers know about old-time soap operas? Well, nothing, but they responded to retro concepts, and what's more retro than old-time radio soap operas?

Developing the campaign on radio

For our college soap opera spots, we decided to turn to radio to spread our message. My agency created imaginary people with imaginary problems and, by using really corny organ music in the background (just like the good old days) and a completely over-the-top actor to read the copy, we introduced each character, his or her problem, and a solution achieved through a quality education from one of our colleges. Here's an example of the copy one of our scripts directed at young adults:

> Emily awoke to the big day. She had spent a year as mustard squirter *(squirt),* then ketchup squirter *(squirt, squirt),* then pickle placer *(one, two, three).* But today, at the pinnacle of fast-food success, she would occupy the drive-through window *(. . . and did you want fries with that?).* This was big, she thought, *really* big. But after a day spent watching other young women cruising through in BMWs, gabbing away on their cell phones, Emily knew that what *she* needed was a *career,* not a job. Especially not *this* job. No education, no career. No career, no BMW.

Simple, huh? She called Silicon Valley's winning education combo — Foothill and De Anza Colleges *(music change, upbeat, jazzy).* With day, evening, and weekend classes, as well as Internet and telecourses available, Emily could get top-quality instruction for just seven bucks a unit. Foothill and De Anza offer an affordable way to earn a college degree or to update job skills for today's competitive job market. Do what Emily did. Get back to school. Enroll now for fall classes at Foothill and De Anza Colleges. Call 555-1212. That's 555-1212.

ANECDOTE

"We want to buy your friendship"

One of the other partners in an agency of which I was a part owner made a presentation to introduce our agency to a small, regional bank — a bank that was having a terrible time competing with the monolithic California financial institutions like Wells Fargo and Bank of America. As creative director, I was invited to attend a get-acquainted session with the bank's flamboyant president. This guy was way ahead of his time. He sported a closely cropped beard and always wore his signature bright-red suspenders (which he proudly showed off by strolling around the bank without his jacket). He was, to say the least, unlike any bank officer I had ever met.

Located in a small regional strip mall in a Bay Area suburb, the bank had come up with a very generous interest rate on savings accounts as a way to attract new deposits. The trick we had to deal with was to tell potential customers about the bank's rate and other good reasons to move money there — and to do so within the parameters of a somewhat limited ad budget. Because the president was such an unusual character, a guy who truly humanized the banking experience, my best idea was to feature him in all the ads.

Coming up with a great, new idea is one thing. In the ad-agency biz, getting clients to agree to the more far-fetched ideas is quite another. In this case, the bank president was just egotistical (and creative) enough to see the logic in, and to go along with, the new headline I invented for

his bank, which was (I change his and the bank's names here), "John Smith, president of Regional Bank, wants to buy your friendship!"

Instead of droning on about the bank and its higher interest rate on money market savings accounts, and then adding all the caveats and details about minimum balances, I thought we should go straight to the heart of the matter. We would tell potential customers that, although John Smith was being a bit mercenary in attracting deposits with a promise of a higher interest rate, he didn't take himself too seriously, and Regional may actually be a fun place to bank.

We did a photo shoot of John wearing his suspenders and used it in all our print ads and in-lobby display materials. We even designed and silk-screened T-shirts with red suspenders in the front and back, featuring the slogan "John Smith Bought My Friendship" and the bank's logo. We also did a series of radio spots (which we ran on economically priced regional stations) in which we went way over the top to explain that Regional was totally different from any other bank.

An off-the-wall strategy, you say? Exactly. And it worked. The bank took in savings-account deposits at a very satisfying clip. This campaign proves that, even if your business is less than exciting, you can write and produce eye-catching (and ear-catching) ads with just a little creativity.

In addition to creating a series of spots directed at teenagers fresh out of high school, we invented other characters and wrote spots directed at adults stuck in go-nowhere, low-paying jobs or eager to return to the job market after long absences — adults in need of an upgrade in skills. We placed our commercials on radio stations specifically programmed to attract our prime audience — everyone from young adults between the ages of 18 and 24, to women between the ages of 25 and 54, or to adults in general. (For more on creating radio advertising, see Chapter 8.)

Assessing the results of the new campaign

The results of our new campaign were more than gratifying. Our clients entered the new radio commercials into various community college creative advertising contests and took several first prizes. More important, enrollments at both colleges went up and our clients remain happy. What more could you want from an ad campaign?

An added bonus is that our spots were very cheap to produce. The most expensive element of the whole campaign was the cost of the actor, who did a superb job of reading (or, I should say, emoting) the copy. All in all, we devised a creative campaign that left most of the client's money available to spend where it would do the most good — on radio stations with strong audiences of prospective students (also known as buyers). For information on how to advertise on a budget, check out Chapter 2.

Incorporating Your Creative Message into an Overall Media Ad Campaign

When a great new idea hits you right between the eyes and the light bulb of creativity suddenly shines brightly, you need to begin incorporating your message into a full-blown ad campaign (or at least as full-blown an ad campaign as you can afford). After you identify all the ways your product is unique and put your finger on a hard-to-resist, eminently logical reason that people should seek you out in order to buy it (see the previous sections of this chapter), you need to find ways to make your idea fit into various forms of advertising.

Often, your creative hook dictates what media you should use — the hook literally drives your campaign:

✔ If your hook is visual, you'll use print, *collateral* (such as mailers, brochures, and so on), and/or television media.

✔ If your concept is audio-driven (a skit between two people or a hook that uses your own voice or a unique music background, for example), radio may be your best bet.

   ✔ If your clever new idea is a catchy slogan or a headline, you can con-
      sider using any variety of media, including billboards and bus cards.

You can't buy a 50-pound ad campaign with a 10-pound budget, so you need
to pick and choose your media and adjust your message accordingly. See
Chapter 2 for more on working within your budget.

The good thing is that you don't need to buy every media outlet in town in
order to get your message across. You can accomplish your goals not only
with a creative message, but also with a creative media buy. So, before you
start designing your campaign, you need to come to grips with how your
message will translate into various media and how much of this media you
can afford. The following sections show you the way and give you tips for
delivering your message in an effective, concise, and affordable manner.

Ensuring consistency of your message in all media you choose

Whatever your unique message turns out to be — whether it's a headline,
sentence, slogan, graphic, or other creative hook — be sure to use that message consistently in all media. You need to apply the same message in all the
forms of media you use in order to establish it as yours and yours alone and
in order to give the consumer a better chance of remembering it. For example, if your radio commercials talk about a half-price sale on a specific item,
your newspaper ads should feature the same sale terms for the same item.
Many small businesses (and a surprising number of large, national advertisers) make the mistake of being inconsistent, and it only serves to confuse the
consumer and to water down the overall advertising impact (and budget).

The good thing about maintaining consistency from one medium to the next
is that translating your message is even easier. If you spend hours and hours
writing a 60-second radio script for an ad, and you decide to augment your
radio advertising with some small newspaper ads, your time isn't lost. In fact,
your job is all but finished, because you can easily edit the same copy you
wrote for radio so that it works for print, thereby creating a cohesive advertising message across both forms of media. One good piece of advertising
copy always leads to another as your campaign begins to take shape.

Keeping your message simple

The real challenge of creating your advertising is to devise a hook that will
cut through the clutter that consumers are exposed to each and every day.
For example, a really clever, creative two-column newspaper ad with a headline that reaches out and grabs your attention can stand head and shoulders

above a full-page, four-color ad that completely misses the mark. Similarly, a radio spot that takes a fresh approach will enjoy much more listener recall than a spot that drones on and on without giving the listener a clear reason to actually hear it.

The best rule you can use as you work toward creating memorable advertising for today's marketplace is summarized in an acronym you won't forget: KISS, which stands for "Keep it simple, stupid."

Why is keeping it simple so important? Because today, more than ever before, consumers are *deluged* with information. Many people are connected to the outside world every minute of the day. Computers, cell phones, Blackberries and other personal digital assistants (PDAs), the Internet, radios, television, and many other electronic devices keep people within reach of information. The amount of data available is overwhelming, and the media throws advertising into this cauldron of information. At the very least, you hope your ads will be noticed; in a perfect world, consumers will remember them and act on what they hear. The key to igniting consumer memory is keeping it simple.

Consumers choose to shop at a particular store when dozens of stores carry essentially the same products because they're captured by an ad that gives them a clear, concise reason to buy — an idea presented in an eye-catching, creative way. Perhaps they desire a great low price, a special that includes a free gift, a discount on future purchases, or any number of things. Whatever the consumers desire, an ad grabbed their attention, and they responded. And, whatever the ad was, I'm willing to bet that the company presented it in a very simple, easy-to-understand manner.

Using words that sell

Certain words and phrases, when used in advertising, have a better-than-ever chance of attracting consumers' attention. You see these words over and over again in ads, but their overuse is a direct result of their effectiveness. Different words or phrases work for different types of businesses, though. Here are some examples of words and phrases that sell in the retail industry:

- ✔ Clearance
- ✔ Discount
- ✔ Everything must go
- ✔ Final closeout
- ✔ Free
- ✔ Going out of business
- ✔ Grand opening

- ✔ Improved
- ✔ Markdown
- ✔ New
- ✔ Overstocked
- ✔ Sale

If ever you needed to use the KISS rule in full-force (see the previous section), it's in the vocabulary you use in your ads. The challenge lies in walking a fine line between using simple, easy-to-grasp words and phrases and writing the way people think (in everyday conversational English). Bottom line: Make your ads simple in their language but creative in their content and presentation.

If you offer a service instead of providing a product, many of the words from the previous list still work. "Free," for example, always gets consumers' attention, as does "new." The following appealing words and phrases, however, are specific to the service industry:

- ✔ Great service
- ✔ Free pickup and delivery
- ✔ On time
- ✔ Trial offer
- ✔ Professional
- ✔ Family owned and operated
- ✔ Guaranteed service
- ✔ Money saving
- ✔ Dependable (or reliable)
- ✔ High quality
- ✔ References available from satisfied customers

Go through your newspaper and look at the ads. Certain words and phrases used by most advertisers will quickly become apparent to you. Now you know what I mean when I say that these words sell. They form a similar thread that runs through most advertising. If you can use any of these words and phrases in your advertising, by all means include them. If they're good enough for the other advertisers in your area, they'll most certainly be good enough for you.

Just as some words really sell, others should scare you off like a rat in a restaurant. Don't use swear words or most slang. And, in general, don't use words with more than three syllables. You can use some four-syllable words (like *incredible* and *absolutely,* as in "absolutely incredible savings!"), but be careful. Keep in mind that most people haven't expanded their vocabularies since high school (which is why most newspapers are written to the sixth-grade reading level).

There are exceptions to these rules, if done creatively. For example, Budweiser created ads some years back that used the word "*Whassup,*" and the ads were fun and memorable.

Delivering your message with clarity

No matter what form of media you use for your message (see Part II for more info on the types of media), be sure to explain your message in clear, easy-to-understand terms. You want consumers to see at a glance what you're selling and then make snap decisions as to whether they want to read or listen further.

Place your most powerful selling message at the beginning of a radio spot or in the form of a headline for printed advertising or Internet banner ads.

For example, if you're having a two-for-one sale, you want to get that information out there right away. Don't drone on for half a radio spot without giving the listeners a reason to actually hear it. Get down to the nitty-gritty and then explain the various details.

Here are two examples of opening copy for a radio spot to advertise a two-for-one sale. See if you can tell which spot is better:

> Smith's Hardware, conveniently located in the Neighborhood Shopping Center, a family owned and operated business for over 50 years, and a store where you've come to expect the very best in top-quality merchandise and friendly, helpful service, is proud to announce its annual two-for-one sale!

> Announcing the annual two-for-one sale at Smith's Hardware — the sale you've been waiting for since last year. Buy one gallon of paint, get another gallon absolutely free!

Both examples include similar information. The difference is that the second example gets the most important point across immediately; the rest of the 60 seconds can be filled with the specifics about convenient location, store history, and other good reasons to visit. The first example may put listeners to sleep within the first couple of lines. Nothing in the first spot makes consumers want to listen.

Following the same rule in a print ad simply means that *two-for-one sale* becomes the headline, with all the other information the consumer needs to know placed beneath it (as briefly and succinctly as possible). In this case, the two-for-one sale *is* the creative hook, because it's the single element of the ad that separates it from other ads for similar stores (see the section "Concocting a Creative Hook to Get Your Audience's Attention" for more on creative hooks).

Part II
Creating Great Ads for Every Medium

The 5th Wave   By Rich Tennant

THE FUTURE OF AD PLACEMENT IN VIDEO GAMES

"Watch out for the Necromancer behind the Toyota with the Snapple in his hand."

In this part . . .

From online ads and your own Web site to print ads in newspapers and magazines, from radio and television to direct mail and billboards — the variety of media available to accept your advertising, and evaporate your budget, is mind-boggling. Whether you can afford a full-blown ad campaign across all media, or you're just looking to find out as much as you can about one particular media choice, you find answers, suggestions, and advice in this part.

Chapter 6

Online Advertising: Maximizing the Enormous Reach of the Internet

*Y*ou've worked to build your business, and now you're wondering, do you need a Web site? The answer is yes, you probably do — especially if your goal is to expand your business. Most consumers have access to computers, even if they don't have one at home — and they're quick to use the Internet for research (though older consumers are still a little behind the curve). For many people, a business isn't real unless it has a Web site. When I need a product or service, I check the Internet even before I open my phone book. It's fast and easy, so a business with a Web site is more likely to attract my attention. Having a simple but well-thought-out site is a great, inexpensive way to advertise your business — even if you don't plan to sell online right away.

In this chapter, I walk you through the steps along the Web site pathway, answering some common questions as I go. What makes a Web site good? If you build it, will they come? Is it easier and cheaper to hire a Web designer? The dirty, little secret is that creating a good Web site isn't as hard as technical people may have you believe — if you know what you want and are willing to commit some cash. The first step is making the decision to do it.

Of course, having your own Web site is just the door (or portal, if you will) to online advertising. You should also consider advertising your business on other Web sites, so the second half of this chapter describes those options: creating banner ads and doing e-mail advertising.

The real question is this: Is a poorly executed Web site better than no site at all? Stated simply, the answer is a resounding *no!* In many cases, a Web site is the first impression a customer has — and everyone knows the importance of good first impressions. A poorly designed Web site with inaccurate information or spelling errors strikes a blow to a business image. If you build a Web site, make it a good one. In this chapter, I show you how.

Measuring the Pros and Cons of Online Advertising

Just like any other advertising medium, online advertising has pros and cons. Here are a few of the advantages to using online advertising:

- **You can easily test the market.** If you create a brochure, you have to print and distribute it before finding out whether your campaign is effective. Response (or lack of response) on the Internet is lightning fast. You can also add a counter to your company's Web site to see how many people visit your site.

- **The ad campaign is less expensive.** Because you don't have the costs associated with reprinting and redistribution (as you do in a more traditional campaign), the overall expense of a change is decreased.

- **The ad works 24 hours a day, 7 days a week, 365 days a year.** It's always nice to know your advertising is working for you around the clock and around the world, so that your customers can view it at their convenience rather than any specific time.

- **You can change your online ad much more easily than you can change ads in other media**. When you need to alter your online ad, no printing or taping is required. Just change the HTML that created the online ad and you're done in a matter of minutes.

- **Your customers can see your ad, shop, and buy, (if you sell your goods online) all without leaving home.** It's hard to beat that sort of convenience.

- **You can target your audience effectively.** The trick is to place your ad where the *right* customers can see it. If you sell exotic teas, you want to place your ad on a site that sells crumpets or cookies, rather than a site that sells motorcycle equipment to bikers. Think like one of your own customers by trying to imagine which sites they're likely to visit. Those sites are where to place your ad.

Although some techies may find it hard to believe, you do have to consider some disadvantages to online advertising, including the following:

✔ **It's too measurable.** You can gather more statistics than a baseball team. Worse, some of the *click-through rates* (the number of times people click on the ad divided by the total number of times people see an ad) are low — often 1 or 2 percent or even less. That means hardly anyone who sees your ad clicks on it and visits your Web site — or buys your product. Online advertising is still in its infancy.

A few years ago, advertisers believed that increasing the number of people who saw an ad would increase the likelihood of a sale. The thinking was that thousands of eyeballs looking at an ad would translate into hundreds of sales. Not necessarily so. A bit later, everyone decided that increasing your click-through rate would increase the number of sales. But that wasn't entirely true either. Currently, advertisers think that the only real measurement of an ad's success is to count the number of people who actually buy a product. The point is that because people don't really understand what works yet, they collect every possible statistic. But not all statistics are useful. As of this writing, nobody knows for certain which statistics will prove to be the most valuable.

✔ **Some major ad agencies (and Wall Street) are losing confidence in online advertising.** The Internet is still so new that the advertising world simply doesn't know yet which advertising methods work best. You do have, however, some good news. Few deny that in the future some form of Internet ads (perhaps combined with TV) will be both powerful and effective. People are figuring it out fast.

✔ **Customers are experiencing advertising overload.** One problem with online ads is the incredible amount of clutter on most Web pages. Every advertiser wants consumer attention, but readers simply have too much information to digest. Often, they choose to ignore ads — and that is what leads to low rates of return.

Even with its disadvantages, the Internet is turning into a tool that surpasses the wildest dreams of ad execs. The radio took 38 years to reach 50 million users. Television took 13 years to reach 50 million viewers. And the Internet took just 5 years to reach the same number of users — a stupendous achievement.

The Internet is a social technology. As your site grows, you can offer chat rooms and e-mail newsletters (not to mention a plethora of other options). Electronic groups are effective and fun as well. People like a sense of community, and the Internet offers that. In the end, all that interactivity means that you can sell people what they want and not just what is left over in stock. That's not just good — it's right. Happy, engaged customers are the Heisman Trophy of the advertising world.

Creating Your Own Web Site

For many businesses, setting up a Web site is the first step toward online advertising. Before you dive into the Web world, though, take a few minutes to consider what you want out of a Web site, and what a Web site can do for you. Here are some of the advantages that Web sites bring:

- ✔ **A Web site improves your image.** Face it — just about *everyone* in business has a site. If you don't, you want to make sure you've intentionally chosen not to do so, and be sure your reasons are sound.

- ✔ **A Web site can help your business — and your customer list — expand.** When you have a Web site, anywhere people have access to the Internet, they can have access to your business. Your customers are no longer limited to the people in your neighborhood.

- ✔ **A Web site can reduce some costs.** You can put information on your Web site that you may normally put in an expensive brochure. People who visit your site can get information quickly, and you save printing and mailing costs. Everybody wins.

- ✔ **A Web site is available around the clock (and the calendar!).** Your Web site works for you even when you're sick or on vacation. When your customers want to buy, your Web site is there to take their orders or receive their questions, which you can then answer when you're online — or you can include answers to "Frequently Asked Questions" on your Web site, which customers can peruse at their convenience.

- ✔ **A Web site offers customers a choice.** They can reach you in person and by phone, fax, e-mail, and now via your Web site. Offering more choices puts the customer in control.

Now that you're sold on the advantages of a Web site, take a few minutes to consider the following drawbacks as well:

- ✔ **Sometimes having a Web site gives visitors the impression that they're able to buy online.** If you don't have an online store, some visitors may be disappointed.

- ✔ **If you include an online store in your Web site, many customers are not willing to send their credit card information over the Internet.** Some people still fear being ripped off. Others prefer shopping in person; they like to see products before they buy, to judge their value.

- ✔ **Having a Web site doesn't ensure success.** You have to work for success on the Web as hard as you work for it in your traditional store.

Deciding on your Web site goals

Establishing goals for your Web site is essential. (How else can you tell whether you're succeeding?) Start by imagining your site in general terms. Do you want to amuse visitors? Then your Web site should be catchy and fun. Are you trying to persuade people to support a political cause? Maybe you want serious articles with just a dash of humor in the cartoons. Do you want people to hire your investment firm? You may want to highlight your credentials in a professional, understated Web site.

Think small. Why? Because it keeps the costs down, and because keeping a site small allows for intelligent growth.

Most people create business Web sites for one of three reasons — to offer information; to offer some form of interactivity, such as e-mail or customer support; or to offer a full-blown online store.

Visit the sites of your competitors. What do you like and dislike? What do they offer? How can you make your site different from and better than theirs? Make a list of competitor services and add to it the things that can make your site more valuable to the customer.

When you're setting goals for your Web site, ask yourself these questions:

✔ **How big do you want your site?** With a larger site, with many pages, you should consider tools that allow people to search your site with ease to find what they need. Unless you have a very large business already, go with a smaller site that can grow with your business.

✔ **How soon do you want your site up and running?** Hiring a Web designer can add weeks to your schedule, so planning ahead is smart. A word to the wise: *Not* hiring a Web designer can add *months* to the schedule, unless you're already a competent designer. Just be sure to put a limit on the amount you're willing to spend (you don't want your designer to get carried away).

✔ **What audience do you want to reach?** If you sell rock music, your site will, and should, look a lot different than if you're selling flowers. Does your audience have access to the latest technology or is it reluctant to try anything flashy? Prepare a list of what your customers want. What is important to them? Don't give them what *you* want. Give them what *they* want.

If you choose to create an online store at your Web site, keep in mind that customers want exactly the same things they want in a traditional store. They want to locate goods easily. They want decent prices and quality merchandise that's in stock. They want to get in and get out as quickly as possible. Oh, and customers want *service,* including guarantees and the ability to return what they don't want. Your customers must trust you, or they won't buy.

Choosing an effective domain name

Your domain name is a very important part of your Web site's success. If you choose a name that's catchy and easy to remember, your customers will come back time and time again. If the name is long or hard to remember, they may forget about it before they even get there.

In general, when you're choosing a domain name for your Web site, pick one that's directly tied to your business. For example, if your business name is Main Street Flower Shop, you could try MainStreetFlowers.com.

Keep in mind that domain names are a very hot commodity. People snatch them up all the time, so the name you want may already have been taken by someone else. Check out www.register.com, where you can search for the domain name you want and see whether it's available. (If it is, you can even go ahead and register for it on the Web site and choose various packages to get your own Web site up and running.)

Saving money (or your sanity): Your Web design

Doing your own Web site design can save you lots of money, *if* you already have the skills. Are you a good graphical designer? Do you know how to transfer that knowledge to the computer? Do you understand HTML (hypertext markup language — the language used to display stuff on the Internet)? Do you know how to create interesting content? Can you take all your beautiful pages and put them on the Internet? Well, then, doing it yourself is the best choice for you.

For the rest of us, only two choices are left: using templates or hiring a Web designer. In the following sections, you can explore these two options.

If you're interested in finding out more about Web site design, check out *Creating Web Pages For Dummies,* 8th Edition, by Bud E. Smith and Arthur Bebak (Wiley).

Using a template

A *template* is a boilerplate pattern that produces a certain type of finished product. Using templates in your Web design lowers costs and ensures consistency throughout the Web site. A Web site template may include such items as a menu, buttons to pass from one page to another, graphics, and sample pages that you can customize. It may have a template to describe your company history, the items you're selling, or special services you offer.

Before using a template, consider two issues:

- ✔ **Templates can provide professional-appearing pages, but you must use only those choices available in the package.** In other words, if you want individuality, templates aren't the right choice.

- ✔ **Many templates take time to figure out.** Templates may be cheaper than a designer in terms of cash layout but costly in terms of time.

You can get templates from some ISPs (Internet service providers), and you can also buy them from Web-design vendors.

Hiring a Web designer

If you don't have the skills and don't want to get the training now, or if you want a professional and personalized site online quickly, then hiring a Web designer is a good way to go. It's also usually — although not always — the most expensive alternative. Chapter 12 provides more information on how to find and choose a Web designer and on shopping for the right ISP to run your site.

Designing a strong Web site

If you decide to go the route of having a Web site for your business, you need to know what makes a site successful. Three qualities of excellent Web sites stand out above the rest. Your Web site must do the following:

- ✔ **Have a clear of purpose.** People go online to accomplish some purpose. The best sites enable people to get what they want quickly. You may be astonished at the number of commercial Web sites that don't explain their own purpose to a visitor. Customers want to know: Are you selling something? If so, what? Are you offering information? Fine, where is it?

Often, you can clarify your reason for existence with a simple tagline under your company name or logo (for example, "Margie's Muffins — Selling pastries to discriminating palates").

✔ **Be easy to navigate.** Easy navigation requires a thoughtful plan, but the extra effort pays off. People become impatient when they click endlessly and never seem to get where they want to be. You can help them by offering no more than a few choices per page. Divide your home page into broad but easily understood categories such as "Products we sell," "Frequently asked questions," "Press releases," and "How to contact us."

A customer who gets lost on your site is a customer who won't return.

✔ **Portray the image you most want to communicate.** Your Web site should carry the same image you portray in all other aspects of advertising your business. Get your logo out front. Project an image that reflects the goals of your business. And get your selling message out there immediately — the customer doesn't have time to be teased.

Although these three qualities may seem simple on paper, carrying through with them can be much more difficult. Often, advertisers know *what* they want to do on their Web sites, but they don't have a clue about *how* to do it. If that advertiser is you, you can benefit from checking out the following sections, where I give practical advice on how to get what you want out of your Web site.

Expressing your message clearly

A person who arrives at your site is interested not only in knowing what you do, but also in what you can do for him. Tell each visitor what benefits you offer — don't make him guess.

Use short paragraphs. Not only are short paragraphs attractive, but few people enjoy wading through an intimidating document full of big blocks of text. Prioritize your content. Put your most important and timely information at the top. Step up and be bold about the most exciting content.

Think of each person who arrives at your site as your one and only customer. Don't make him do all the work. Keep it simple. Avoid confusion.

Focusing on content

Content is the single most-important reason people visit a site — they want information. Give it to them freely. Offer something of value.

Here are some guidelines to making your Web content first-class:

- ✔ **Omit needless words.** That's what Strunk and White said years ago (in *The Elements of Style* [Longman]), and it's still terrific advice today. All content should have a reason to be on your page, so get rid of fluff.

- ✔ **Stay current.** Customers love knowing the latest tips and the most current information, and they're more likely to return to a site when they're fairly certain the content changes regularly. The best sites clearly state when and how often the Web site content is updated.

- ✔ **Highlight what's going on with your business.** Have a Web page devoted to press releases. If you don't have any, write some, or hire a local writer to whip up a few for you. Then you can e-mail them to newspapers and put them on your Web site. A press release helps reporters find out exactly what you do. Put your newsletters on your Web site, too.

- ✔ **Say it visually.** Visual clues are helpful in communicating time-sensitive information to your audience. If your site features articles on a certain topic, make sure the date is displayed prominently. You may want to post a red arrow next to new information to alert the consumer. You don't want to be flashy (using blinking neon lights, for example), but you *can* use bold colors with discretion. Good sites also often have an area called "What's New." That's a good spot to highlight promotional information or future events.

Making your site a door, not a window

You want your site to be inviting (like the reception area or lobby of your own business), instead of chaotic or confusing, which only creates a slew of window shoppers (who *rarely* come in to buy). In order to create an appealing Web site, consider some of the following suggestions:

- ✔ **Offer a visitor no more than four or five choices.** When visitors arrive at a site, they immediately try to make sense of it. But they stop trying if they have more than a handful of choices on a single page. Let them know the point of your site right away. Invite a customer in.

- ✔ **Don't make any single page too long.** A page is too long if people have to scroll down to find relevant information. If you have a lot of information to share, split it up and put a healthy chunk of information on each page. Each page of content should contain a single conceptual nugget of information. Not six nuggets — one. Clearly, some exceptions to this guideline exist, but on the whole, a single page of information is a reasonable goal.

- ✔ **Check and recheck your spelling and grammar.** You want your site to reflect your business's competence and professionalism. Botching the nitty-gritty grammar stuff can be quite the turn-off to many potential customers.

✔ **Be consistent.** Carry a theme throughout your site. Make sure each page has the same background and the same buttons to help visitors navigate your site.

✔ **Choose a solid background.** A one-color background is simply easier to read than if you have wild graphics floating behind your text — no matter how subtle you think they may be! You should also keep in mind, though, that dark words on a dark background will also be tough for people to read, so make sure the colors you use complement each other well. Look at other sites to find what you think is easy to read. Finally, the colors on your site can look different depending on the software people use. Ask your friends to view your site to make sure it's attractive on other software.

I learned a lesson the hard way about trying too hard to impress people. Once I designed a cool background for a friend, and it looked great on my machine with my software. I took it to her home, put it on her computer, and was appalled. My beautiful dark blue background looked garish and ugly on her machine. Different Internet browsers display colors differently, so beware.

Cutting down on graphics and audio

Visitors want fast-loading pages, and graphics slow things down considerably. So every graphic on your Web site must earn its place. Is it worth the extra time it takes to load? Using the newest new thing isn't always the *smartest* smart thing. Some people still don't have fast Internet connections. Others don't want to buy all the software necessary to display graphics and audio and movies. Make your page one that loads quickly.

What is a fast-loading page? One that appears in just a few seconds. Bear in mind that some people do have broadband, cable, and DSL connections and enjoy sophisticated graphics. So design your site for the appropriate audience.

Be careful before adding audio to a site. Many people don't like having music blare at them unless they choose to listen. Some people surf the Web in their cubicles at work. They (and their bosses) aren't happy if loud noises suddenly scream out. So skip the audio unless it's important to your business — if you sell music, for example, or speech-recognition software. And always offer a visitor the choice of whether to listen or not.

Making it easy to contact you

You may be surprised at how many sites forget this simple piece of wisdom: Make it simple for customers to find you. Sprinkle your phone number, address, e-mail information, business hours, and so on throughout your site.

Also add a link to your homepage saying, "Contact Us." When readers click on that link, make sure all your contact information is available for viewing. *Remember:* You're advertising your business, so do it well.

Tell your customers how you can support their needs. Can buyers send e-mail to you? Should they call? Do you have a toll-free number? Reassure customers that you're a real business.

Also, ask your local chamber of commerce to have a link to your Web site. Reporters look at city pages to see what's new and interesting from a local angle. If your site is there, they're more likely to visit it. Finally, make it easy for reporters to contact you. Have your phone number and address prominently displayed on your Web site. Some businesses even have a special phone number for reporters to call for an interview.

Maintaining and updating your site

A good site has links that work. Clicking on a link only to find yourself on a page that says, "Information not found" or "Site under construction" is just plain annoying. Having broken links can damage your reputation and give customers a reason to question your ability to provide whatever service you're promoting. Remember that the work on a Web site doesn't end when the page is placed on the Internet. Keep your links and all other information accurate and up to date.

Promoting Your Site

If you build it, will they come? Having a Web site does no good if nobody can find it. You can promote your site in a couple ways — online promotion and offline advertising. And you need to do *both* to get the word out. In the following sections, you can figure out how to do just that.

Online promotion

A *search engine* (or directory) is a tool (such as Yahoo! or AltaVista) for combing the billions of Internet pages to find the information you need. One problem with search engines is that they're so incredibly thorough. Even the simplest search can return millions of *hits* (sites that fit your search criteria). Another problem is that no single search engine covers the entire Web. That means you can receive different answers to the same question on different search engines. You can view that as an annoyance *or* as an opportunity. I choose the latter outlook, because it gives me more chances to succeed — to get my site listed in such a way that anyone can find it.

Gleaning wisdom from Goldilocks: Web sites should be just the right size, too

People hate clicking and clicking and clicking while never seeming to arrive anywhere useful. They will stay on your site if you give them the information they want within a few clicks. Never force anyone to work too hard to find what they want.

A piece of magic is involved in creating a good Web site, and it's this: People are just like Goldilocks — they don't want too much information on a page, and they don't want too little. They want just the right amount.

How do you know the right amount? Observe yourself or your kids surfing the Internet. What makes you impatient? Slow-loading graphics and long, dull pages, I bet. On the other hand, if the pages don't contain enough information, you're forced to click too often. You don't want that either. Visit other sites to develop a sixth sense about what is too much and too little. Finding the right amount isn't a riddle that technology can solve; it calls for common sense and clear thinking. A good general guideline to shoot for is no more than three clicks before viewers find what they're looking for.

Don't worry about getting your site listed on more than eight or nine search engines. Almost everybody has a favorite search engine anyway, and people aren't going to check 47 search engines to find you. Each person may check one or maybe two of the major engines, so don't bother with the little ones.

Each engine ranks sites using different criteria — and those criteria change frequently. The formula used by the search engines to rank sites is highly secret, but some common elements never change. Search engines rank sites high in any given category if the site follows a set of rules. This ranking system is why finding a Web site developer who understands how to optimize your site for the search engines is so important. If you run a furniture store specializing in antiques, you want people to be able to look under the words furniture and antique and antique furniture and have your business appear near the top of the list. A good Web designer can make sure this happens.

To make it easy on your Web site developer, tell him to optimize only for the following search engines and directories: AltaVista, Excite, Google, Lycos, webCrawler, and Yahoo! Search engines take six to eight weeks to index new sites, so you have to be patient. Make sure that your Web site developer submits your URL (web address) as soon as possible to decrease the wait.

Curious about the costs attached to buying key words on search engines? Feel free to flip over to Chapter 12.

Offline promotion

You can do a lot offline to let people know you have a Web site, too. Put your URL on everything: brochures, business cards, direct mail, newspaper ads, radio and TV commercials, stationery, t-shirts, pens, tiepins, magnetic refrigerator stickers, your storefront sign, even your answering machine or voice mail message — in other words, everywhere you would put your phone number or street address. It's just as important to your business's success.

Give people a reason to visit your site. Offer something free, whether it be information about an amazing diet or a free t-shirt. Most people who see your URL on a billboard won't rush home to view your site unless something is in it for them. Offer convenience. Offer online ordering. Offer *something*.

Setting Goals for Online Ads

The Internet has sped things up, but the basic rules of good advertising haven't changed. Whether you're first or last to market, you need to sustain the basics to succeed — customer service, communication, commitment. Personalized service just about always leads to happy customers. Amazon.com greets consumers by name and offers reading and video suggestions tailored to the individual. People love the notion that someone is looking after their needs and interests.

The first step is to determine your own online advertising direction. Speaking generally, you can choose from three strategies in an online effort:

- ✔ **Branding campaigns,** in which the goal is to get people to recognize your product or company name

- ✔ **Click-through campaigns,** in which you get people to click on your ad in order to be taken to your Web site

- ✔ **Sell-through campaigns,** in which you get people to buy right away

You can design different banners depending on your goals — the same banner just won't work for all three strategies. Choose one goal per banner so that you meet your objectives. Use a good mix of the three campaigns, which I describe in detail in the following sections.

Ads that build awareness

Branding means getting people to recognize your name (in a positive way, of course). The idea is that if someone sees your name enough times, he'll remember it later when he thinks about purchasing. For example, a person seeing an ad on TV for a certain type of toilet paper doesn't leap out of his chair and rush to the store. But he may remember the brand some day when he's *in* the store. The same is true for Internet ads.

A recent study shows that the primary reason for advertising on the Internet has, in fact, shifted toward branding — and away from Web site traffic-building and sales generation. This strategy makes a lot of sense when you realize that sales resistance is strong when a user is intent on buying something else.

The drawback to advertising for branding purposes is that the success of a campaign is difficult (if not impossible) to measure. Because of this, some companies decide that branding-type banners aren't for them. But I think that's a mistake, because your competitors are out there with their online ads building brand awareness. It's a mistake because branding — whether online or offline — takes time. If you don't make an effort to impress your name on visitors, you lose valuable weeks and months. A person online has thousands of choices, and you want that person to remember your name. The only way to do that is to get it out there.

Ads that encourage click-through

Click-through simply means that when a user sees your ad, he clicks on it and is taken directly to your Web site. When a user clicks through to your site, it means that your ad was so compelling that the user stopped what he was doing on another site and went to visit yours. That's powerful stuff.

The purpose of a click-through campaign is to build traffic to your Web site. One excellent way to think about that is to remember headlines in a newspaper. Headlines don't tell you the whole story; they just tell you enough to pique your interest. That's exactly the goal of a click-through campaign: to generate enough interest that your viewers click on your ad and visit your site.

Selling your product is one obvious goal of click-through campaigns (before a customer buys, she has to get over to your site). Another reason may be Web-traffic generation. Perhaps you've sold advertising space to another company, and you've promised that a certain number of visitors will go to your site. Click-through campaigns are also effective if your plan is to build a database of individuals to whom you plan to sell your product in the future. Many businesses currently build such a consumer list by asking people for their e-mail addresses. This list is the best sort of customer database, because everyone on the list has asked to be there.

Ads that encourage sales

The point of a *sell-through* campaign (or one that encourages sales) is to drive a sale immediately. Suppose you see an ad for an office supply discount site, and that ad promises useful items on sale for remarkable prices. If you visit that site and buy *only* the items on sale . . . well, that's a sell-through ad that didn't work. The goal is to get you to go to the site, shop around, and buy something else in addition to the sale items. More than that, the ad was probably designed to encourage you to become a regular customer.

To induce a purchase in a sell-through campaign, you have to offer an extraordinary bargain, which is known as a *loss leader*. Sell-through campaigns are appropriate when you want to generate revenue in a hurry. You may think sell-through ads are the only ones worth having, but they really are a short-term strategy, because they require you to always offer amazing sales. Think twice before you settle on this as your one-and-only ad campaign.

Choosing Among Online Ad Formats

In the dim, dark online past (a decade ago), your Web site was your ad — your only ad. Not much was actually sold online, but an Internet presence gave a certain cachet. Businesses placed their sites into the search engines, people came because it was cool, and if they liked what they saw, they called or visited your brick-and-mortar store and bought goods in the traditional way. Web sites in those days tended to be *brochureware* — a simple conversion of product information to language that a Web site could display. No animation, no rich media, nothing. Plain vanilla. But it didn't work very well, largely because customers faced choices that bewildered them and because Web sites couldn't target the right customers.

Here's a piece of trivia for you: The first banner ad appeared on Hotwired. com in October of 1994 — it was an ad by AT&T. Hotwired wondered what the response would be from visitors to its site, and, to its surprise, it didn't receive a single complaint. Banner ads were born. Shortly thereafter, someone realized that you could advertise effectively by sending e-mail to people who wanted to know about your products. Electronic newsletters appeared out of nowhere, and a second form of online advertising hit the big time.

Online advertising guidelines

Here are a few common-sense guidelines as you advertise online: Be truthful. Don't mislead consumers. Substantiate your claims. Be fair to consumers. Make necessary disclosures clear and conspicuous.

For example, if your banner ad promises a free dinner at Charlie's Steak House, you must mention — within the banner — that the purchase of two airline tickets to Florida is necessary before the free dinner is awarded. You can't force someone to click to your site before knowing that a purchase is involved in the "free" dinner. If you offer a free dinner (or some other giveaway) on your Web site, you must place the disclosure close to the offer. You can't make someone scroll down endlessly only to discover that she must buy something first; place the disclosure nearby. Make sure the disclosure is clear and easily understood.

You can find other ad models for online advertising, but banner ads and e-mail are the main ones you need to understand. I cover them in more detail in the following sections.

Creating banner ads

Placing a banner or *button* (a small banner ad) on someone else's site offers two benefits: It drives visitors to your site, and it gives your product or company visibility on the Web. Banner ads are helpful in building brand recognition. The Interactive Advertising Bureau (www.iab.net) provides guidelines for different sizes and styles of banners, buttons, skyscrapers (which are essentially vertical banners), and other formats. Figure 6-1 contains an example of an effective internet banner ad.

In the following sections, I describe the characteristics of a good banner ad (you don't want to create a bad one, do you?) and give you some pointers on how to find a banner designer if you decide you don't want to do this yourself.

Knowing what makes a banner good

One thing advertisers have figured out is that rich-media banners (ones that have graphics with audio, video, and other technology components beyond mere animation) work well. They're simply more interesting than static banners — ones that don't have all these extra features. Rich-media banners also take a long time to load (appear on the screen), so you don't want the designer of your banner to pile huge amounts of technology into one little ad. If you choose to go with a rich-media banner, be sure the *interactivity* (the bells and whistles) are related somehow to what you're selling.

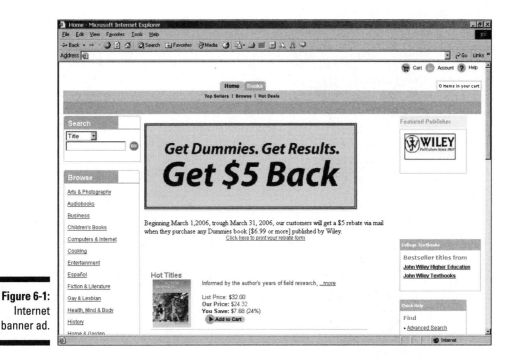

Figure 6-1:
Internet
banner ad.

You can drive traffic to your site with cheap tricks, but doing so is unfair. Recently, a certain company designed a banner that looked very much like the error message you receive just before your computer crashes. "Click here," said the ad. People clicked. Many of them thought they had to click or their machine would crash. Instead, they were taken to the Web site of that company. I'm not prepared to say their intention was dishonest, but that idea resulted in a trick that made people feel foolish. My advice is to sell honestly.

Determining the quality of a banner depends largely on which ad strategy you have chosen. You want a different sort of banner depending on whether your goal is branding, building Web traffic, or selling. If your goal is to build brand awareness, you want something attractive and catchy so people will remember. You want your company name and/or product prominently displayed. You want something simple and short. Find a good slogan so that your ad pops out of the Web clutter.

If you're aiming at a click-through campaign (that is, you want to drive traffic to your site but not necessarily to make an immediate sale), you want to pique interest fairly. You can, for example, put up a banner that advertises free dinners, and in doing so, you can have a phenomenal click-through rate. Millions will visit your site, but that's one of those cheap tricks — unless you're actually prepared to give free dinners to everyone who visits your site. Figure 6-2 shows an example of a Web page containing a simple yet effective click ad.

Figure 6-2:
Web page
containing a
click ad.

For a click-through ad, keep in mind the following tips:

✔ **Remember to say "click here" in your banner.** You would be surprised at the number of banners that fail to tell a viewer what action to take.

✔ **Make it short.** Don't bore customers with all the grimy details. Viewers don't have time to wade through your long copy in the myriad ads that bombard them. Get to the point — and fast!

✔ **Use the word *free* in your ad.** Free can always catch someone's eye — no matter how focused he is on some other task. Just remember to follow through on your promise of something free. Customers won't come back if you trick them.

✔ **Pose a question.** Questions encourage people to click, but you want it to be a compelling question, such as "What three things do all best-selling novels have in common?"

✔ **Be sure that people feel as if they can get something they want by clicking on your ad.** "Click here to get a free personalized estimate of your social security benefits with private accounts" is much better than "Click here for information about social security." People don't want to merely visit another Web site; they want to feel that a click can bring them value. Give it to them.

✔ **Make your banner interactive.** We all like to be involved, and your viewers are no different.

✔ **Change your banners frequently.** If a user hasn't clicked after three visits, he isn't likely to do so in the future.

✔ **Create a mystery.** Curiosity is an extraordinary motivator. Suppose you're in the computer peripheral business, and you sell keyboards. Of course, we all know that the top row of a keyboard contains these letters: QWERTYUIOP. Now to create a mystery in your ad, ask people to guess the longest word that can be typed using only those letters. I know a lot of people who wouldn't be able to resist clicking over to your site to find the answer, but I'm sure *you* would never fall for such a silly trick, now would you? (By the way, the answer isn't *typewriter*. Oh no, that would be too easy. It's *Rupturewort,* a West Indian plant.) People love to discover intriguing facts — and they'll click over to your site to do just that.

If your banner ad is part of a sell-through campaign, you need a fast-loading banner. The point of a sell-through campaign is an immediate sale. How can a slow-loading graphic accomplish that goal? It can't. Create a sense of urgency. The words "Last day of sale" help. For a sell-through campaign, do all the things you would do for a click-through campaign, except don't create a mystery. You want good strong information so someone will buy as soon as he reaches your site.

Finding a banner designer

Before you start looking for someone to design your banner ad, be sure to find a few samples of banners that you like. Let a designer know what you want to do. In the same regard, know whether you want a branding campaign, a click-through campaign, or a sell-through campaign. To find a designer, ask your ISP for references; check out the list of banner designers at www. bannertips.com/designersForHire.shtml or search online by entering "professional banner design" into a search engine.

Are banners and buttons effective?

If you get a 1 or 2 percent conversion rate, your banners are performing at or above normal. That's dismal, you say. Well, yes it is, but consider the whole story before rushing to judgment.

When so many dot-coms failed that we started to call them dot-bombs, online ad impressions still increased exponentially and reached an all-time high in December 2000 — the height of the panic.

Plus, with so many more ads out there now, the conversion rate is bound to be lower. Not all

companies spend the time or effort to care about the right kind of banner put in the right place to do the right job. So good banners and buttons can be very effective.

Banner bashing is popular. Maybe it's right, too. I can't guarantee you that banner advertising will wind up being the online ad model that works. But I do think incorporating banners into your overall advertising strategy makes sense.

Doing e-mail advertising

E-mail is the sweetheart of the current advertising models. It's cheap. It's fast. It's effective. Recently, response rates for *permission-based advertising* (where you ask the customer before sending e-mail) beat the heck out of banner ad click-through rates.

Why is e-mail so successful? Because it's a form of dialogue. Your customers can respond to you, a real human being, instead of watching a Web page.

Think of an e-mail campaign as being an extension of your other advertising strategies. You don't want to replace them entirely, but you can add the hottest sizzle in town by using e-mail. The reason e-mail is hot is that you can target so effectively. You can be wildly creative — embedding audio and video and interactive capabilities in your messages — for relatively little expense.

In the next sections, I offer pointers on the best way to do e-mail advertising. I tell you how to compile — and/or buy — good lists of people to send your e-mail ads to. I also advise writing and sending your own newsletter via e-mail to prospective customers.

Collecting lists

If you want to use e-mail in your ad campaign, you're going to need e-mail addresses of people to send your messages to. Start by asking your regular customers for their e-mail addresses. Those who want to receive ads from you will comply — and you don't want to bother the people who don't want to give you their e-mail addresses.

You can also collect information from those who visit your site by asking them for their feedback. Inquire about their interests. Ask them for their e-mail addresses. Offer discount store coupons or tickets to a local show to people who give you information. *Remember:* The data people give you is valuable, so you may want to give a little something in return for the information they give.

You can also buy lists containing thousands of e-mail addresses. But I hate this method because the people on those lists haven't asked to be there. If you send unsolicited advertisements, you're sending *spam* (unwanted e-mail). Spam is unkind, unfair, and counterproductive. Plus, response rates on these kinds of e-mails are low.

Publishing newsletters

E-mail newsletters are an increasingly popular Web phenomenon. Offer a newsletter on your Web site and allow people to sign up. Then, once a week or once a month, send out information about your business — information that can help the customer. Be generous with your tips and information pertinent to your business. Word will get out that you offer good value, and people will come.

A holistic veterinarian I know started her newsletter over a year ago, and it's a winner. Each month she sends out a newsletter via e-mail that is chock full of tips for animal health. And her business has increased dramatically.

Using e-mail successfully

E-mail can be a strong part of your overall advertising campaign. In order to make this happen, be sure to follow these tips:

- ✔ **Ask for e-mail addresses — never send unsolicited e-mail.** People don't like to have e-mail forced into their mailbox, piling up without an end in sight. Make sure the e-mail addresses you obtain are given voluntarily from customers who really want to hear from you.

- ✔ **Keep records of all registrations forever.** Sometimes, years later, people tell you they never signed up. With great courtesy, show them their original registration and the date you received it.

- ✔ **Always offer a chance to opt out.** In each e-mail, tell people how they can stop receiving the mail (*unsubscribe*). Make the instructions clear and prominent.

- ✔ **State your privacy policy.** Tell people that you will never share or sell their e-mail addresses. And keep your word.

✔ **Appoint a real, live person to handle problems and inquiries.** Your goal should be to respond to each e-mail within 12 hours. Sooner is better. Another good idea is to have an automated reply that is sent immediately and lets the person know you received his message. Be sure to follow up with a personalized reply as soon as possible. Many (if not most) ISPs offer the ability to respond automatically.

✔ **Keep your list secure.** Make sure that the recipients can't see each other's e-mail addresses. You can figure out how to make an alias list and put that list in the blind carbon copy (BCC) area when sent.

✔ **Check the e-mail you send out for typos, misspellings, and so on.** Put your best foot forward.

✔ **Choose your subject line with care.** Make it provocative — and make it sound like something other than an ad. "Make money fast," *doesn't* work. "A unique opportunity to improve your business," *does* work.

✔ **Avoid closing down communication.** I once had an e-mail correspondence that left me infuriated. I was about to buy a new car, and I wanted my new baby to be perfect. I requested (by e-mail) a certain color that I had seen on another model by the same auto manufacturer. I received an e-mail in response that stated I couldn't have my car in that color. Well, okay, but the infuriating part was that her note had a postscript that read, "Have a nice day!" With that one line, the salesperson declared the conversation over and closed down communication. *Never* close off communication with a customer.

Chapter 7

Using Print Ads: Small Spaces with Big Audiences

In This Chapter

▶ Creating print ads that cut through the clutter

▶ Writing and designing an ad that grabs your readers' attention

▶ Making sure your ad includes all the required elements — and nothing extra

*B*ecause television is more fragmented by the numerous cable channels now available, radio formats and magazines are more tightly targeted to very narrow audiences, the Internet is a more popular alternative to traditional media, and consumers have increasingly more media choices, advertisers have a difficult time reaching their entire target audience with a single medium. For this reason, you also need to consider advertising in newspapers, locally published magazines, and the magazine sections of your local newspaper. Print is a tried-and-true vehicle for advertising, and if you use it well, print ads can work for you, too.

Your print-buying options are many and varied, but in this chapter, I focus primarily on newspaper advertising. The good news is that the formula for designing and writing an effective print ad remains the same across the board, so whether you decide to use your print ad in a medium other than newspaper, you can use this information just as well.

Exploring the Advantages of Print

Despite the fact that newspaper readership has been declining steadily for years, papers still have a lot going for them. They cover the entire demographic spectrum, and their flexibility allows you to stretch your advertising budget. You don't need to buy a full-page ad — newspapers can sell you ads in an infinite variety of sizes. By designing small-space ads, you can buy more frequency and more audience, and, in many cases, you can get great position on the page.

As a general rule, the smaller the ad, the lower the cost per view. However, the ad size you choose should match the "size" of the news announcement in your ad. For example, if you're advertising a giant once-a-year sale, a larger ad better communicates that message. In contrast, a weekly special at a small restaurant is better suited to a small space ad. Larger ads are more often seen than smaller ads, but ad space is sold by the column inch, and the relationship between size and true impressions isn't linear.

Also, you don't need to run four-color ads (even the large, national advertisers and their ad agencies rarely spend their money for that luxury), because newspapers are, essentially, still a black-and-white medium. Even though *USA Today* forever changed the face of newspapers by being the first to publish a color paper back in 1982, costly four-color ads are still very rare in most dailies (although four-color process is used in editorial content and news photos all the time).

Another advantage to advertising in newspapers is the fact that they are printed in sections, each one targeted to a particular interest — from sports to entertainment to business. Buying space in the section that has been formatted to reach the greatest number of persons in your primary target audience demographic gives your ads a better chance of being read by your prospective customers, which, in turn, helps you spend your budget more effectively. Newspapers are the pickup trucks of advertising — solid, sturdy, no-nonsense, and unglamorous — but they get the job done.

Print advertising isn't limited to newspapers, though. Your local newspaper may also include a locally focused magazine section. If you live in a large metropolitan area, several locally published special-interest magazines will be happy to sell you ads. You can also buy ad space in regional editions of major magazines, such as *Sports Illustrated, U.S. News and World Report,* and *Time,* which, although still a bit pricey, are often affordable (and always prestigious) to the local advertiser. Finally, the community papers, college papers, entertainment guides, classified advertising papers, auto-seller papers, and countless other advertising media are options you may want to consider (although some of these publications make better fish wrap than advertising vehicles, so be careful).

Recognizing What Makes a Print Ad Successful

Advertising legend David Ogilvy was famous for writing print ads that contained literally thousands of words. He assumed a certain intelligence and curiosity in his readers, and he gave them an incredible volume of facts about the various products he was selling. But that was in a different, less hectic time. Ogilvy's approach probably won't work in this day and age, when the average American is exposed to about 250 ad messages every day (which includes TV, radio, and print). In my opinion, today, brevity is the soul of print.

Having said that, there is still a place for long-copy ads, depending on the market you're trying to reach and the type of ad you're running. For example, most advertising to older consumers requires more copy (but legible copy!), because seniors tend to be willing to read and want complete information before letting go of their hard-earned cash. Another reason to use long copy is when you're doing direct selling or seeking an order directly as a result of an ad, which requires a more-complete sales message and is therefore best suited to a long-copy approach.

In addition to copious amounts of *white space* (white background without any graphics or type, like the margins on this page), an effective print ad must include three main elements:

- ✔ A strong headline
- ✔ Brief sell copy
- ✔ An arresting graphic

Anything else, other than your logo, is clutter, and the average person just doesn't have the time to sift through the mess. (For more on these three elements, check out the section "Writing and Designing an Eye-Catching Print Ad.")

Some advertisers design *reverse ads* (a black background with white letters) in their effort to attract the readers' attention. But I don't think this technique works any better than a nicely designed, clean ad with lots of white background.

Most print ads are so muddled with copy, headlines, subheads, banners, graphics, prices, and logos that the reader's eye moves right past the ads, because deciphering what the heck the ad is trying to sell is nearly impossible. The ads are such a blur that they appear to be in motion! It's as if the advertisers, who spend a lot of money for the ads, want to squeeze as much information as possible into the space to get their money's worth. Unfortunately, a page filled with confusing, poorly designed ads is a page to quickly turn, and that's exactly what the readers do.

The ads that grab your audience's attention, the ones that make an impact and have a chance of being read, are the ones that are attractively designed and invite your audience to stop for a moment. Good ads are uncluttered and have clever headlines and interesting graphic elements — they're reader-friendly.

On the other hand, *some* cluttered ads can still be attractively designed to make them easy to read and simple to grasp. If your business has multiple locations, extensive inventory, or numerous products, you may *need* to include a lot of information in your ad. For example, my wireless client uses newspaper to advertise certain cellular offers. These offers can be very complicated, requiring extensive explanation and disclaimers. He also has dozens of store locations that must be included in his print ads. But his ads (which are designed by Pulse Media, a very talented local graphic design firm) never appear cluttered, even though they are rarely larger than 4 columns wide by 12 inches high. Even with all the elements he has to include, his ads still have ample room for white space. This achievement is a testament to thoughtful, clean design — something you, too, should strive for.

Figure 7-1 gives you a look at a cluttered print ad that worked. (It's from my *For Dummies* friends, so you know it worked!) This ad could be surrounded by other ads and *still* jump off the page. A lot of information is packed into this ad, so it could easily have been a hodgepodge of clutter. But instead, the ad is clean and easy to understand, even though it contains the following elements:

- ✔ 8 photos — and a cartoon!
- ✔ A headline, promising a rebate
- ✔ The fill-in-the-blank coupon
- ✔ Instructions on how to fill out the coupon
- ✔ The company logo
- ✔ The terms of the deal, in tiny type

Figure 7-1: A newspaper ad that successfully gives the reader a great deal of information and the ability to order the product.

So what keeps this ad from appearing cluttered? The ad uses bold graphic elements and typography. The first things the eye sees are probably the pictures of the books, then the headline ("Buy any Dummies book and get $5.00 with a mail-in rebate"). Those elements are the foundation of the ad and the primary hooks to attract new customers: Who doesn't want to save money?

If you must include multiple products and/or numerous complicated elements in your print ads, you can still create a crisp, uncluttered look by paying careful attention to the design and layout. (For more on this, see the sections "Generating your graphics" and "Don't forget the layout!".)

Writing and Designing an Eye-Catching Print Ad

Newspaper and magazine readers (your prospective customers) don't care nearly as much about your business as you do. As a matter of fact, they don't care about your business at all. So for this reason, your ads must be clear, succinct, informative, and inviting. Your ads need to give readers a reason to be interested in your business. They can't be pompous and assume, through complicated copy or confusing graphics, that the readers understand everything there is to know about your business and the products or services you're selling. In fact, your print ad has just a split second to attract attention and quickly explain why your product or service has some lasting benefit to those who read about it.

When you sit down to write a print ad, keep in mind that those who read it aren't going to spend a lot of time doing so. Plus, your ad, especially a newspaper ad, will very likely share a page with many other ads, each of which is vying for the reader's attention. And you will probably have no control over the page on which your ad is inserted or the position of your ad on that page. Therefore, *brief copy* and a *clean design* are the soul of print, and to achieve the best possible retail ad, you must give careful attention to the three basic elements (from the previous section) of a good print ad. In the following sections, I cover each of these elements — plus some — so you can use them effectively.

Hammering out your headline

In nearly all cases, the *headline* is the single most-important element of a print ad. The headline has no more than a split second to grab the reader's attention. It's often the largest element on an ad, is generally placed at the top of the ad, and is the first thing — sometimes the only thing — a reader sees. Research says that 90 percent of body copy goes unread, so your head-line had better be good. If the headline is clever, informative, and inviting, it can stop the reader dead in his tracks. If the headline is long, drawn out, and boring (or if it doesn't even exist), the reader will skip right past your ad without giving a moment's thought to all the money you spent putting it there.

Strive to be clear and concise in your headlines. Avoid the temptation to become so "creative" that your meaning is lost or obscured.

Think of your ad headline the way you do the title of a book — for example, *this* book, *Advertising For Dummies,* 2nd Edition, pretty much sums up what this book is about and what level of experience you need to have to benefit from the information in it. That's how succinct your ad headline should be. In con-trast, we could have titled this book something like *An Easy-to-Read and Helpful How-to-do-it Guide to Advertising Your Business (Whatever it May Be, Whether You're Selling Products or Services) for People Who Don't Have Any Background in Advertising.* But that title takes too long to read and figure out — even though it offers more information than our pithy title. Keep that in mind when you're writing your headline: Keep it short and to the point. (See the sidebar "It's an ad, not an encyclopedia," in this chapter for more on headline length.)

The headline is worth some extra work on your part because it may be the only element of your ad that anyone reads. When I write a print ad, I probably spend 90 percent of my time devising the headline. When the light bulb finally goes on and I'm satisfied that the headline is as good as it can be, the body copy falls quickly into place. And if the headline is well written and descriptive enough, it can either stand alone or pull the reader's eye to the *body copy* (the copy that sells the product, as described in this chapter's sec-tion "Building your body copy").

Your headline usually works together with your graphic element, and vice versa — the headline and graphics usually go hand-in-hand. The *head* (that's ad speak for headline) and the graphic, whether it's a photo or a drawing, set the tone of the ad and should be able to stand alone, whether or not anyone gets around to reading the body copy. The head and graphic must create the uniqueness of your ad, the extra something that separates you from all your rivals who are advertising in the same print media.

Often, an ad consists of nothing more than a headline, a subhead, and a logo. An ad for a clothing store may have a headline that reads, "ONE DAY ONLY SALE!" and a subhead that reads, "Hurry! All suits, sports jackets, and slacks reduced 50 percent this Saturday only." Add the store logo, the address, and a phone number, and the ad is complete — it contains all the information the reader needs.

Where the headline is placed within the ad is as important as what the headline says. You need to make sure that the headline *dominates* the ad so it can be quickly understood. Too often, the headline, which includes the most important information within an ad, is lost in a muddle of too many type fonts, graphics, and other elements. The reader's eye isn't drawn to anything, the ad is ignored, and the advertiser's money goes down the drain.

Shaping your subheads

In addition to the main headline, a *subhead* is used to impart secondary information. The headline must grab readers, but the subhead can explain the deal further. Keep your headline brief and clever, and use the subhead to be a bit more expansive with your information. For example, if you're selling a product, the headline may read, "The Deal of the Century!" The subhead could follow with, "We're having a store-wide clearance sale." If you're selling a service, the headline could be, "Don't Pay Your Taxes!" The subhead could read, "Until you talk with Smith Accountancy."

Not all ads require a subhead, but this element, generally set in smaller type, is there to give the reader additional information without cluttering up your ad.

Building your body copy

The *body copy,* also known as the *sell copy,* is where you can explain your offer in detail. But, like everything else in a good print ad, you need to keep the body copy brief — and possibly not include it at all. A good ad can get by without body copy, using just a well-written headline and a solid subhead.

Don't expect rapt attention and deep involvement from the reader. (Ninety percent of the time, body copy goes unread.) The reader doesn't have time to sift through mounds of information in order to find a reason to respond. Squeezing 50 pounds of copy into a one-pound ad is a mistake. When writing body copy for a print ad, regardless of the size of the ad, invoking the KISS Rule — keep it simple, stupid — is a good idea.

Link the headline, key visual, and opening line of your body copy. Readers are much more likely to make sense of your ad if the headline and key visual work extremely well together. It also helps bring the reader into your ad if the copy lead is consistent with the premise of your headline and key visual.

It's an ad, not an encyclopedia

The primary mistake made in many print ads is verbosity. The philosophy seems to be: Why use 5 words when 500 words will do? Readers aren't interested in how to *make* a fine Swiss watch. They're only interested in how much money they can save if they buy the watch from you.

A brief headline is particularly important. A headline reading, "50 PERCENT SAVINGS" is better than one reading, "Everything storewide has been marked down 50 percent." Making your headline brief, intriguing, and easy to grasp, most certainly, enhances your ad's effectiveness. Trying to fit too much information into the headline can be self-defeating. Use the subhead or the body copy for the nuts and bolts of your sales pitch.

Keep your body copy brief and your graphic elements relevant and bold. That way, you make it easy for your readers to grasp what you're trying to say and what you're striving to sell. Just because you've spent a fair amount of money to buy the ad space doesn't mean that you have to fill it wall-to-wall. An ad that's easy for the reader to understand may be rewarded with the reader dropping into your store or contacting you, credit card poised and at the ready!

Do what I do: Write your ad, and then go back and see how many superfluous words you can eliminate until your copy is as tight as it can possibly be. In print copy, less is more!

Generating your graphics

Whether it's photography, fine art, line art, cartoon, or typography, the *graphic element* of your ad is there to attract the readers' eyes and interest them enough to read your body copy. Your graphic, together with your headline, is there to encourage readers to invest a little time to actually absorb what it is you're trying to sell. The graphic element usually calls attention to, or complements, the headline — the two elements work together to create the overall ambience of the ad.

Make sure your graphic element is relevant to what you're selling. A photo of a girl in a bikini isn't the best way to sell anything except bikinis. Health and fitness spas are always using bathing suit babes as their central graphic. (Are some people really dumb enough to believe that those women are actually members?)

If your ad is for a straightforward, no-holds-barred clearance sale, your graphic element may be nothing more than a very large headline spelled out in a bold, readable typeface that says, "Get In Here!" If, on the other hand, your ad is meant to announce a new product, then a quality photo or drawing of that product, along with a subtle headline, will do nicely.

Getting the help you need

The artists who work in the retail design and layout department of your local paper are probably overworked, underpaid, and not always diligent in their efforts. But they *are* capable of doing good work if you insist on it (if they didn't have talent they wouldn't have been hired by the publication in the first place). Ask for their help, and don't accept an ad that you feel could have been done much better.

Remember: Don't be adversarial in your dealings with the newspaper staff, but do let them know that you have definite ideas on what a good ad layout is. These artists, like anyone else, would rather do work they can be proud of.

Newspapers can sometimes mangle a good photograph in the printing process — and unless you're paying big bucks, the graphics will probably be black and white. When a photo is reproduced in a newspaper, it always runs the risk of appearing too dark, too light, or too cloudy (especially if one of the pressmen has neglected to re-ink the rollers). Newspapers do strive for good quality in their printing process, but to avoid frustration and irate clients, I usually avoid using photos in newspaper ads. A black-and-white line drawing usually reproduces much better.

Lines, shapes, borders, symbols, and clip art are available to you on your computer right alongside a few dozen different type fonts. You shouldn't have any trouble creating a good print ad complete with a clever headline and an arresting graphic by using nothing more than your word-processing program. Of course, if you aren't all that comfortable with a computer, you may want to employ the services of a good graphic designer. Hiring a professional to do a professional's job, regardless of what the job is, always pays in the long run. But whether you're able to hire a pro depends on your budget.

The newspaper in which you're advertising can also provide you with design help. If you feel comfortable with their abilities, you may want to just let the newspaper's design department handle the whole enterprise of producing your ad. This service is called *pub set* (which means the *pub*lication *set*s the ad), and it's usually free. Keep in mind that, as with anything in life, you get what you pay for.

Don't forget the layout!

The design and layout of an ad is everything. Print ads are often very poorly designed. These ads are easily ignored because they don't attract the eye to any particular feature or element, and they certainly don't sell anybody anything.

Figure 7-2 illustrates a sample layout for a magazine ad. If you stick to this kind of layout, you can't go wrong.

In this plain-English guide, forensics guru and crime fiction consultant
Dr. D. P. Lyle demystifies the science of crime scene investigations, from
fingerprints and fibers to time of death and DNA.

"Dynamic, entertaining,
and educational ...
blows the lid off the
science of crime."
—KATHLEEN ANTRIM, author
of *Capital Offense*

0-7645-5580-4 • 384 pp.
Available wherever
books are sold.

Figure 7-2:
Layout is
an all-
important
part of your
print ad's
success.

Wiley, the Wiley logo, For Dummies, and related trademarks,
logos, and trade dress are trademarks or registered trademarks
of John Wiley & Sons, Inc. and/or its affiliates.

FOR
DUMMIES
A Branded Imprint of ⊛WILEY
Now you know.

You can do good print advertisement designs by using various computer art
programs. But if you're not sure whether you're the best person to handle the
layout of your ad, hire a professional to do it for you. The extra money spent
will come back to you in the form of increased attention to your ad and customer response. If you're using the publication's designers, stay on top of

Image is everything

A clean, well-designed, and orderly print ad can go a long way in telling readers that your business is also clean, well designed, and orderly. By making your point in clear, concise terms, you're doing the readers a favor. They can see at a glance whether you're selling something they need. You haven't taken much of their time, and they appreciate that.

Whether you're buying a full-page or a one-column two-inch ad, your ad must focus the reader's eyes on the most relevant information as quickly as possible. Every other ad in the publication is competing for the reader's attention. Your ad may even be stacked atop the ad of your direct competitor (if it is, get the newspaper to give you a *make good,* in which you get another ad free of charge). Give yourself a chance by designing and writing a superior ad that cuts through all the clutter and gives the reader a reason to stop for a moment.

them until they bring you an ad layout that adheres to all the prerequisites in this chapter. Don't hesitate to insist on good design, even though you're getting it for free. To find freelance professional designers, you can look in your local Yellow Pages under "Graphic Designers" or "Graphic Services." Another possibility is to ask some of your local printers for references.

Chapter 8

Radio: Effective, Affordable, and Fun

Sitting before a blank piece of paper or an empty computer screen and attempting to write a 60-second radio commercial that can effectively and memorably motivate listeners to buy *your* product or service can be an intimidating task. How do you separate yourself from the herd? What magic words can you use to describe all the wonderful reasons why consumers should hire you or buy from you instead of from the dozens of other businesses out there trying to convince them of the same thing? How can you turn hard facts into clever copy that cuts through the clutter and stops listeners dead in their tracks?

Writing radio ads is a process, like anything else, and it gets easier the more you do it. In this chapter, I lead you through the process one step at a time and, with any luck whatsoever, by the end of this chapter, you'll be writing spots like a pro. To pack a thousand seconds of information into a 60-second bag isn't as hard as it appears if you follow these guidelines.

Summarizing Your Business in 60 Seconds

You may think it's a daunting prospect to tell your customers everything they need to know about your business within the limited time frame of one minute. But a minute is quite a long time, actually. Look at your watch and let a full minute go by. Tapping your fingers or fidgeting in your seat isn't allowed. Concentrate on the second hand (or the seconds ticking off on your digital watch). See what I mean? A minute is a long time. Sixty excruciatingly slow clicks. Just think of all the wonderful information you can squeeze into a spot within that *huge* amount of time.

The trick here is to concentrate on the *relevant* information you want to impart and to discard everything else. You simply can't summarize an encyclopedia's worth of information in 60 seconds, but you can tell the world quite a lot about yourself in that length of time. Writing *radio 60s,* as they're called, is good practice for you because, if you're ever interested in writing ads for television, you need to do this in 30 seconds — or even 15. Whew!

So what information do you need to convey in your ad? Okay, here it comes, folks, a professional copywriter's secret, a revelation so incredible, so astute, so amazing that you'll likely say to yourself, "Humph! I knew that!" It's the same basic informational formula used by journalists — namely: Who, what, when, where, and why (otherwise known as the *five Ws*).

When arranged in a radio spot, the five Ws don't always fall in a particular order, of course. Including them all is a good idea, but you can arrange them any way you like — within reason.

In this section, I uncover how the five Ws apply to you and how you can use them to create memorable radio ads.

Who are you?

The first thing you want your listener to know is *who* you are, so you need to mention the name of your business within the first line or two. I hear commercials all the time that drone on and on and never seem to think that the sponsor's name is important enough to mention until somewhere around the last five seconds. This format is a big, fat, money-wasting mistake because by then it's too late. Listeners *never* hear every word of your commercial. It doesn't matter whether they hear it 20 times, or even 100 times, they don't listen carefully to each and every word. Instead, they hear bits and pieces of it. They may recall some elements of it. They know they've heard "something" that appeals to them. They may even respond to it (at least you hope they do). But listeners are never able to recite your ad word for word. So telling them who you are *immediately* is very important.

What are you selling?

The next thing you want listeners to know is *what* you're selling. Which of your products or services are you featuring in this spot? Don't try to sell your entire business in one 60-second spot. It just doesn't work — you can confuse listeners even more than they already are.

Instead, target your message to one or two important elements. Give the listener a fighting chance to remember what the heck you're talking about.

If you have too much information to squeeze into one spot, write two different spots and rotate them 50/50 on the air.

Consumers are being deluged with advertising information, both audio and visual, each and every waking moment of their lives. The first thing they see in the morning is advertising on the toothpaste tube, then on the cereal box and milk carton, then on the coffee can, then on the labels of their clothes, and only then, after subliminally absorbing dozens of advertising messages, do they pick up their newspapers, or turn on the radio or TV, all of which bury consumers in advertising.

All you're trying to do in your spot — all you can *hope* to do — is get your foot in the door with one juicy tidbit of information, so your audience recalls at least *something* of what you're saying. Target your message very carefully and succinctly. Narrow your message to simple, hard-hitting, important facts that listeners can remember and act on.

When do you want consumers to act?

You can't expect your listeners to act if they don't know when to do it. When does your special sale price take effect? When does this offer go away? When is your store open? This *W* is a great area into which you can insert your calls to action, such as the following:

- ✔ "This offer absolutely ends midnight Saturday."
- ✔ "Hurry in today!"
- ✔ "Call now!"
- ✔ "We're staying open until 10:00 every night to keep up with customer demand."
- ✔ "Sale ends Thursday."

If you can insert an element of urgency into your commercial, you give listeners just that much more to think about and a good reason to act.

How can customers get in touch with you?

You definitely want to tell your listeners *where* you are and how they can find you. Although this sounds rather basic, you may be amazed at how many spots wait until the end of the ad to mention it — or even forget this all-important information altogether!

You want to include your phone number (preferably, a toll-free number, so customers won't have to pay for the call!) so customers can call for information or for directions to your nearest store.

For your business location, give the address and phone number, but be careful here: Listeners can't be expected to remember too many numbers or complicated directions. Chances are they hear your spot while driving or doing something else, and they aren't inclined or able to jot down any information. When was the last time you were so blown away by an advertising message that you pulled your car off the road and wrote down the advertiser's name and address? Probably never.

The simpler, the better. Include a phone number rather than an address. Be sure to repeat the phone number a minimum of two times. If you absolutely must include an address, write something like, "Located on Main Street near First," instead of expecting anyone to recall "36452 East Main Street."

If you have a Web address, use it in your spot *instead of* the phone number. Don't mention them both — remembering that many numbers and letters is just too much to ask of your listeners.

Why should customers hire or buy from you?

And now the most important of all the elements of a commercial, the *why.* Ask yourself the following questions before drafting your copy:

- ✔ Why should the customer buy from you rather than from somebody else?

- ✔ Why should the customer hire you or your company instead of someone else?

- ✔ Why is your deal the very best deal that customers are ever going to find?

- ✔ Why should anyone go out of his way to seek out your product or service when buying it somewhere else may be much more convenient?

Sell your expertise; a great price and terms; a friendly, family-like atmosphere; a closeout price that's irresistible; or any number of other points. The *why* part of your ad is very likely the reason you're advertising in the first place. It's your *hook,* your reason for being, your unique product difference. This area separates the successful businesses from the also-rans.

Putting the five *W*s to use

If your head is spinning from the thought of incorporating the five *W*s into one radio spot, here's an example of how you can even incorporate them into one sentence that opens a 60-second radio commercial:

> CALIFORNIA DINETTES *(Who)*, PURVEYORS OF FINE CASUAL DINING FURNITURE *(What)*, IS HAVING ITS ANNUAL SPRING DECORATING SALE *(Why)* BEGINNING FRIDAY *(When)* AT ITS BEAUTIFUL SHOWROOMS IN SAN JOSE, SAN CARLOS, AND PLEASANT HILL *(Where)*.

This sentence would be a good opener to a 60-second spot because it tells listeners nearly everything they need to know right off the bat. It also leaves 50 seconds in which to get more specific (for example, to add a broad description of the furniture items on sale, what the prices and terms are, the telephone number, the sale deadline, and so on). But if listeners only hear the first few words of this spot, the first sentence gives them all the truly important information about this furniture sale.

This spot is also a completed 10-second spot, which stations sometimes call *billboards, I.D.s,* or *promos.* If your media buy includes 10-second spots (which are often included at no charge), then this spot is what you want to air. Listeners may not even hear your 60-second spot, but they may hear one of your billboards. Try to include everything they need to know within those first ten seconds.

You can expand this spot into the complete 60-second version as well. Add more specific information and dress it up with adjectives and a call to action. See if you can identify the five *W*s in this spot. They're all there — and more than once.

CALIFORNIA DINETTES, PURVEYORS OF FINE CASUAL DINING FURNITURE, IS HAVING ITS ANNUAL SPRING DECORATING SALE BEGINNING FRIDAY AT ITS BEAUTIFUL SHOWROOMS IN SAN JOSE, SAN CARLOS, AND PLEASANT HILL. WE'VE BEEN BUSY GRABBING UP FABULOUS DEALS ON CASUAL DINING FURNITURE FROM THE NATION'S BEST MANUFACTURERS. RIGHT NOW THE CALIFORNIA DINETTES SHOWROOMS AND WAREHOUSE ARE BULGING. WE NEED TO GET THIS FINE FURNITURE OFF OUR FLOORS AND ONTO YOUR FLOORS RIGHT AWAY, SO WE'VE SLASHED PRICES. CHOOSE FROM THE LATEST DINETTES IN IRON AND GLASS, NATURAL WOODS, AND LAMINATES — WITH ELEGANT TABLETOPS OF GRANITE, CORIAN, AND WOOD INLAYS — ALL AT 15 TO 50 PERCENT OFF! NEED BARSTOOLS? ALL BARSTOOLS REDUCED AN EXTRA 30 PERCENT. SO FOR SUPER DEALS, COME AND GET 'EM DURING SPRING SAVINGS DAYS AT THE CASUAL DINING SPECIALISTS — CALIFORNIA DINETTES, CONVENIENTLY LOCATED IN SAN CARLOS, PLEASANT HILL, AND SAN JOSE. HURRY IN TODAY FOR BEST SELECTION!

Notice that the complete 60-second spot mentions the name of the store three times and its locations twice. It describes what furniture is on sale, lists the many whys, and inserts two calls to action ("Come and get 'em" and "Hurry in today for best selection!"). If listeners hear only the first sentence or the final sentence, those listeners have heard enough to know that something interesting is going on at California Dinettes.

You must always find the magic *why* in order to have any hope of listener response to your commercials. For example, your listener can buy a can of paint anywhere, from any hardware store. But *your* business, your products, your prices, your terms, your convenient location, your incredible customer service, your friendly employees, your free gourmet coffee and your plush, posh, golly-gosh waiting room are so much better than anyone else's that he'd be a fool not to rush right in and give you his business. That's the *why*. And, to the ultimate success of your spot, the why is everything.

Deciding on the Format for Your Ad

Radio ads are there to get the attention of your listeners — people you want to become customers if they aren't already. Before you sit down and start writing, consider: If you want your radio ad to be effective, it needs to do the following, all within the span of one minute (or between 180 and 200 words):

- Grab the listeners' attention
- Tell them something they want to hear
- Sell them something they may not need
- Mention the name of your business several times
- Get your phone number or Web address indelibly written into their brains
- Motivate them with a *call to action* (something that tells your reader what to do, such as "Call today for the best prices!" or "In stores now!")

Knowing what to include in your ad is one thing, but an equally important part of creating your ad is knowing how exactly to communicate that message. In the following sections, I cover some common formats for radio spots. Within these different formats, of course, you may discover endless room for creativity. So flex those creative muscles!

Due to the ever-changing world of technology, each station has its own requirements for your advertising materials. You can't find one exact form to use when submitting broadcast copy, so be sure to check with the station to make sure your materials are up to par.

Talking it up: Dialogue

Dialogue is a common form of radio spots, but like fingernails on a blackboard, it makes me cringe. The problem with dialogue radio spots is that they're usually poorly written. Can you think of any radio commercials more ridiculous than a poorly written, poorly acted dialogue spot?

You know the ones I mean — they're the spots in which two people are doing or talking about something totally unrelated to the product being sold, and then they awkwardly bring the product *sell* (or message) into the dialogue. For instance, the spot opens with the sound of a golf ball being hit, and the following dialogue takes place:

> **Jim:** "Wow, great drive, Bill. I've never seen you hit the ball *that* far before."
>
> **Bill:** "Thanks, Jim. I'm seeing the ball a lot better since I went to Dr. Fishburn's Laser Eye Center, where I had both eyes done for just $2,495."
>
> **Jim:** "Gee, Bill, do you mean that if I undergo major eye surgery at Dr. Fishburn's Laser Eye Center, and spend only $2,495, I can hit the ball farther, too?"
>
> **Bill:** "No doubt about it, Jim. You'll improve your game and improve your life at Dr. Fishburn's Laser Eye Center. Just call 1-800-555-1212 and make an appointment."
>
> **Jim:** "What was that number again, Bill? Did you say 1-800-555-1212?"
>
> **Bill:** "Yep, 1-800-555-1212. Call them today."

The reason I hate these kinds of radio spots is that nobody talks like that in real life! These spots just cry out to be ignored, if not laughed at, because they're completely unbelievable. Even the major advertising agencies do this stuff, especially for pharmaceutical clients — and they should know better.

I stay as far away from dialogue spots as I can, and I think you should, too. In my opinion, nothing is more effective on radio than a single-voice read of good, believable copy. Don't offend or insult your listener with a premise and copy that is unbelievable, contrived, confusing, and just plain dumb. If you do, you have no one to blame but yourself when that listener reaches over, punches the radio button, and makes you instantly disappear.

While consumers are listening to your spot on the station you just spent a bunch of money to buy, you owe it to yourself and to your listeners to capture their limited attention spans with some good, clear copy — copy that gives them a reason to listen and a reason to buy your product. If you confuse the issue with an unrealistic concept and improbable copy, you lose them.

Amusing (and schmoozing) the masses: Comedy

Like dialogue spots, a poorly conceived comedy premise and badly written copy do a lot more harm than good — so tread lightly. Setting up an amusing idea, including some copy that actually sells your product in an entertaining manner, and then delivering a good punch line in the span of 60 seconds is difficult. The sad number of unfunny spots on the air that are trying to be comical is a testament to the difficulty inherent in comedy writing.

When it comes to good comedy writing, you've either got it, or you don't. I don't think that you can be taught to write good comedy. Personally, I've had good success with comedy writing, and I've used it in many radio spots. But very few products and services lend themselves to this genre.

Including some tongue-in-cheek styling to your copy, maybe poking a little fun at yourself, or at least not taking yourself too seriously is okay. But, unless you're very proficient at it, leave the comedy writing to the pros because comedy is very serious business. That's one of the reasons you may want to check out Chapter 16 on "Deciding Whether to Hire an Ad Agency."

Avoid punch line humor. Radio is a frequency medium, so punch lines get old very fast — and after they do, nobody will want to listen to your ad. The best style of humor for radio is *situational humor*. In this style of humor, the situation is focus of the comedy: The *Seinfeld* TV show is a classic example of situational humor.

Giving just the facts: A straight read

A single voice reading 60 seconds of clear, concise, fact-filled copy that motivates and sells listeners is always a good bet. No frills. No jokes. No unrealistic dialogue. Just the offer — the selling proposition — read by a good, strong, male or female voice. You may want to toss in some background music or even some sound effects (see the sidebar "Sound effects and music tracks" for more information). I prefer this format when writing and producing direct-response broadcast advertising. To me, a *straight read* is the most effective copywriting method you can use to convey a selling message. And it's the easiest, which, if you're new to the game, may be the best reason of all to employ it.

When writing a straight read, you sit down and write a wonderful 60-second spot with a clear message and a compelling call to action. Then you hand this script to the voice talent who records it, the engineer adds some appropriate music or sound effects, and the station puts it on the air. Voilà! Your ad campaign is out there beating on the ears of your potential customers. It's not a cute spot. It's not even a fancy spot. But it's on the radio getting your message out to listeners who, if you've followed the writing instructions I outline in this chapter, are banging on your door, calling you, or checking out your Web site any minute now.

TIP

Sound effects and music tracks

Want to jazz up your spot? This may be a good time to touch on the wonderful world of effects. Sound effects (SFX) and music tracks (MX) are the magic that makes radio "the theater of the mind." The sound effects and music tracks of the old-time radio shows put listeners right in the middle of the action. And that's what they can still do for your listeners today. Do you want 500 wild horses to gallop through your commercial? Go for it. Do you want your announcer to read your spot while standing on the starting line of a noisy racetrack? No problem. Do you want your entire spot to take place in a driving thunderstorm or in the middle of a battlefield? Be my guest.

Most radio stations and all production houses have huge collections of stock sound effects and music for use in commercial backgrounds. Pick a sound, almost *any* sound, and they are sure to have it — and it can be woven seamlessly into your spot. Then choose some appropriate music and mix it into the backdrop of your spot. With these production tricks, even if you're only producing a straight read, you can enhance your ad with effects and background music to help it cut through the clutter.

Determining Who Should Read the Script

After you have your radio spot written, you need to find someone to read it. And the possibilities are numerous. You can read the spot yourself, have a studio announcer (someone who works for the radio station) read it for you, or hire a professional voiceover talent. I cover each of these options in the following sections.

Doing it yourself

I'm generally against clients voicing their own spots on radio or getting in front of the cameras on TV. Everyone wants to be in show business; everyone wants to hear her friends say, "Hey, I heard you on the radio today!" But, generally speaking, reading your own radio spots is not a very good idea. When you read your own spots, it usually comes off as amateur night.

Generally, you're much better off using a professionally trained voice talent who can give a spot the believability and sincerity it needs, rather than standing as an inexperienced rookie in front of a microphone and hoping for the best. Of course, two of the best-known exceptions to this very flexible rule were Frank Perdue of Perdue Chickens and Dave Thomas of Wendy's, both of whom brought a unique, charming talent to their commercials and were completely believable.

ANECDOTE

The exception to the rule

Having issued all my warnings about reading your own radio spots in the section "Doing it yourself," I want to share with you the story of one client I have who is the exception to the rule. His name is Matt Fidiam, and he's the general manager of Parrot Cellular, a major Northern California wireless retailer.

My agency had been trying unsuccessfully to get the Parrot Cellular account for so long that I finally just admitted to myself that it wasn't going to happen and had just about given up. Happily, my business associate, Marnie Doherty, did *not* give up. She simply wouldn't take *no* for an answer and kept after the account like a pit bull. In a final attempt to attract the client's attention and, hopefully, to secure the business, she and I went to a micro-brewery and whipped up a batch of our very own beer. Then we bottled it, complete with custom-labeling Marnie had designed. Knowing that Mr. Fidiam has a fondness for the occasional exotic beer and a well-developed sense of humor, we packaged several bottles into a lovely wooden gift box with an outside label reading: "You may be shocked to learn we are *not* above using bribery!" We then placed the gift box of custom brew on the doorstep of Matt's corporate offices early one morning before anyone arrived for work. Hey, we had nothing to lose.

It worked. He called us that very morning and said, "If you guys are as good at advertising as you are at sales, I've got to give you my account."

After having a few meetings with Matt (even before we secured the account), it was immediately apparent to me that he would be his own best on-air talent. He's a very animated, articulate, enthusiastic guy with a great sense of humor and a very unique voice. It was obvious

that with properly written copy, he would be the best person to project the personal enthusiasm he had about his own products. And, in the process, we would have a one-of-a-kind voice on the air in the Bay Area selling Parrot Cellular stores. That revelation made me sure that we could do a great job on the account in the first place and what kept Marnie Doherty tenaciously pitching the business long after I had given up. We knew that, given a chance, our idea of putting him on the air would work for him. And we were right.

After finally landing the account, we didn't have to talk too hard to get him to agree to do a few spots as a test. I wrote several spots in the first person ("Hi, this is Matt Fidiam for Parrot Cellular . . ."). We then went into a recording studio, put him in front of a mic, and he was, as I had hoped, a natural. Oh, he stumbled a bit here and there, but even the pros do that. And, because the recording process is digital these days, we were able to cut and paste the spots so he didn't have to go back to the beginning each time he flubbed a line. He wasn't a pro (not yet, anyway), but the final commercials were great.

Now, hundreds of commercials later, Matt Fidiam's voice is one of the most recognizable on Bay Area radio, which is precisely what I was after in the first place. He and I once attended a hockey game together, and while we were chatting in the concession area, a stranger walked up to him and asked, "Hey, aren't you that guy who sells cell phones on the radio?"

I've written so many commercials for Parrot Cellular that I've begun to think like my client. I know the words he likes to use and the ones he stumbles over. I know the phrasing that he prefers and how to insert just the right amount of sarcasm and "edge" that have become his trademark. And now, when we go into a recording studio, Matt is there for no more than ten minutes. He reads the spots, usually straight through on the first take, and then he leaves. He has become the consummate professional voice talent.

Matt has been so successful with radio advertising that he has moved nearly 80 percent of his advertising funds into broadcast and has grown, since I first started working for him, from 11 local stores to 70 stores throughout Northern California. Parrot Cellular now accounts for nearly 25 percent of the total new telephone activations of Northern California Cingular Wireless. And, today, Parrot Cellular *owns* Bay Area radio.

Even the most gregarious, enthusiastic, vivacious person can be reduced to a blubbering bowl of jelly when you put him into a sound-proofed booth and flip the switch on a mic. The same person who is the life of the party and the best joke teller in the world, the one who has more personality than five people, is suddenly reduced to a monotone robot. Nothing is worse than a spot that sounds like it's being *read*.

On the other hand, you may have exactly what it takes to come across as believable and memorable on the air (see the sidebar "The exception to the rule" for more information). If you're a natural voice talent, by all means go for it. No one can possibly sell your products and services better than you. But be objective when you critique your final commercial. Don't just play it for people who are only going to tell you what you want to hear, such as friends and family. Instead, play it for vendors and customers and watch them, especially their eyes, carefully while they listen to your spot. They may be able to lie to you, flatter you, but their eyes (and their body language) can't. Of course, in the final analysis, you must make the final decision.

Listen to your finished spot very objectively and try to hear it through the ears of John or Jane Doe driving down the road being bombarded by commercial message after commercial message. As you listen, assess your commercial by asking the following questions — and answer honestly:

- ✔ Does your copy give the listener a reason to act?
- ✔ Does your voice and delivery motivate listeners?
- ✔ Is your finished commercial memorable?
- ✔ Do you sound excited, sincere, and believable?
- ✔ If I heard this spot, would I be motivated to respond to it?

If the answer to any of the above questions is no, you probably need to admit that you're not the next Ed McMahon and move on to the following section.

Using a studio announcer

Another option when you're looking for the right voice for your radio spot is to rely on the station-employed studio announcers (disk jockeys or on-air personalities). The advantage to this route is that it's the cheapest way to go. The service is usually free of charge as part of your media buy. You only have to pay a talent fee if you use a studio announcer who works for a station other than the one the spots air on. By and large, studio announcers do a good, if not always enthusiastic, job on most commercial copy they read. Another advantage is that because these on-air personalities are familiar, listeners are more likely to trust them or at least pay attention to what they have to say.

Just handing your script to each station you want to advertise on and having the spots read by various station-employed studio announcers immediately negates one of the most important elements of a successful broadcast campaign: continuity. Listeners tend to bounce around from station to station and, if you're lucky, they may hear your spots on more that one. So you need to be sure they hear the same message regardless of the station they happen to be listening to at the time. Plus, if you use a studio announcer, your commercial may wind up sounding just like all the other spots on that station. After all, your ad isn't the *only* one those announcers are reading.

Hiring a professional voice talent

If you're willing to pay a little more to make your radio spots top notch, you can hire a pro to read them for you. Your station sales rep, the production manager at most stations, or even your Yellow Pages (look under "Talent Agencies") can steer you toward professional voices in your area. These people don't work for any particular station; instead, they're freelance talents or voice actors who make their livings doing commercial voiceovers, radio and TV spots, corporate sales videos, and anything else that requires the talents and abilities of someone who is better than most of us are at simply reading.

Depending on the size of the area where you live, you may have a harder time finding a good voiceover talent, but they're out there. Your local radio or TV station's creative and production personnel can put you in touch with talent agents or voice talent outside your area, all of whom can do a great job for you from a distance and send you the finished copy on a CD (or even send the spots electronically directly to the stations).

Finding and funding union professionals

Some professional voice talents (usually the very best of them) are members of the Screen Actors Guild (SAG) or the American Federation of Television and Radio Artists (AFTRA). In other words, they're union. Being part of a union means that they get paid a union minimum fee to record the spot and grant you the use of it on the air for 13 weeks — plus they earn residuals if the spot stays on the air longer than that or returns on a later *flight of commercials* (which are the schedule broadcast dates). And the really high-powered talent can ask for, and get, far more than the union minimum. You may not want this.

Working with union voice talent gets very expensive, but by employing union talent, you're making the trade-off of a higher fee in exchange for a better finished product. And the whole point may be moot anyway because you, as a client, must be what's called a SAG or AFTRA *signatory* in order to employ these union members in the first place (although, and I'm not trying to get anyone into trouble here, I've worked with union talent who waived their residual rights in exchange for a flat fee just to get the extra work). If you've employed an ad agency, don't sweat these details; it can handle this stuff for you.

For example, my ad agency uses the same six or eight male and female voice talents for a variety of accounts, because these people have the ability to bring something fresh and new to everything they do. Even if their spots for different clients run back-to-back on a station, listeners never know they're hearing the same person, because the content of each spot sounds so different.

So if you're going to do a lot of broadcast advertising, hook up with some professional voice talents. Then pay them promptly so they're always available when you call.

A pro usually charges a flat fee to voice (record) one 60-second radio spot, and a different fee to voice a 30-second television spot. You want to hire a voiceover talent on a *buy-out basis,* which is simply a fee for service, with no strings attached. The talent does the spot for a previously agreed-upon price, you give the actor a check, and she gives you full and unlimited rights to the finished spot for as long as you want to air it. In other words, you own it and can do with it as you please.

Be clear about the terms of your agreement with a voice talent from the beginning so you have no confusion.

If you're considering hiring professional voice talents, you should shop around, because costs may vary significantly from one market to the next. For example, prices in New York City are based on the time the talent spends recording, charging nonunion talent around $500 for the first hour, and anywhere from $200 to $250 for every extra half hour. However, you can most likely hire talent for almost $100 less outside of the Big Apple.

Ask your station rep what the going rate is in your area for both nonunion and union (see the nearby sidebar) talent. Get an upfront quote from the talent and go from there. Be sure you know what you're getting into before committing to a voice talent.

Setting It All in Motion: How to Get Your Ad on the Radio

You've written your spot. It's perfect. It's interesting. It sells. And it even includes some clever effects. You've had it recorded and produced by a top-quality voice talent (or, in the interest of frugality, you've done it yourself), and you're ready to put it on the air. You've bought advertising schedules on several radio stations. You're ready to go. Now what?

First you need a few copies of the *master* (the original that likely remains in the custody of the radio station that produced it). I always take a copy for my agency's archives and leave the master on file with the station. (Who needs the extra responsibility of archiving a master copy?)

Help is available

The process of getting your spot on the radio can seem very technical, complicated, and even overwhelming. But your radio station's sales reps can help lead you through the actual process one step at a time. Believe me, if the station rep has gotten a foot in your door and you've placed a buy with him, the radio station wants everything to go smoothly for you. The folks there want your spots to be successful so that you continue to place buys on their station. So they help in any way they can to ensure that your advertising works.

Don't be afraid to ask questions and to request your station rep's expert assistance in giving your advertising flight (schedule) the best possible chance to succeed. *Remember:* Your station rep, the person who is actually calling on your business, is especially interested in your success. He is paid on commission. He wants your spots to work, your business to prosper, and customers to beat down your door, so you stay with him month after month, year after year. He helps you get copy written, spots produced, traffic instructions submitted, dubs sent to other stations, and whatever else it takes to make you happy (at least he does if he's any good).

You need one copy for yourself and one for each radio station on your media schedule.

Label the copies (or the boxes they come in) with your company name, the spot title, the spot length, and the production date of the spot. If you want to get really fancy, order some custom audio labels. But your standard company mailing labels work just as well.

Don't send out anything to the stations on your buy that isn't carefully labeled. Radio station traffic or continuity departments have enough problems without trying to find your unlabeled dub (copy of your ad) in a sea of commercials. The traffic or continuity department schedules and runs the correct spots at the correct times for each and every advertiser the station has on the air. That's hundreds of commercials every day — which can make for a very hectic and high-stress environment where mistakes can, and do, happen. So make your instructions to the traffic department very clear to eliminate confusion.

Here is a sample of good traffic instructions, ready to send with your radio spot to the radio station's traffic department:

> **Your Company Name, address, phone, fax, e-mail, and any other contact information**
>
> **Date:** August 15, 2007
>
> **Traffic Instructions to:** [LIST STATION CALL LETTERS HERE]
>
> **ATTN:** TRAFFIC DEPARTMENT
>
> **For:** Your Company Name
>
> **Flight date:** September 1 through October 15, 2007
>
> RUN "FALL CLEARANCE SALE:60," @ 100% OF SPOTS SCHEDULED (PER YOUR STATION'S CONTRACT) BEGINNING SEPTEMBER 1 AND THROUGH OCTOBER 15, 2007
>
> Put any special billing instructions here.
>
> Put your name, title, and phone number here so the traffic department can contact you with any questions.

Note: A radio schedule is called a *flight.* Notice on the traffic instructions that I call out the flight date. This section alerts the Traffic Department that, at the end of this flight, this particular spot will no longer run, and new copy and instructions will be forthcoming (or your radio schedule concludes).

Chapter 9

Demystifying TV Commercials: They Don't Have to Win Awards to Be Effective

. . . .

In This Chapter

▶ Creating a quality television spot on a budget

▶ Writing the audio and thinking visually

▶ Working with a production crew to shoot your spot

▶ Getting your spot edited to perfection

. . . .

*Y*ou've probably seen TV commercials from local advertisers and small businesses that have distinctive advertising that made a name for their businesses. Just because you're not a Fortune 500 company with a million-dollar advertising budget doesn't mean you can't do effective TV commercials.

Many small businesses feature the owner or another family member, or even an employee, if that person is more comfortable in front of the camera and would make a good spokesperson for the business. Others use a consistent theme, piece of music, location, actor, or a premise — this consistency in all the company's commercials helps build familiarity with the business. While you can build a distinctive image in any media, TV is highly successful for brand building and rewards advertisers that employ continuity.

Continuity is the key when designing an ad campaign. You don't want to water down your budget by advertising different messages on various media. And the foremost element you want to keep in mind as you write your TV spot are your visuals — think visually and consider your production budget as you create your spot.

Although you want your TV commercials to be consistent with your radio spots, TV spots should be more than just radio with visuals. Think about the TV commercials you not only like but that persuaded you to buy (or at least investigate) a product being advertised — and keep that in mind when you're developing your own TV spots.

The best TV commercials are ones that grab viewers' attention, making them want to look at the screen and see how your product can be used, or what your store looks like and the variety of products you sell, or your earnest appeal for how your service can help them. TV commercials are even more effective if they have substantial entertainment value.

In this chapter, I walk you through the process of actually writing your own TV commercial — from the audio to the visual to the computer graphics. I also help you find ways to cut costs to stay within your budget. And I let you know what to expect when your commercial is actually shot and edited. Producing a TV commercial can be a daunting task, but in this chapter, I demystify it so that you can put TV to work for you.

Designing Your TV Commercial in Layers

When you set out to create an effective TV commercial, you can easily become overwhelmed by the various aspects of the job. But keep in mind the three basic elements to a TV spot: audio, video, and computer graphics. If you divide your commercial up into these three elements, the job is much easier to accomplish.

Every television spot doesn't necessarily include all three elements, but most good spots do, so consider designing your spot to include all of them. I break down these three elements in the following sections.

Start with a big idea or campaign theme, and then work on your three layers from that overall concept. If you don't have a theme, you'll just develop a series of unrelated ads — which won't help you build name recognition for your company or attract customers to your business. And that's your goal, right?

Audio

Audio is the sound track that augments and enhances the visuals, the sell copy, the description, and the story that you want to tell. The audio can be a *voiceover* (a voice — maybe even yours — doing a sales pitch from off-camera) or an on-camera actor. The audio track may also include any music or sound effects you select.

Video

The *video* is the visual component of the commercial. These pictures are what the viewers see — they're what capture the eyes and the attention of potential customers. The video can be anything from you doing an on-camera sales pitch, to product footage provided to you by your supplier, to video you shoot in your store, to anything else you can think of.

Don't get too carried away with elaborate visual elements that not only add dramatically to the look of your spot, but also add greatly to the cost of it. You can create visuals that are effective but cheap — particularly with the help of computers — it just takes a bit of thought. Instead of you standing on-camera pitching your business as a herd of wild horses gallops through the scene, the sound effects of a herd of wild horses galloping by off-camera (and someone off-camera kicking up copious amounts of dust) can do quite nicely. Viewers may swear they saw a herd of horses go by as you stand there selling them your products.

Computer graphics

The final element of a TV commercial is the computer graphics (CG for short). CG is the lettering (or possibly price numbers) that appears on the screen to drive home certain points you want to make. It can be made to flash on and off, wipe or crawl across the screen, spin into the frame, explode into the frame, or do any number of eye-catching effects.

You can also use computer-generated effects, which can be entire scenes made to fly into the frame, spin, explode, appear out of infinity, and perform other interesting tricks. The computers that are available to television editors do amazing things these days. When you get into the actual production process, you can enhance your commercial greatly with these wonderful effects.

While you're writing and planning your commercial, meet with the art director or creative director of the production facility you're using so you can see the computer graphics and effects that are available to you. If you're going to spend some serious money on a schedule with a station, you should get a tour of its production facility and a demonstration of all the state-of-the-art tricks that you can insert into your spots. Don't be satisfied to just do another mundane spot if you can use the latest in computer technology to enhance and improve your spots and make them into something interesting and memorable.

Computer graphics by themselves don't rescue a poorly conceived and badly written spot. (Garbage in, garbage out.) Start with well-written copy and a sound, creative premise and go from there.

Professional help is available to you

You are the best person to write the preliminary draft of the script for your TV spot, because you know your merchandise better than anyone. At the very least, you should be the one to write the *fact sheet* (the list of relevant facts and features that should be included in your spot). You are also the best person to decide *where* you want to shoot the commercial — in studio, at your place of business, outdoors on location, or wherever — and what merchandise or materials you want to feature in it.

But the TV station from which you are buying the airtime has all sorts of professional creative help available to walk you through the process. The station has copywriters, art directors, producers, directors, and editors who are there to make sure your commercial is as professionally done as possible. They all want your spot to generate business for you so you stay with their

station. They want their viewers to respond positively to your spot, not to tune it out. Because they don't want an amateur production going onto the air, they assist you in many ways to make sure your commercial looks professional. They also throw in their two cents when it comes to creative content, so be sure to listen to them. They've done this thousands of times before.

If you're looking for higher quality (and can afford it), you may want to employ an independent production company and professional director to do all this stuff for you. Most TV station production departments are certainly capable of doing good work, but independent houses, in an effort to build their own résumés, often bring a higher level of creativity and production skills to the job.

All this computer technology brings with it another, less-obvious benefit: It cuts your production costs dramatically. Nowadays, the computers make the entire editing process so fast and painless that you can get in and out of the editing suite quickly and, therefore, cheaply.

Bringing the Audio and Visual Together

When you're writing a TV commercial, you need to think visually. Try to picture in your mind's eye what you want to appear on the screen as the words you write are spoken. If you're selling furniture, for instance, and your copy opens with a description of a cherry wood bedroom set, does your scene open with the bedroom set, a wide shot of your entire store, or a beautiful cherry tree in full bloom? Or do you imagine using all three of these shots in quick succession? Personally, I would choose the image of the cherry tree, opening the spot with a shot of the tree and all its pink blossoms, then cutting to the bedroom set you're featuring, and then zooming out to show the size of your showroom, or cutting to a shot of the showroom. Or you may even get really ambitious and place the bedroom set in front of the cherry tree for a lovely outdoor opening shot.

Keeping your budget in mind

Before you go crazy with creative opening shots, or any shots for that matter, consider your budget and try to calculate what it will cost you if, for instance, you must pay for a video crew, their equipment, their truck, and a location shoot in order to show that cherry wood bedroom set sitting outdoors in front of a tree. If you can afford it, go for it. But an infinite variety of other shots may work just as well and cost you far less in production charges.

Discuss production charges with your TV station sales rep and haul out the old calculator as you create your script. I've done location shoots that cost very little in comparison to the final result, so going outdoors to shoot footage shouldn't intimidate you. You can't expect to create a TV spot as inexpensively as a radio spot, but with some advance planning, you can keep the costs within reason.

Shooting the entire spot in the station's studio costs far less than having to go out on location. And not having to shoot any footage at all is cheaper still. If, like automakers, your vendors have footage or still photos available to you, take advantage of it. Then, by adding a few hundred dollars per hour to pay for an editor and the

rental of an editing suite, your TV commercial can be ready to go.

All but the tiniest TV stations have editing suites where you can cut and paste factory footage (vendor-supplied footage) or still photos into a finished spot, but not all TV stations have studios or remote capabilities (with trucks filled with equipment for on-location shoots). Check with the station you're dealing with to see what production facilities it offers, and, of course, how much those facilities cost.

Video editors can be your best friends when it comes time to make a TV spot. These people are well acquainted with working with rookies and, with a combination of professional talent and patience, they guide you through the various complicated steps required to produce a finished spot. I've gone into an editing suite with some very definite ideas in mind and tossed them out when an editor pointed out a better, more creative, way to do what I wanted to accomplish. Video editors know how to make the best product possible within the budget guidelines set before them. Listen to them, watch them, and soak in their expertise.

Your opening scene is all-important because it's the first thing that greets the viewers, the first thing that either grabs the viewers or causes them to leave the room to grab a soft drink. When you're working with a limited budget, you aren't able to show a supermodel sitting on the edge of the Grand Canyon as your opening scene grabber. But you can, with a little thought, come up with some elements that are creative and eye-catching enough to at least give your spot a fighting chance at capturing the attention of some prospective customers.

Keep your budget uppermost in your mind. All sorts of creative thoughts come to you as you begin to write a commercial to sell your product or service, but you likely discard many of these as being too unrealistic and expensive to actually include in your spot. Wild horses cost a lot of money, but the *sound* of wild horses doesn't. (For more on your budget, check out the sidebar "Keeping your budget in mind" or Chapter 2.)

Finish the script before going back and adding the visual elements. Squeezing everything you want to say into 30 seconds of clear copy is hard enough without also worrying about what's appearing on the screen. Do one thing at a time. Write the copy, then go back and fit the pictures and graphics to the soundtrack.

To help you write your TV spot, here's a sample first draft script showing the *audio* (the spoken words) in all caps, the *video keys* (TV production speak for lettering that appears on the screen either over the footage or as its own element), and the *video* (the camera and staging directions; how you visualize what needs to happen on the screen as the voiceover talks in the background) squeezed in between. (*V/o* stands for *voiceover,* which is just a voice speaking from somewhere off-camera.)

> **Video:** *Automatic doughnut machine shot through store window*
>
> **V/o:** MAN HAS BEEN BUYING AND EATING DOUGHNUTS FOR CENTURIES. YUM, YUM.
>
> **Video:** *Close up of doughnuts being flipped in oil bath*
>
> **V/o:** BUT, UNTIL NOW, IT NEVER OCCURRED TO DOUGHNUT MUNCHERS THAT THEY WERE BEING CHEATED.
>
> **Video:** *Wide shot of doughnuts being sprinkled with cinnamon and sugar*
>
> **V/o:** YES, CHEATED. BECAUSE THE DOUGHNUTS THEY WERE BUYING HAD GREAT BIG HOLES IN THE CENTER!
>
> **Video:** *Close up of variety of decorated donuts*
>
> **Video Key:** *Fresh *Delicious (actual printed words appearing on screen)
>
> **V/o:** WELL, NOT AT SMITH'S DOUGHNUTS. SMITH'S DOUGHNUTS ARE ALWAYS DELICIOUS, ALWAYS FRESH. AND, IN A BOLD INNOVATION THAT IS SURELY AS EARTH-SHATTERING AS PAVED ROADS OR SLICED BREAD, SMITH'S DOUGHNUTS HAVE SMALLER HOLES.
>
> **Video Key:** Smith's Doughnuts (logo)
>
> 1234 Main Street (in the Acme Shopping Center)
>
> **V/o:** DON'T ACCEPT BEING CHEATED BY BIG DOUGHNUT HOLES. ALWAYS GET YOUR DOUGHNUTS AT SMITH'S DOUGHNUT SHOP IN THE ACME SHOPPING CENTER.
>
> **Video Key:** *Tiny little holes *Tiny little prices
>
> **V/o:** TINY LITTLE HOLES. TINY LITTLE PRICES.

This sample is a *first draft script,* the initial pass through the various elements that ultimately become a finished spot. At this point in the writing process, the video keys and the video camera directions that you call out are really only suggestions — they often change in the editing suite as you and your production team consider better ideas.

Deciding What to Feature in Your Commercial

Are you a good enough actor to star in your own commercial? Do you even *want* to? Is your place of business interesting and unusual enough to feature in your commercial? Or would it be a better idea to just put a camera on the products you're selling and let it go at that? The choices are endless — but I cover the basics in the following sections.

Appearing in your own commercial

You've probably seen many spots in which a store owner steps in front of the camera and does her own commercial. These kinds of commercials can, more often than not, be a very uncomfortable, even embarrassing, experience for all concerned — the store owner as well as the viewers. Nothing is more excruciating than watching someone look foolish for a full 30 seconds, but that is what some business owners choose to do every time they star in their own commercials.

On the other hand, you may be a natural and, if you are, then by all means, go for it. No one else could possibly bring the enthusiasm and expertise that you can to this endeavor. No one else can ever be as good as you at selling your business. If you have a strong desire to be your own spokesperson, practice, practice, practice. Have someone shoot some home video of you doing your script, and do an objective critique of the finished product. Without stars in your eyes, ask yourself the following questions:

✔ Are you believable?

✔ Do you look comfortable?

✔ Does your presentation make your audience want to visit your store and buy something?

✔ Do you look ill at ease and sound as though you're reading a script?

Above all, be honest. Only you can decide whether you're a good enough actor to pull it off.

If you choose to stand in front of the camera and deliver the pitch yourself, keep in mind that the best opening scene for your spot is probably *not* a close-up of you. A close-up only makes you yet another *talking head,* something that viewers get far too much of on the various news and entertainment shows. Instead, find an opening scene that may be a bit more creative than a headshot of you (even if you do have a million-dollar smile).

If you decide that you're not the best person to be the spokesperson for your business, first see if anyone else who works with you could do the job well. Obviously, this way is a much less expensive than hiring a professional actor, which requires you to decide what type of person would be best to promote your business, find the right actor, and have the budget to pay him or her! If you don't have someone who fits the bill, keep reading.

Promoting with a professional

You may figure out that neither you, your employees, nor anyone else in your family can sell your business the way you envision. It may be time to call in a professional. While you do have to fork out some extra cash, a professional actor may be just what your business needs.

So how do you go about finding acting talent? The best place to start is to ask the TV station you're working with. You can also check out any local acting agencies by looking in your phone book.

Before you decide on an actor, be sure to ask yourself what type of person you want to advertise your business in a way that attracts your target audience. For example, if you own a beauty salon, hiring a burly construction worker-type to try to sell your recent manicure special may not the best idea. However, you must also know what type of commercial you want to shoot as well. If you're going for more of a comedy, the construction worker advertising manicures may just work if done right.

Highlighting your place of business

Hiring a remote crew to come to your place of business and shoot the spot puts your business front-and-center. If your store looks really good, if it's nicely decorated and inviting to prospective customers (and, as a matter of good business, it should be), why not? Plus, shooting footage inside your store, showroom, studio, office, or gallery may be a lot easier than hauling a bunch of your products down to a TV station studio or to a remote location — especially if you're selling large, heavy merchandise like the cherry wood bedroom set I mentioned earlier in this chapter. (For more information about shooting your spot at your business, flip to the section "On location.")

Focusing the camera on your product or service

Go ahead and cut to the chase — immediately show the products you want to sell with this TV spot. Instead of getting too fancy with long shots of your location or close-ups of your spokesperson (whether it's you or a hired professional), you may be better served by getting right down to business and featuring the items that are going to make you some money.

You can never go wrong by showing an item and price in a TV spot. For example, if you're selling power tools, line them up in an attractive display, lay in some computer graphics to show the prices (video keys), and use a voiceover to explain why your store is the only store to sell these power tools so cheap. Nothing too complicated. Just a good, hard-sell spot that can generate some business for you.

If you opt to focus on your product, you can still use voiceover talent to read a script highlighting the important features.

Figuring Out Where to Shoot

When you've purchased a fairly hefty schedule on one of your local TV stations, and you've written a script and outlined the visual elements you want to include, you're ready to go into production. You have two basic options: a location shoot or an in-studio shoot. In the following sections, I outline what you can expect from both options.

On location

If you're going to shoot on location, the first thing you need to do, of course, is to find the location. It could be the interior or exterior of your place of business, or it may be a scenic park or point of interest in your area. For example, I've done location shoots all over Northern California, including at the local zoo, shopping centers, restaurants, parks, and upscale neighborhoods. The location you choose depends on what you're selling and what kind of place can add something to your commercial.

Where to find great ideas

Some of the industry's best directors, producers, camera people, lighting specialists, sound technicians, and editors are working on music videos. Creative ideas on staging, backgrounds, editing, computer graphics, and computer-generated effects are offered up 24-hours a day, and you can discover a lot by simply watching a few music videos. You can see the cutting edge in video-production techniques — which you can then emulate and incorporate into your own video productions.

Especially observe their editing techniques, how they use different effects when they cut or dissolve from scene to scene, and how they sometimes go from color footage to black and white with wonderful effectiveness. You can make your own TV commercial a thing of beauty if you use some of these state-of-the-art effects in your production. Computers make it not only possible, but also very inexpensive.

Another great place to find new ideas is in the commercials produced for national advertisers — the commercials you see every time you turn on the TV. If you see something that really attracts your attention, some effect or editing trick that jumps out at you, by all means talk to your station creative people about it. Chances are they can help you incorporate the idea into your spot.

Shooting at many locations isn't always free, and you may have to go through a bit of bureaucratic nonsense in order to shoot there. You may need signed permission to use certain locations such as public parks and some shopping centers. Many public facilities also charge you a rental fee to use their locations in a commercial. Don't just show up at your local zoo with a video crew and start shooting. You may get into trouble and end up costing yourself a lot more money than you would have by going through the proper channels. If you're using an independent production company, it usually takes care of these details for you. But don't expect a television station crew to care one way or another.

In the following sections, I give you some tips on how to get ready for shooting your commercial. I also describe what you can expect from the video crew and the process of actually shooting your TV ad.

Preparing for the shoot

Scout the location for camera positions and backgrounds before your video crew shows up. They're charging you by the day, the half-day, or the hour. So don't waste their time (and your money) scouting the location after they arrive — have these details all planned in advance.

Drive or walk around the park, or whatever locale you've selected, and choose scenes that are attractive and that allow access for the video crew and their van. Keep in mind that the crew comes complete with a van that holds all the electronics, a generator, video monitors, sound equipment, and so on. The van is a self-contained, traveling production facility, and during the shoot it must be very close to the camera, so you need to take this into consideration when scouting your location.

Introducing . . . your crew

The video crew for a location shoot usually consists of a director, a director of photography (DP), also known as a *shooter* (the cameraperson), a sound technician, and perhaps a couple of grips. *Grips* are responsible for setting up and moving equipment and for holding reflectors to aid the cameraperson in lighting. Interns or some other entry-level people may also be along on the shoot as *gophers* (as in "go-pher this, and go-pher that").

Getting down to business

The crew arrives in a van at the location you've chosen and spends the first half-hour or so wandering around sipping their coffees or soft drinks. The director (who may be doubling as the shooter) wanders around with you to see where you want to shoot the various scenes. He makes some mental notes about camera angles and lighting.

Whether the star of the commercial is you or a professional talent you've hired, the crew wires your talent with a miniature microphone, a battery pack, and a transmitter, or the sound may be recorded from a distance on a directional mic held by a sound technician. The sound technician in the van, through earphones, tests all of this gear for clarity. If the shoot has a really big budget, the crew may also include a makeup artist and a hairstylist to make the talent look as good as possible.

The talent is asked to stand in the first selected scene, and the grips are directed to set up the lights or *reflectors* (aluminum-foil-covered panels that are used to direct available sunlight onto the talent). The shooter sets up the camera on a tripod, and the grips anchor it with canvas bags filled with lead shot. The camera is focused. And you and the director, on the monitors inside the van, can study the view through the lens. The talent's voice level is given a final test and, when all things are ready, the first scene is laid down on videotape or film.

If you've selected more than one scene, the entire process must be repeated until the whole spot, scene by scene, has been shot and is, in the vernacular, in the can. Each scene is not necessarily shot in order. You may begin with the final scene and work your way to the beginning — this decision is the director's call and often depends on the layout of the location you've selected.

In order to avoid confusion later on, each scene is *slated* — the grip holds a board on which is written the spot name and scene number in front of the camera lens for a moment (that's the black board with a clapper you've seen in movies when the director calls, "Action!"). Another way to indicate the start of a scene is for an engineer in the van to write a brief description of each scene and its position on the recorded tape on a sheet of paper. Either way, this helps the director and video editor identify each scene when it comes time to do the final editing back at the studio.

In the studio

Shooting your commercials in a studio is much less expensive than shooting on location, and it may make a lot of sense if you need to shoot multiple commercials or rotate new spots in on a regular basis. In the studio, you also have much more latitude with camera setups than you do on location. For instance, the camera can be set on a *dolly,* which is a platform on wheels that runs on tracks. The grips pull the dolly slowly along the tracks as the shooter rides on top of the dolly. The effect is a smooth lateral movement that adds interest to an otherwise static, boring camera setup.

In the following sections, you can familiarize yourself with what's involved when shooting at the studio so you can determine whether it's a good option for your own TV ad.

Sizing up the studio and its crew

The studio most television stations use for shooting commercials is a very large space with a very high ceiling from which hang rack upon rack of lights. You probably can't see any sharp corners where the walls meet the floor. Instead, this space is gently coved and is called a *cyclorama* (or a *cyc* for short). This smooth edge where the walls meet the floors creates the illusion of infinity, a space with no beginning, no end. The floor is cement and is usually polished. The studio may also contain the news program set — the set you see each time you tune into the station's local news programs.

The production crew consists of the director (a station employee); a cameraman (called the *shooter*); a sound technician; two grips to handle props, move background scenery, set up camera dollies, and so on; as well as any makeup artists or stylists.

Outlining the process

Prior to the shoot, the entire script is transcribed to the *teleprompter,* a screen that sits just slightly above the camera lens. The talent can then read the copy while appearing to look directly into the camera. Your favorite newscasters, while dramatically shuffling through stacks of paper placed before them on a desk, are actually reading the news stories off of a teleprompter.

Props that you want to use in the spot are placed into the scene, the talent takes her place, and a piece of tape is stuck to the floor where the talent can stand. This place is called the *mark*. The teleprompter is manned by one of the grips who rolls the copy up or down in synchronization to the talent's reading speed, the camera is brought to the correct speed, and everyone is ready for the first take.

If you have a well-rehearsed professional doing the read, one take may be all you need, but I've always done five or six takes just for insurance. When you take the tape into the editing suite, you may see something you missed while doing the actual shoot, so it's good to have several backup takes just in case, especially if the talent has gone home and you don't have a chance to shoot another take.

The makeup artist, with her box of magic brushes and powders, usually stands by in the studio ready to touch up any blemishes and to dry off perspiration on the talent caused by the banks of hot lights.

This process is repeated as often as necessary until the director, the producer (that's you — or the producer you've hired), the shooter, and everyone involved are satisfied that the spot is complete, that it's as good as it's going to get, and that it's ready for final editing. The process is very creative every step along the way, and you can have fun doing it — I know *I* do. I've shot hundreds, if not thousands, of retail TV spots, and it's a kick each and every time I do it. The people you work with are experts in their fields and are there to help you. They're a very creative bunch, so listen to their suggestions and follow their directions. Your final product will be that much better because you did.

Producing Your Commercial

When you produce a TV commercial, you can either use the TV station's production department or you can hire an independent production house to do it for you. I cover both options in the following sections.

Using the TV station's production department

Chances are the TV station from which you're buying a schedule of advertising time has a fairly good production department. If for some reason the station doesn't, you may want to buy your schedule from a different station. You're going to produce a commercial, and you may not want to incur the expense of using an independent production house. Even if the station you select doesn't have all the latest electronics bells and whistles, it's probably capable of putting together a good local commercial for your business.

How to get free production

The media director for my agency has been able to get free production for our retail clients so often that they almost expect it every time. How is this done? Simple. It's called *negotiation*. When we make a substantial buy on a station, we always grind the sales rep and sales manager a bit in order to get the best deal possible. We rarely buy a schedule as it's initially presented. We always look for something extra, whether it be more spots for the same dollars or our spots running in better *dayparts* (time periods) than were initially offered. And the one area where we always try to get something extra is in production. If we buy a hefty airtime schedule, we always ask for a *production credit* so we're able to cut the cost of producing our commercials. The production credit is money that may or may not cover all the expense of producing commercials, but it usually makes a huge dent in the overall cost. Most stations cave in to this request if it's the difference between getting the airtime schedule or not.

Quite frankly, production charges from local TV stations aren't that high. As a matter of fact, they're usually quite reasonable, and my clients hardly notice the costs when added to our monthly invoices. I've never had a client complain that these charges were out of line. But if you can save the cost of production and then pass along the savings to your clients, why not ask?

Often, in the case of cable TV stations and some small independent broadcast TV stations, free production of one commercial is offered as part of the schedule — you don't even need to ask. The station can hardly sell you a spot schedule if you don't have a commercial to put on the air, so it throws a production session into the deal. They may not bring a lot of enthusiasm or creativity to the event, however, so be sure to stay on top of them when it comes time to actually do the shoot and the editing.

When you sign the contract to buy an airtime schedule, arrange to get a tour of the station's production facility and make sure you get to meet the two most important players, the two creative-types who help you produce your commercial:

- ✔ **The Retail Production Manager** is the person who oversees all the commercials produced for the retail clients of the station. It's this person's job to arrange studio and editing times; assign and schedule shooting crews for studio and location sessions; arrange for props, studio backdrops, makeup artists, and hairstylists; and assemble all the many pieces that go into a production session. Everyone who works in the production department answers to this person — you want to be very nice to the Retail Production Manager.

- ✔ **The Video Editor** is the person with whom you ultimately share the dark and claustrophobic confines of the editing suite. It's this person's job to stitch together all the pieces of your commercial — the video, soundtrack, computer graphics, special effects, and so on — into a coherent and concise 30 seconds of brilliance that viewers actually notice and remember. This person knows which buttons to push to make commercials look wonderful, and video editors typically overflow with ingenious ideas to make commercials better.

Hiring an independent production house

If you need something extra in the way of production capabilities, something that the production department of your local TV station simply can't offer, find an independent production company. The Retail Production Manager of your local station may be able to point you in the right direction. Or you may find a few possibilities in your local Yellow Pages under "Video Production Services." Avoid the ones that list themselves as wedding specialists or specialists in some other field, because they won't be equipped to handle commercial jobs.

Interview the companies you find, tell them what you're after, and have them show you their *sample reel* (an example of their work), so you can judge whether they have the skills to create television commercials from initial camerawork through the final editing process. Also, be sure to get a quote in advance. If you're like me, you hate surprises.

Editing Your Commercial

The editing suite is grandly named, but it's actually just a small, dark room into which tons of electronic equipment has been jammed. Somewhere behind the video editor, you can find a chair for you, the producer. You have a good view of all the monitors and are able to control (or at least participate in) all the action.

The video editor, who has edited commercials thousands of times before, has a copy of your script and, with nonchalance, assembles all the pieces into a finished 30-second commercial that you can be very proud of. Most importantly, the video editor is there to make you look good (as are the director, the shooter, and all the other people involved with your project). Listen to your editor's suggestions. Watch and learn. Nothing drives an editor crazier than clients who think they know more about the process than the editor does. Video editing is a very technical and precise talent — a talent that takes years to perfect, years of sitting in that claustrophobic, little, dark room pushing buttons and winding tape. So do yourself a favor — give the editor free rein and enjoy the final result.

First, the sound track (the audio) must be inserted into the master file (which becomes your final commercial). Then, all the videotape you shot, either on location or in the studio is, after having been digitized, brought up on one of the monitors in front of the editor. The editor rolls through the footage, and you both select the takes that comprise the final commercial. Each selected take is timed and inserted into the master file piece-by-piece until a full 30 seconds is stitched together into a finished spot. If you want any of the scenes to fly or spin into the commercial, these computer effects are selected, designed, and inserted.

Any computer graphics — prices, product features, important copy points — are then typed by the editor and inserted into the spot, as is a music background (if any) and your logo, which appear at the end of the commercial along with your phone number, address, directions, or whatever you want. If the spot requires a disclaimer of any kind, this too is typed by the editor and inserted into the spot in the appropriate place. You may help select the fonts, sizes, and colors of the graphics, or at least put in your two cents' worth.

When you add up the writing time, the shooting time, and the editing time, even though most of the process is done using the most powerful computers, the entire procedure of producing a 30-second TV commercial can actually take days. But, at the end of the editing session, you walk out of the editing suite with a finished commercial in the can, ready for air — and ready to entice customers into your business where they will, you hope, spend lots of money. Have fun with it — producing TV commercials can be very exciting!

Chapter 10

Collateral Advertising and Direct Mail: Brochures, Flyers, Newsletters, and More

*W*hen you invest your money into writing and designing business-collateral materials, you invest in a first impression. *Collateral materials* are the brochures, mailers, flyers, and newsletters you produce for your business, all of which make an impression on your customers — and *potential* customers. Whether the impression is a good one resulting in increased business or a bad or ambivalent one that ends up being a gigantic waste of your money is entirely up to you.

Although many businesses use collateral materials to introduce a business or product, unlike other forms of advertising, you can also use it later in the sales cycle, usually when you've identified your prospective purchasers and you're making contact with them. Collateral advertising often supports the sales of your product or service as well. These sales aids are intended to make the salesperson's job easier and more effective.

You can distribute collateral ads to your customers in a variety of ways, such as through direct mail or as flyers that you can leave in public places that accept such materials or in your customer's bags. For a creative mind like yours, the options are innumerable.

As with all advertising materials, the creative ideas and production values you put to use in your collateral materials make the difference between success and failure. Do it right and you reap the rewards. Do it wrong, as so many businesses do, and you'll wish you'd saved your money. This chapter gives you the information you need so you can start a collateral ad campaign that best suits your business needs.

First Things First: Planning Your Collateral Campaign

A sizeable portion of the hundreds of advertising messages everyone is exposed to on a daily basis comes in the form of collateral materials. You open your mailbox every day and find a fresh pile of brochures, catalogs, newsletters, and flyers. Why do you read some of it and throw the rest away? If you're like most people, you're more likely to pay attention to the materials that are provocative, with a clean design. And if the piece is easy to read and simple to navigate, all the better. But the run-of-the-mill stuff, the direct mailers and postcards that don't display the slightest creativity, that don't instantly give you a reason to open and read them, go out with yesterday's newspaper.

As with any form of advertising, when it comes to collateral, you need to plan your work and then work your plan. Invest your time and effort into the planning of your collateral advertising — plan it as carefully as you would any important endeavor. The amount of time you put into the planning stage is the best investment you can make toward the ultimate effectiveness of the piece. Chapter 5 gives you more detailed information on planning your campaign, but for collateral advertising in particular, it's important to remember this: Don't just toss together a bunch of words, prices, pictures, and a "Hurry on down" or "Contact us now," and hope for the best. It doesn't work that way.

Before you sit down to create a piece of collateral advertising, plan by doing the following:

1. **Define the purpose for the ad.** Are you trying to reach *new* customers or to inform *existing* customers?

2. **Determine what you can do within your budget constraints.** Rough out a design and get estimates from printers so you can figure out what you can afford. See the section "Watching Out for Collateral Budget Busters" in this chapter or Chapter 2 for more information.

3. **Organize your message and crystallize your design.** Don't expect much involvement from your readers. Make your design and copy clear, informative, and, above all, *brief* (see Chapter 4). After you've done this, it's time to shift your tasks from planning your ad to creating the ad.

4. **Write and rewrite your headline and copy until it's as concise as it can be.** Make sure no extraneous words are in your headline; make sure it has *sell.* (Check out Chapter 19 for some tips on writing ads.)

5. **Toss out any superfluous elements from your ad that only distract from your message.** Be as objective as possible when tightening your design and copy. Include only those elements that are absolutely necessary to getting your message across.

6. **Do sketches and rearrange the elements until the design is a good as it can be.** Don't just toss your various elements together helter-skelter. Be thoughtful in your design. Make it attractive and easy to grasp.

7. **Make sure your copy and content flow in a logical sequence.** Don't be pompous, ponderous, and boring with too much copy or irrelevant information. Your target audience doesn't have time for it.

8. **Be objective.** Is the piece reader-friendly? Does it quickly communicate a benefit? Would *you* read it if you found it in your mailbox?

Keep in mind that creating collateral advertising is very similar to creating print ads. See Chapter 7 for more information that you can apply to your collateral advertising.

If you write and design your brochure sequentially and if you take it one step at a time and make sure you complete each step with precision, then your finished piece stands a good chance of success.

Watching Out for Collateral Budget Busters

If you keep your collateral plan in place (as I discuss in the preceding section), you can go a long way toward keeping your advertising affordable. The more elaborate the piece, the costlier it is. So you need to ask yourself, "What can I afford?" And then stick to that budget. Chapter 2 gives you information on how to establish your budget and stay within it.

If your business or location doesn't allow you to easily distribute or mail collateral ads to your customers on your own, you should also make sure you set aside part of your budget for a direct-mail provider. I cover that in the section "Handing Off the Dirty Work: Direct-Mail Houses" later in this chapter. For now, though, I concentrate on the budget of your ads themselves.

As with all advertising, if you get carried away designing something that, in the final analysis, has a printing cost of $5 a unit and you can only afford $1 a unit, you probably have to go back to the old drawing board. In collateral advertising, two items in particular can overinflate your budget in a hurry if you aren't careful: color and printing costs.

In the following sections, I unravel the costs of color printing and offer some less-expensive solutions. I also break down the various types of printers to give you a better idea of what can work for you (and your bottom line).

Adding a little (or a lot) of color

Today, buying a personal color printer can cost as low as $500, but if you add just one color to your collateral advertising, you may add a few more zeros to your overall printing costs. Add two or three more colors, and you may be in for a serious dose of sticker shock. In addition, paper costs alone have skyrocketed over the years, and professional printers have never been embarrassed about charging a lot of money for their work. Be sure you know what you're getting yourself into before you design something so elaborate that you can't afford it. I talk about color in more detail later in the chapter, but you really do need to know up front: The more color you use, the bigger your budget should be.

You can get away with producing a very nice and relatively inexpensive piece in just one color: black. If what you're saying is strong and if what you're showing is interesting, then black ink on a white background may do the job nicely.

I receive postcard-size mailers on a weekly basis from local real estate agents showing off their listings. They include a photo of the house, a brief description, the asking price, and a photo of the agent. These pieces of collateral advertising are well-designed with easy-to-understand copy, and if I were in the market for a new home, they would be quite effective in arousing my interest. They're all printed on glossy card stock in black and white. Nothing could be simpler — and the costs are relatively low, too.

Printing cheap: No such thing?

Printing isn't cheap — unless you do it yourself, and even then, you have the cost of investing in a high-quality paper and toner cartridges, which increase considerably if you buy a color printer. The number of pages, colors, photos, die-cuts, and clever folds you design into your piece is in direct proportion to your blood pressure when you get the cost-of-printing estimate. As a rule, quick print jobs usually cost a few cents per copy. The major-league brochure jobs cost a few dollars a copy. Be sure you remember these dollar signs before you even begin to design your ad.

Also keep in mind that the type of printer you use affects costs, because printing prices vary widely according to the capabilities and equipment of each printer. Check out the following printing options:

- ✔ **National chain shops:** The national chain copy shops (FedEx Kinko's, Staples, and Office Depot) have given small businesses many more printing options. These quick-print specialists are very good at producing small jobs where cost is more important than quality. You can either visit your local branch or check out their services online, simply by uploading the document you want printed.

- ✔ **Large printing firms:** Large printing firms that have presses that cover a square city block are capable of doing the most exquisite work — if you have the budget for it.

- ✔ **Printers specializing in small to mid-size jobs:** Other printers are experts in small to mid-size jobs, such as letterheads, envelopes, and business cards — they're also qualified to do brochures, flyers, mailers, and the like.

The key is to pick the type of printer who can handle (at a cost you can afford) the type of printing you need. I use one local printer for my company newsletters, corporate image items, and one- or two-color mailers. Located in a small strip mall, this printer does great work and charges a very reasonable price for smaller jobs. But for full-color, multi-page extravaganzas, I go to a large firm that has a huge press and the binding capability (collating and stapling the pages together) that is required when producing large brochure jobs.

Another factor affecting costs is how many prints you need. Typically, the per-unit cost goes down the more items you print. For that reason, printing 5,000 units is often more economical than printing just 1,000.

If you only need 1,000 copies for a particular mailing, you can save money in the long run by printing 5,000 and then, at a later date, imprinting the additional pieces with information relevant to a future sale or announcement. With advance planning, you can save a lot of money on printing costs. For example, I have a client who does regular mailings to his list of current customers — about 2,500 people. We generally print 10,000 pieces, which are designed with space for updated copy that can be printed in one color later. By printing 10,000 units the first time around and then sending the brochure with updated copy and a new sales message in four separate mailings, this client saves a ton of money on printing bills.

Although printing services are everywhere, good printers are a little more rare. To find a suitable printer, ask other small businesses in your neighborhood which printers they use, thumb through the Yellow Pages, or if you hire a graphic designer (see "Hiring a pro to do the design work for you" later in the chapter), let the designer advise you.

Digital printers: When you have the need for speed

Digital printing is printing a finished product directly from a computer or a CD. Years ago, you had to create a *paste-up* (a hand-assembled, full-size facsimile containing all the elements of your finished brochure) or *film* (a picture of your final paste-up) and take it to a traditional offset printer for printing. But printing has evolved so that most printing is now done digitally, where all you need to do is give a disk or upload an electronic file to a printer or copy shop. Digital printing offers you the following advantages:

✔ **You get a quicker turnaround time.**

✔ **Making changes (even at the last minute) is less expensive, because you can change your file so easily.**

✔ ***Short runs*** **(a relatively small number of finished pieces) are more affordable.**

✔ **You can print ads on any paper stock.**

✔ **You can merge the ad with a mailing list to print addresses directly onto the pieces.** Your computerized mailing list is fed into the press, and each address is imprinted on the individual mailing pieces as they run through the press. This process eliminates the need for later affixing mailing labels to each printed piece and saves money at the mailing house.

Digital printing has become crucial to businesses that may want to test the waters with a particular brochure without printing zillions of copies and spending huge amounts of money. Last-minute digital printing of jobs such as trade-show flyers, price lists, and pamphlets has bailed out many a company with the need for speedy, last-minute collateral pieces or multiple copies of a new press release. Turnaround time for the average digital printing job is measured in days, not weeks, and they can sometimes be done in 24 hours.

The single most-important factor to any printing project is the final proofing of the artwork before you release it to the printer. Even though you have the opportunity to see a final proof from the printer prior to the actual press run (usually called a *blue line*), any changes or corrections that aren't on the original artwork are charged back to you at a premium rate.

If you decide to buy your own color printer, you need to know the volume of pages you'll be printing per month, then check the number of pages per minute that your printer can handle: For example, one model of Brother printer can print 30,000 pages a month. Also check the paper stock the printer can handle, depending on what you want: Heavy stock can sometimes be difficult, so if you need to print on heavy paper, you'll need to get a printer that can handle that (not all printers can). Finally, check the resolution (the number of *dpi,* or dots-per-inch). Remember, you want your collateral advertising to look *great.*

Designing the Best Collateral Ads for Your Business

Collateral advertising has numerous purposes — and the different kinds of collateral advertising at your disposal are numerous as well. You should research carefully, always keeping your budget in mind, to determine which form of collateral advertising best suits your needs. Types of collateral ads include:

- **Brochures:** These can be anything from a single sheet, folded in two or three, to a stapled booklet that's almost a mini-catalog, either in one color printing or more. You can leave brochures behind with prospective clients at the end of a sales presentation. You can also keep a stack of them on the counter at your place of business or send them as direct mail. You can also send out brochures to people who request more information about your business.

- **Postcards:** Just like the 4-x-6-inch cards you send from vacation to your family and friends back home, these postcards are typically a picture of your product, your service in action, or some other aspect of your business, with brief info on the back, perhaps announcing an upcoming sale or other news. These puppies are ideal for reducing cost and getting read without having to be opened. Postcards can be sent to current customers to announce an upcoming sale, perhaps including a perforated coupon or return card good for a preferred-customer discount. Figure 10-1 shows an example of a very effective postcard.

- **Newsletters:** These can be as simple as a page (kind of like those typed letters you get from long-lost friends at holidays, telling you what everyone in the family has been doing during the year) to 4 pages or even 16 pages. Many small business owners (and consultants) write their own newsletters, to keep their company's products and services uppermost in their customers' minds. Your newsletter could provide information on trends in the industry; news and reviews of new products or services — either your own or others'; or just fun-to-read articles that your customers may enjoy.

- **Business cards:** These need no explanation: They're an evolution of the old-fashioned "calling cards" that provide your name, your business's name, address, phone number, fax number, e-mail address, Web site, and any other contact info you want to include. Some people include their photo — a great idea for customers who are more likely to remember your face than your name. Or you might include a picture of your storefront or office on the front of the card, with your contact info on the back. Anything that makes your card stand out from the rest in the Rolodex is helpful!

- ✔ **Electronic direct mail:** Whether via e-mail, Web content, or text messaging, electronic direct mail is the fastest-growing area of direct mail. Check out Chapter 6 for more info on Web-based and e-mail advertising.

- ✔ **Freebies and samples:** These tchotchkes are small, dimensional devices relevant to your business, product, or ad campaign. They can include a product miniature, a free sample, a toy, or another creative element.

Figure 10-1:
A promotional postcard. The back (not shown) is large enough to allow for the customer's mailing address and a small order form.

Whatever you're trying to accomplish, a collateral piece, in one or more of its many forms, can do the job. How *well* it does the job is up to you.

Even though collateral advertising should be a stand-alone advertising vehicle and must contain selling points and a call to action, it hardly ever makes a sale on its own. Instead, it's an integral piece of the overall advertising puzzle. A glossy, well-designed collateral piece can say a lot about your business (for example, that you're a classy business that sells classy products or provides a luxury service), and, if it's done right, it can play on the emotions of your customers and generate increased sales.

Striving for a simple design and clear copy

You have a message you want to communicate, but hundreds of advertising messages bombard the consumer everyday. So how do you accomplish the former in spite of the latter? Through the simple, interesting design and a clear message that are essential to a good collateral piece.

Paying attention to what you read

A good place to start when deciding on a collateral ad design for your business is to ask yourself, "Why do I read some of the collateral advertising I receive, and why do I toss the rest?" What is it about the design and layout, or the written promise, of some pieces that grabs your attention, and even compels you to respond? If you can answer this question, you're on your way to designing your own successful piece, because the design and copy elements that work on you may also work on your customers.

If you find a brochure that you really like, save it. As a matter of fact, collect all the ones you like and make a file. I'm not suggesting you plagiarize these, but they can be a great source of inspiration. For example, I have a client who's saved nearly every direct-mail piece, in-store promotional piece, brochure, pamphlet, and flyer he's come in contact with for decades. The guy uses direct mail on a regular basis and always needs new ideas. He keeps huge scrapbooks of this stuff to use as references when he's preparing his own collateral pieces. He doesn't copy them verbatim; he uses them to *jumpstart* his own imagination.

If you can train yourself to do some subjective analysis of the design and copy of brochures and pamphlets that appeal to you, you can then put this newfound design sense to work in your own advertising.

Just as with broadcast commercials (see Chapters 8 and 9) or print ads (Chapter 7), the collateral material you use as part of your overall advertising strategy must make an instant impression on the recipient — a positive impact that compels the consumer to open, read, and respond. Writing and designing these materials isn't any big mystery. The same elements you strive for in other media are the ones you should strive for in this media as well: an interesting design; clear, concise copy; the promise of something to benefit the consumer; and a call to action.

You can't expect much involvement from the reader in your brochure — actually, you can't expect *any* involvement, only a cursory glance at best. So the simpler your message, the better.

Deciding what to include in your ad

Whether you're preparing an elaborate multi-page, multi-color collateral piece such as an overview of what products or services your company offers or a simple black-and-white postcard destined to be mailed to a preferred customer list, the rules are the same:

✔ Keep it attractive, relevant, simple, and, above all, reader friendly.

✔ Don't expect the recipients to give it much time (they're on the receiving end of tons of this stuff, just like you are).

- Use interesting graphics and a provocative headline to interest them enough to at least give the piece a fighting chance at being opened and read.

- If you have room anywhere in your ad, and if you're selling a product that can be shipped to the customer, it's helpful to include an order form, like the one shown in Figure 10-2.

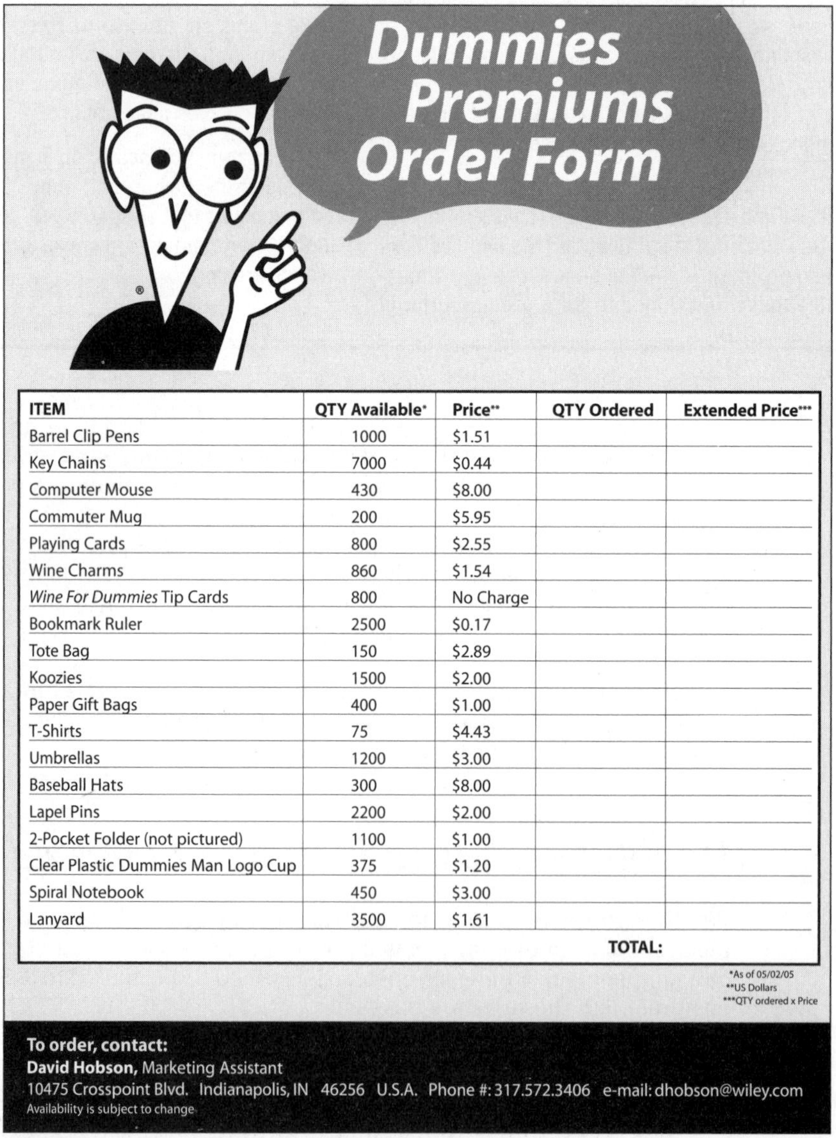

Dummies Premiums Order Form

ITEM	QTY Available*	Price**	QTY Ordered	Extended Price***
Barrel Clip Pens	1000	$1.51		
Key Chains	7000	$0.44		
Computer Mouse	430	$8.00		
Commuter Mug	200	$5.95		
Playing Cards	800	$2.55		
Wine Charms	860	$1.54		
Wine For Dummies Tip Cards	800	No Charge		
Bookmark Ruler	2500	$0.17		
Tote Bag	150	$2.89		
Koozies	1500	$2.00		
Paper Gift Bags	400	$1.00		
T-Shirts	75	$4.43		
Umbrellas	1200	$3.00		
Baseball Hats	300	$8.00		
Lapel Pins	2200	$2.00		
2-Pocket Folder (not pictured)	1100	$1.00		
Clear Plastic Dummies Man Logo Cup	375	$1.20		
Spiral Notebook	450	$3.00		
Lanyard	3500	$1.61		
			TOTAL:	

*As of 05/02/05
**US Dollars
***QTY ordered x Price

To order, contact:
David Hobson, Marketing Assistant
10475 Crosspoint Blvd. Indianapolis, IN 46256 U.S.A. Phone #: 317.572.3406 e-mail: dhobson@wiley.com
Availability is subject to change.

Figure 10-2:
This order form appears on the inside of a folding flyer.

When you're designing a collateral piece, include only those elements that are essential to your message and avoid the temptation to incorporate too much information. Think about whether a particular graphic element focuses your readers' attention, or whether it only confuses them. If you've included something in your collateral advertising that is pure ornamentation and is, in fact, a distraction, toss it out and start again. For example, as mentioned, a picture of you or your business or products is helpful (for customer recall), but artwork that's only used to break up text isn't.

In the following sections, I outline the various elements of a good collateral piece and show you how to make each element help to deliver your all-important sales message.

Putting the important copy points at the top

When you're organizing the words (or copy) that go into your ad, imagine a stepladder. Put your most important copy points on the top step, the next most-important points on the next step down, and so forth. Make a list of the various components that you want to include in your brochure, ranking the elements from the most important to the least. Then feature the most-significant points more boldly in order to make an instant impact on the reader.

For example, if you're creating a piece announcing a sale or other special event, get right to the point and make the line at the very top of your ad say what's most important: "Sale!" Don't get cute and make the first thing the reader sees something like, "Due to continued customer demand. . . ."

Write an eye-stopping headline and brief, succinct body copy. Don't confuse your readers with a long-winded explanation of how to build a watch; just tell them, in plain English, why they should buy a watch from you. The difference between having your piece read or having it tossed into the garbage is the split second it takes for your recipient to be either intrigued or bored.

Don't be reluctant to throw out unnecessary copy the brochure can live without. Pare down your list of copy points to the bare-bones selling message. Get rid of the superfluous and concentrate on the important. The less work you create for the recipient, the better. Make it easy for potential customers to instantly grasp your message.

Using the right typeface

Use a typeface that best expresses the tone of your brochure. Look at the different fonts in your computer word-processing program, and see what options you have. For example:

> ✔ If the piece is meant to be humorous and whimsical, find a typeface that's silly or goofy. Keep in mind, though, that the type you choose needs to be very *readable,* so make sure you choose a large-enough version of these fonts so that the type design doesn't interfere with your message, which is the most important factor.

> ✔ If your piece is serious, like an announcement of a presale open house for your preferred customers, choose a typeface that's dignified and solid.
>
> ✔ If you're sending out a mailer to announce a big sale, use a typeface that is big, bold, and direct. You can find lots of examples of these — but beware of using type that's *too* bold, because that's distracting for readers. Use boldface type judiciously, to call attention to the most important message in your advertising piece.

Don't use more than two or three different typefaces in your collateral advertising. Numerous typefaces tend to confuse and distract the reader's eye rather than focus it. Also, where possible, avoid underlines, boldfaces, italics, outlines, borders, stars, bars, and any other visual distractions. These cutesy elements only add clutter and distract your readers from your message.

Including graphic elements

Your graphic choices are many and varied — everything from photographs to full-color drawings, black-and-white line art to a clever typeface treatment. Choose the graphic element that best conveys the essence of what you're trying to sell, and what you're attempting to accomplish with the printed piece you're creating.

If you're showing a particular product that is now on sale, then a photograph (either one supplied by the manufacturer or shot by a local photographer) may be the way to go. Show the item, give the price or the call to action (for example, "This dress marked down 50 percent this weekend only"), and make sure these elements jump off the page quickly.

Use graphics if they add to the *sell* of the piece. Don't include graphics purely as design elements if they just distract from the message. Don't clutter your design with multiple graphic images unless each of them has some relevance to the piece. The biggest mistake made by retail advertisers is trying to fit too much information into a single ad. Jamming too much information into a single piece only confuses the reader.

Considering color

Here again, multiple colors increase your printing costs. And, although color does add interest and impact, it's not always necessary. You can do many effective brochures and mailers in black and white. The message and design is what makes or breaks your sales piece, not the addition of several colors. You can also print one color on a contrasting color paper. Printing papers come in nearly infinite varieties and colors. A nice shade of blue ink on a cream-colored paper may work as well as four-color process on white paper if your message and design are well planned and executed.

On the other hand, certain brochures simply cry out for four-color process. If you're selling something — food, clothing, fine art — that must be shown in all its multicolored glory, then you want to go the full-color route. A prospective customer may have trouble picturing the beauty of a painting, for instance, if you did your sales piece only in black and white.

Choosing the right paper

Printing involves more than color and ink. Printing papers come in numerous colors, textures, weights, and finishes. Coated paper (which is usually slick and glossy) gives more depth and brilliance to your piece and reproduces photographs much better, even if it's only printed with black ink. Soft-finish, textured papers are perfect for a classy brochure or for letterheads and cards that require a solid business image. You can also save a tree by using recycled paper (and then tell the world about it in little, tiny type inside your brochure), but keep in mind that some recycled papers cost more.

The different *weights* (thickness and heft) of paper give you multiple choices when you produce collateral. You can use heavy weights for postcards and brochure covers, light weights for mailers stuffed into envelopes, and so on. Paper samples come in small demonstration packets prepared by numerous paper companies. Your printer trots out paper samples until you're cross-eyed with confusion, and then he hauls out a bunch more. You may want to find out which papers are available to you before you get too far in your brochure design. Paper is an integral part of the brochure-design equation. A paper with a rich appearance and feel adds greatly to the ambience of your finished piece. Your printer can help you make your choice.

Getting help with your design

You can safely say that anyone can design a brochure. You could design one. I could design one. Even your kid — the one who shows great aptitude for drawing lovely pictures or coloring within the lines — could design one. But, why send out a piece that looks amateurish and a bit rough around the edges when you can create something to be proud of with just a little advanced planning and careful thought?

When creating collateral ads, weigh the costs of hiring someone with the skills (such as design) or equipment (color printers and so on) to help you versus doing it yourself. For example, a concert promoter who did a mailing a few years ago designed her own brochure, using photos she obtained from the musicians who were performing. She chose to do this herself because she's a creative, talented person with a good eye for design.

She had a local copy shop print her brochure on heavy stock because her own printer couldn't handle that weight of paper. The copy shop also scored and folded her mailing piece, printed her logo on envelopes, and printed her labels (which can sometimes be tricky because they're sticky and can ruin your toner cartridge if they get stuck).

Finally, she stuffed all the envelopes and labels and applied all the postage herself. This mailing was a small, though, going out to only about 300 people. If you're mailing to thousands, you probably need help; fortunately, you can outsource all these tasks (check out the section "Handing Off the Dirty Work: Direct-Mail Houses") — or you may find it more cost effective to invest in a color printer and color toner as these costs continue to become more affordable.

A collateral piece, whatever form it takes, is a reflection on you and on the quality of your business. It's worth some time and effort. I've always hired professional talent to do the jobs that I'm either incapable of doing or don't have the time to do right, and I think that's good advice for you to heed as well. In the following sections, I cover the various ways you can create a quality collateral piece. The process involves much more than just typing information on paper.

Using design software you may already own

You have access to some excellent collateral-material design templates on various software programs, and you may already have them on your computer. For example, Microsoft Publisher has a huge variety of templates for brochures, mailers, postcards, greeting cards, letterheads, and so on. Software programs also include step-by-step tutorials that are supposed to transform the design klutz into the design pro. Even if you have no experience in design, software can be of enormous value. Think of software as sort of a high-tech paint-by-numbers set. You're given multiple choices at every step along the way (cover art, photos, backgrounds, colors, layouts, type fonts, folds), and you end up with a mailer, brochure, or other item of business collateral. You can also use these design programs to help you create print advertisements and signage.

One caution here: By using these built-in computer design programs, you run the risk of creating something that may have been done by another company, perhaps even one of your competitors. The choices on these programs may look endless, but they have a similar look and feel, and, for the most part, they're not very original.

When you're finished designing the ad, save your final draft to a disk in the specific file program requested by your printer. Then hand the disk to your printer, tell him how many copies you want, and take the rest of the day off.

Some cautions on buying art and printing

If you're working with a graphic designer, she can quite likely have a good idea of the look and feel of your finished printed piece, and she also has some definite thoughts as to which printer she wants you to use. Ask your designer to provide you with an official Request for Estimate form, including all the specifications of your printing job. Important information includes:

✓ **Quantity:** The number of pieces to be printed

✓ **Flat size:** The size before folding

✓ **Finished size:** The size after folding

✓ **Stock:** What quality and color paper the job is to be printed on

✓ **Ink colors:** Which colors will be used

✓ **Screens:** The degrees of color

✓ **Half-tones or color separations:** The number of photos

After your designer gives you this completed form, you can then send it to a few reputable printers via fax or e-mail. With all the job's specs clearly defined on the form, and after determining the number of pieces you need, you can ask for printing quotes. Then you can further negotiate with the printers after you receive back all the quotes. Some printers may substitute a particular paper your artist has called for with a house stock (papers they keep on hand) in order to offer you the lowest price possible. Confer with your artist regarding any variances found on the estimate forms.

Hiring a pro to do the design work for you

The best way to get the best possible design is, in most cases, to hire a professional graphic artist to handle these chores for you. A professional designer can help you with the creation of the piece and also assist you in making the many printing decisions required — all in all, a good investment. Graphic designers cost money, but not nearly as much money as a few thousand poorly conceived, badly designed mailing pieces that no one bothers to read.

Your printer can likely recommend talented graphic designers in your area, and you can also look in your good old Yellow Pages under "Graphic Designers." In my local Bay Area phone book, this list is seven pages long! Call one or more of your local designers, invite them to your business, and ask each of them to bring their *book* (a collection of the designer's work samples). A quick scan of the designer's work can help you choose the right person for your particular job.

Ask for a copy of the terms and conditions from your designer. Make certain you have a complete understanding of ownership and what is financially expected of you in order to receive your final artwork and your final printed pieces. Some designers expect to be paid again if their artwork is used to create more than one piece, or if you reuse their artwork to print the piece again at a later date. Negotiating and agreeing upon a flat *buy out* (where you own all rights to the finished artwork) is best. That way, should you choose to reuse the artwork at a later date, you won't incur additional charges.

Handing Off the Dirty Work: Direct-Mail Houses

Though it certainly isn't the only method of getting collateral ads to your customers, direct mail is the most-common means. The appeal is easy to understand: With the proliferation of copy shops in the last decade, it's easier than ever to have someone else handle all the details for your direct-mail campaign, such as envelope stuffing, folding, sorting, postage, and so on.

In addition to a traditional mailing house, Staples, Office Depot, FedEx Kinko's, and most local copy shops now offer this service (onsite and online). You simply take your finished printing to them, or have your printer deliver it to them directly, and they take care of the rest. They also furnish you with the mailing list you require, print the labels, affix the labels to your mailing pieces, add the postage, sort the pieces by zip code, box them up, and deliver them to the post office. It sure beats licking envelopes yourself — though you should weigh the cost of paying someone versus the cost of your own time if you do some of these tasks yourself.

You might also consider combining your collateral ads with your e-mail or Web advertising efforts (see Chapter 6 for details). Keep in mind, though, that you should only contact those customers by e-mail who have expressed interest in receiving e-mail from you, so that you don't get banned for spamming people. And if you're attaching collateral materials — either a postcard or a brochure or a newsletter — to your e-mails, make sure the format you're using in your collateral is something that can be easily opened and read by your customers. Sending an attachment that doesn't open or takes forever to open will only frustrate your customers and make a bad impression — which is not the way you want to advertise your business!

Asking the direct-mail provider some important questions

If you use a graphic artist to design your ad, then she probably knows of a good mailing house, but just in case she doesn't, you can locate one using the Yellow Pages. The only difference from one mailing house to the next is the quality of their mailing lists. A well-qualified, up-to-date mailing list is the most-important part of the direct-mail equation. For this reason, ask the mailing house the following questions:

> ✔ **When was the list last updated?** You don't want to spend your hard-earned money sending out the direct mail only to have them returned by the post office as undeliverable. Look for a house that updates its lists

monthly, quarterly at the very outside. On average, most reputable direct-mail houses update their lists every six weeks.

✔ **Is the data on the mailing list presorted by carrier routes or 9- or 11-digit zip codes and certified for accuracy of address information?** You want your lists to be at least presorted by zip codes so that you receive postage discounts. And the more extensively a mailing list is detailed (zip code digits, carrier routes, carrier route sequence), the larger your postage discounts are. And certification of accuracy is important so that you're sure you're getting what you paid for.

✔ **Will a summary report that breaks out the counts by zip code and other information be made available to me?** The summary report gives the list buyer (that's you) a snapshot of the list capabilities and detail (income level, gender, education, and so on) before you make a list purchase decision. The mailing house offers this report free of charge in most cases.

✔ **Is there a minimum charge?** When you decide to buy a mailing list, the summary report may inform you that a total of 2,200 names are available on this particular list, and that the cost is $75 per 1,000 names but with a minimum charge of $250. List companies set a minimum charge on all lists. What you want to look for when buying a list are minimum charges buried in the small print.

✔ **Is the list charge for one-time or multiple usage?** Typically, a multiple-use list costs you about three times the cost of a one-time-only use. The multiple-use list *isn't* updated prior to each use, so, if you're uncertain about using the list more than once, or if your second or third use of the list will be at a much later date, buy it for one time only.

✔ **What is the charge for output?** Your mailing house shows you a price list for the various forms of mailing labels. In simple terms, a *continuous form* (also referred to as *chesire*) is the typical (old-fashioned) computer paper with slotted tracks on either side that comes in boxes and is used on dot-matrix printers. A computer program prints multiple addresses on this paper, and a machine at the direct-mail house cuts and glues the labels to the mailing pieces. Chesire is the cheapest label form. Sticky labels need to be affixed by hand and may be more expensive. However you choose to get the job done, the list company either mails you a computer disk or sends the list to you or your direct-mail house electronically (via e-mail).

✔ **What are my label printing options (laser, inkjet, dot matrix, and so on)?** You can use either traditional sticky labels, or you may decide to have the addresses printed directly on the mail piece, as many direct mailers now do, making the mail appear to be more personal so your readers are less likely to perceive it as "junk mail."

✔ **Can I include a secondary message on my labels (for example, "preferred customer")?** These secondary messages, generally with a double- or triple-spaced separation, go above the recipient's name and address.

✔ **Will I receive a verification of mailing from either the post office or the mailing house?** This verification is either the official United States Postal Service Form USPS 3602 or a form created by the mailing house, which the USPS then stamps and signs to verify that the mailing was delivered as ordered.

Form 3602-EZ is a simplified postage statement designed specifically for small business mailers who are mailing standard mail cards, letters, and flats and paying via permit imprint. Keep in mind, though, that if your mail pieces weigh more than 3.3 ounces each (which means that you pay a piece rate for each piece in the mailing, plus a pound rate for the total weight of the mailing), then you can't use this form.

You can easily purchase mailing lists online through various Web sites such as www.infousa.com or www.salesgenie.com (both of which claim to own proprietary databases of 210 million U.S. consumers and 14 million U.S. businesses). Another Web site, www.polk.com, specializes in automotive-oriented lists. You can also type "mailing lists" into an Internet search engine to find what you're looking for. These companies provide you excellent, in-depth research capabilities — before you even purchase a list.

I receive direct-mail pieces that are so far off base that I wonder how in the heck my name ever found its way to that particular list. Case in point: I receive mail each month from a singles club inviting me to parties and other social events where I can meet and mingle with other singles and have a high old time. Sounds like a lot of fun to me. Of course, the fact that I've been married for a thousand years would seem to indicate that my address on this list is a gigantic waste of the advertiser's money.

Mailing lists: Something for everyone

Mailing lists are increasingly more sophisticated and informative. Mailing houses have these lists broken down by demographics (age, race, and so on), geography (zip codes, ethnic neighborhoods), income, buying habits, home value, swimming-pool ownership, the works. Name your requirements, and chances are a mailing house has the list you're looking for.

Added to the incredible mix of information is the term *psychographics,* which can pinpoint certain people (for example, "condo-dwelling, SUV-driving, techie"). You can probably find more information in the form of mailing lists than you want or need to know.

Remember: Any direct-mail house can stuff envelopes. It's the *quality* and *timeliness* of their lists that you should be most interested in. Because people move from one place to another, change their marital status, modify their buying habits, increase or decrease their income, and change all sorts of things, mailing lists must be purged and updated often — every six weeks is optimum. If you want to send a mailer to households earning $100,000 and up, you can find a list that can get the job done. How up-to-date the list is, however, makes the difference between all your mailers hitting the correct homes and a whole bunch of them being returned.

A good result from a direct mailing is a return of 2 to 3 percent. That's not much. If you send 1,000 mailers, that means you may get *responses* from only 20 or 30 people, and *converted responses* (sales) from even fewer. But if a few of those 20 or 30 people spend a lot of money with you, and if their added business pays for your printing and mailing costs, those 20 or 30 people may be enough — especially if they become return customers. But the fact that a good direct-mail campaign brings you only a maximum 3 percent return puts that much more meaning into the validity of the list to which you're mailing. You can never be 100 percent certain that the list you're buying is completely current. But you can pressure the direct-mail house to give you assurances that the list is as valid as it can make it.

Planning your postage

Your good credit allows you to be billed for the design work, printing, mailing list, and mailing services, but you have to pay for the postage upfront. The cost of postage is the one item for which the direct-mail house requires you to pay in advance or, as we say in the agency business, *CIA* (short for *cash in advance*). The direct-mail house must pay for the postage when it delivers the material to the post office, or it will have had to pay upfront to load postage into its postage meter. One way or another, the company wants your check before your mailing moves out its door.

After going through all the trouble and expense of sending out direct mail, you may be stunned at the number of direct-mail missives that are returned to you stamped "non-deliverable as addressed." No matter how good the list, some of your mail is destined to make a quick roundtrip. You never know how many people actually read your direct mail, but you sure as heck know how many people never received it in the first place. Direct mail is likely one of the more-measurable media, because the returned items just sit there, in an ever-increasing pile, mocking you. For this reason, most direct-mail houses use their own return addresses rather than the clients'. That way, you don't have to see how many items get returned.

Chapter 11

Opting for Outdoor Ads: Billboards, Posters, Ads on Buses, and Other Signage

*O*utdoor advertising is likely the earliest form of advertising. Before the billboard became a freestanding structure, advertisers plastered their snake-oil logos and slogans on rural barns and on the sides of downtown buildings. And long before that, in an age when most of the population was illiterate, stores and businesses displayed signs that were pictorial (often carved) representations of what they were selling — a mortar and pestle for a drugstore, a tankard of beer for a tavern, a big bloody tooth for a dentist, a hammer and anvil for a blacksmith, the scales of justice for an attorney, and so on.

Outdoor advertising (also known as *out-of-home advertising*), which includes billboards, bus shelters, subway posters, street furniture (bus benches), stadium displays, mall and airport signs, bus cards, taxi tops, shopping carts, and a multitude of other forms, has high visibility. Of the hundreds of messages advertisers expose daily to consumers, I'd guess the majority of them are outdoors.

Outdoor advertising is relatively small on the advertising food chain, behind direct mail, television, radio, newspaper, magazine, Internet, and even Yellow Pages advertising. Still, it's not insignificant: According to the Outdoor Advertising Association of America (OAAA), in 2005, advertisers spent $6.3 billion on outdoor advertising, which was 8 percent more than the previous year. And it can be a highly effective (and affordable) medium when the basic rules of good advertising are applied — namely, an eye-catching design and clear, concise copy.

In this chapter, I clue you in to whether outdoor ads are right for your business; what your options are in terms of all the different formats and placements; and how you can design the most effective outdoor ad, given the large size of this medium but also the fact that it doesn't really support a lot of copy. In the sections that follow, I'll show you how and when to THINK BIG and still get your message across.

Recognizing the Advantages of Outdoor Advertising

Outdoor advertising is on display 24 hours a day, 7 days a week, 365 days a year. It isn't surrounded by editorial content and competing advertisements the way newspaper ads are; it doesn't compete with programming and other commercials the way radio and TV ads do; it doesn't interfere with what someone is doing when browsing the Web, the way online ads pop up; and you can target it to reach very specific audiences by board location and neighborhood. Outdoor is exceptionally effective at reaching various ethnic groups, because you can choose which neighborhoods you want to advertise in — if you want to reach a Hispanic audience, you can place your ads on boards in predominantly Hispanic neighborhoods, and so forth.

Outdoor advertising is ideally suited for

- ✔ Building recognition of your name, logo, package, or other icons associated with your brand
- ✔ Targeting an audience geographically
- ✔ Assisting prospects and customers with directional information

You can't throw outdoor advertising out with the trash, reach over and turn it off, close it out as an electronic intrusion on a computer, or use it to line the bottom of a bird cage. It sits up there — big, bold, and impressive — to be read over and over again by passing motorists and everyone who lives in the neighborhood. It gives you continual exposure, like a 30-day-long commercial — and that's just what you want.

ANECDOTE

H&R Block hits a nerve

H&R Block developed a very effective outdoor campaign a few years back. Capitalizing on the utter confusion of a tax form, one of the company's billboards read: "Subtract line 64 from line 56 if more than line 56 . . . or call us."

Although this board used more words than I believe is optimal, the board worked because it was humorous and struck a nerve. People remembered the ad, even though it was long, because it was so creative.

Outdoor advertising includes billboards, posters, airport ads, bus signs, mall posters, bus shelter ads, stadium signs, bench advertising, shopping cart and gas pump advertising, blimps, banners towed by airplanes — the list is endless.

Who uses outdoor advertising? Here are just a few businesses that do outdoor ads:

✔ Radio stations are among the largest buyers of outdoor ads, because the people viewing the boards are in their cars and are quite likely listening to the radio — and that's a great time to remind them of your station.

✔ Cell phone companies are one of the fastest-growing buyers of outdoor advertising.

✔ Fast-food outlets use billboards to attract hungry motorists to specific locations at highway exits.

✔ Automobile manufacturers and local dealers use outdoor ads to reach consumers who are, when they see the ads, sitting in their cars and trucks.

The top 10 industries that use outdoor ads, according to the OAAA, include the following:

1. Local services and amusements
2. Media and advertising
3. Retail
4. Insurance and real estate
5. Public transportation, hotels, and resorts
6. Financial
7. Restaurants
8. Communications
9. Automotive: Dealers and services
10. Automotive: Auto access and equipment

Altoids's refreshing boards

Altoids, the "curiously strong breath mints" from England, made a big splash on the outdoor scene a few years back with its wonderfully creative copy. One board read: "Mints so strong they come in a metal box." And another winner said: "Refreshes your breath while you scream." Very little copy, but a whole bunch of creativity. It was a billboard campaign that put Altoids on the map in the United States without, as far as I know, any other media support.

But outdoor advertising isn't *limited* to these types of businesses. Small to mid-size businesses that have more modest budgets than the types of companies listed above can use outdoor ads successfully. Small businesses can make their media buys more affordable by selectively choosing board locations that are near their stores and businesses. Outdoor advertising allows you to advertise your products where the ad can be seen by anyone who drives in the vicinity of your store or business location.

The audience for outdoor advertising is growing steadily as people spend fewer hours at home with traditional media and more time on the road and in their cars. What better way to reach people in their cars than with a big, fat billboard alongside the street or a clever ad on the rear end of that bus that's blocking the road up ahead?

Measuring the Effectiveness of Outdoor Ads

Because people spend fewer hours at home, where TV, cable, magazines, newspapers, books, and the Internet all clamor for attention, billboards may be the way to go when it comes to advertising. People are in their cars more than ever — daily vehicle trips continue to climb, and the number of cars on the road seems to grow exponentially. With so many people sitting in traffic jams, drivers and passengers are stuck with radio and billboards as their only media options.

So how do you know for sure how many people are reading your ads? Billboard cost-effectiveness is measured by the Traffic Audit Bureau, which sends out spotters to sit near billboards and count passing cars. Although many advertisers are local retailers, national sponsors are increasingly using the medium to build their brands. Why? Because outdoor advertising is effective and affordable, and it just sits there pumping out the message 24 hours a day.

Outdoor has been called a pure advertising medium, and that may be true. Billboards stand alone without the editorial, programming, and competitive advertising distractions found in newspapers, magazines, radio, and television.

Choosing Among Your Outdoor Advertising Options

Outdoor advertising takes on many forms. Here are many examples (but not all of them) of the outdoor vehicles for sale. It makes you wish you had unlimited funds, doesn't it?

- **Off-premise outdoor advertising:** This outdoor advertising format encompasses any outdoor sign used to advertise your business that is located alongside a road or freeway, in a mall, on a bus, or flying overhead being towed by a biplane. It is not the sign on the front of your store or your office door.

- **Permanent paints:** Permanent paints are huge structures on which the message is painted on the face or printed on vinyl, which is then attached to the face of the structure. As you can imagine, these ads are big and expensive.

- **Rotary bulletins:** These ads are the largest of the standard billboard structures, measuring 14 x 48 feet. The advertising copy for rotary bulletins is printed on vinyl or painted on panels, which are rotated or moved between many locations during the term of the contract. They offer the largest impact in the marketplace and are not only big, but costly.

- **Posters:** The industry standard, also called *30 sheets,* posters are the signs you see everywhere. Copy is printed on posting paper and pasted to the face of the sign. Posters measure 12 x 24 feet. Several posters may be purchased and displayed throughout the market to achieve what is known as a *showing* (the number of boards you have purchased and the length of time your advertising appears on them). Depending on the size of your showing, posters can be quite affordable. See Figure 11-1 for an example of a poster that can be used either indoors or outdoors.

- **Junior posters:** These posters are approximately 6 x 12 feet. They're the same as posters, just half the size (hence the name *junior*). Unfortunately, they are *not* half the cost.

Other outdoor media formats

The number of different outdoor advertising methods you can choose from are almost infinite. In addition to the ones covered in more detail in this chapter, you can also advertise in the following places:

✔ Airships (blimps)

✔ Bus benches and shelters

✔ Bus interior cards

✔ Gas pumps

✔ In-mall kiosks

✔ Parking meter cards

✔ Rest areas

✔ Restroom walls

✔ Shopping carts

✔ Stadiums or arenas

✔ Subway and commuter rail ads

✔ Taxi tops

And that ain't the half of it. Outdoor advertising takes on so many forms that it can, at times, become overly intrusive. If you call a local outdoor advertising company, you can get a full list of what's available to you. I'd need another book this size to describe them all.

✔ **Bus shelter ads:** Bus shelter ads are 48-x-68-inch posters in backlit frames that are integrated into bus shelters. They provide 24-hour exposure in heavy-traffic areas.

✔ **Bus-side advertising:** This form of advertising is available in four sizes:

- **Super Kings:** Available only in select markets, you can usually see these ads located on the traffic-facing or left-hand sides of buses and extending from wheel well to wheel well.

- **Kings:** You can affix these ads to the traffic side of buses, but they are somewhat shorter in length than the Super Kings.

- **Queens:** Check out these ads on the curb sides or right-hand sides of the vehicles.

- **Tails:** As the name implies, the Tails (short for *taillights*) bring up the rear and are quite good for reaching a captive audience (such as you when you're just sitting there inhaling the diesel fumes).

✔ **Aerial banners:** Aerial banners are in-your-face outdoor advertising at its apex. You're watching a football game, minding your own business, when you look up and see an airplane towing a banner that reads: "Eat a Heap Cheap at Joe's." Aerials are flown over sporting events, other special events of every description, and even at beaches — areas where other forms of advertising are nonexistent. This mode of outdoor is also good for birthday surprises when you really want to show off.

Figure 11-1:
This poster can be hung outside a building, in a window, or from a store ceiling.

Designing Memorable Outdoor Advertising

The number of options for outdoor ads may seem overwhelming, but the processes for designing them are identical in most cases. When deciding how to set up your campaign, the important thing to keep in mind is, exactly what makes a great outdoor ad campaign? How many words should you use? What colors work best to attract the attention of passing motorists? Should you use graphics or just stick with hard-hitting copy? Ask a dozen experts, and you may get a dozen different answers. It's the beauty (and the bother) of the business.

But in my opinion, you need to know two primary measuring factors for outdoor advertising:

✔ **Impact:** The ability to grab a viewer's attention in a matter of seconds.

✔ **Appeal:** Persuasiveness and positive response by the viewer to the creative content.

Figure 11-2 shows a sign used inside a bus terminal. The ad was a success because it immediately caught viewer attention with its simple message, bold color, four-word header, and colorful product images. Viewers didn't need to engage in a lot of reading to get the message, learn the product name, and know how the product would benefit them.

Eyeball-popping creative content, readability, simplicity and clarity of message, and, of course, memorability (just like creative content of any advertising media) are the keys to a successful outdoor ad. The fact that an outdoor ad, at least on a billboard, must be seen, read, and remembered while the viewer is otherwise distracted with driving a car down a hostile freeway makes simplicity and clarity of message the most important part of the equation. You only have a couple of seconds to grab the viewer by the eyeballs, so your copy had better be brief and very fascinating. If you're using a graphic element, it too needs to be unique, relevant, and easy to understand.

Outdoor is one medium where simple visuals and word puns are appropriate and highly effective. In your outdoor ads, strive for simple, readable, and creative ads, a welcome diversion to the monotony of travel.

I honestly believe that if you can encapsulate your message onto a really good billboard advertisement; if you can project your message quickly and with clarity; if you can generate some truly creative copy (a message that's brief, perhaps funny, and eye-catching), you've designed your entire ad campaign. If you can boil it down to six or eight perfect words, then you, my friend, have made it so easy on consumers that you can hardly miss getting their attention. The ad you've written to create a memorable billboard can translate beautifully to any media. It is for this reason that your outdoor advertising copywriting effort deserves serious time and attention.

The following sections cover how to make your outdoor ad readable, clear, and memorable — which is all you need to get your message across to potential customers!

Pursuing potential customers

Before you can come up with an award-winning slogan, you must know who your target audience is. Who is most likely to buy your product or use your service? Of course, this is true of ads in any medium: Check out Chapter 5 for a refresher course to make sure you're targeting the right people for your business — and that you can reach them via outdoor ads.

Figure 11-2:
A successful bus terminal ad.

Getting help with your outdoor ads

Getting started with outdoor advertising is easier than you may think. For starters, check out the Web site of the Outdoor Advertising Association of America (OAAA), the trade organization for the industry and the epicenter of reams of information about who, what, when, and where. Find this complete informational source at www.oaaa.org. Or call 202-833-5566 to reach a live person at the OAAA who is happy to answer your questions.

You can also call outdoor advertising companies that are operating in your area, accessible through another great source: SRDS Media Solutions's *Out-of-Home Advertising Source*.

This book can not only steer you to the right outdoor company, but it also gives you a list of the company's rates. The book is available for sale in hard copy or electronically at www.srds.com (click on "Subscription and Product Information"); you can also call to order the book at 800-232-0772, ext. 8020 (or you may find it at your local business library). You can do a search of local companies in a number of ways: by type, geography, or company name. These companies can help you through the complete process — from concept to creation, from printing to posting, and even to tracking your results.

Making your ad readable

If customers can't read your outdoor ad, then what's the point? Your design should be connected with a simple, clean text in a very readable type font. Prioritize the keywords of your copy and keep your copy short and full of punch. Use humor, but get to the punch line quickly. Vary the font size, avoiding copy set in all capital letters. People are used to reading text in a combination of uppercase and lowercase, so outdoor ad copy should conform to this format.

Six words is the most favorable number for billboard readability, but keeping your message that short is often impossible. Try eight words if you must, but any more than eight could be dangerous to the health of your ad budget.

If you're using a graphic element — a picture, drawing, or logo — make it big and keep it simple. Don't force your viewers to search for the message. They don't bother. So make it clear immediately. How many billboards have you seen that, like so many poorly designed newspaper ads, contain enough information to fill an encyclopedia and the advertiser's logo so small you can't read it with binoculars? The message is lost in a jumble of words, type fonts, graphics, and a cacophony of background colors. Viewers drive right on by with only a confused glance at the ill-conceived board. The ad is a total failure. And the money is wasted.

Be sure to use colors wisely. Strong color contrasts between the background and the copy and graphics is absolutely essential. Use primary colors — yellows, reds, blues, and good-old black. Use bright shades of colors rather than darker tones, which retreat from the viewer. A bright yellow background and black letters would be the optimum combination (hey, the publishers of this book knew what they were doing, didn't they?). Using colors isn't complicated — just shoot for the best possible readability from a long way off, because that huge billboard looks like a postage stamp from a distance.

Keeping your ad clear

Viewers don't want to be teased; they want to be informed. And with a billboard, they need to be informed in a split second, so don't get too cute. Be clear, concise, and direct. Relate your message to familiar experiences and situations. Emphasize your product or service as the answer to the viewer's prayers. If you're showing the product, make it big, bold, and brazen.

Also, make sure you limit the number of elements in your ad. A graphic, logo, and headline only gets more complex — and therefore easier to ignore — if you add elements such as the hours you're open, your address, phone number(s), and URL. Less is generally more, so add other information with care and restraint.

Clarity is more important than cleverness. Don't make the joke so subtle that no one gets it — that only causes annoyance. And if you do use humor, be sure it's relevant to the experiences and knowledge of your target audience. Don't use East Coast humor on a California billboard. And try to create a tight connection between your product's benefit and its relevance to the viewer's life; create a problem and solve it in eight words or less.

Making it worth remembering

When your goal is to create a memorable ad for any media, imagery is often more important than words. The use of a hard-hitting visual element can generate more memorability for the viewer. Use images that are easily recognizable — like the beer mugs, anvils, and bloody teeth that comprised the signs for saloons, blacksmiths, and dentists hundreds of years ago. Include light-hearted, spirited elements that generate excitement, but try to ensure that the viewer can relate to the person or situation being depicted. Possibly your best solution is a bold display of your slogan, package, storefront, or logo.

When all else fails . . .

The sign companies with which you do business have design and production departments whose only goal in life is to make your outdoor advertising successful. They know how to design a board, how to write brief, hard-hitting copy, and where to place your outdoor ads for the optimal impact. The creative specialists in outdoor, like the specialists in any media, understand what works in their particular field.

You certainly have your own ideas of what you want, and you likely have at least a copy outline. But you may do well by letting the professionals put the final touches on your creative strategy. This design service is, by and large, available to you at no extra charge. My advice? Take advantage of it.

The San Francisco Zoo did a series of billboards that was very memorable, including one that featured a large photo of an anteater and, in black lettering on a white background, the copy: "Eats 30,000 termites per day. Sorry, not available for rent." Now that's creative!

Above all, make the message simple and easy to recall. Use bright, eye-catching color and brief, well-written copy. You only have a few seconds to make an impact on someone who is already preoccupied driving a car.

For more tips on how to create memorable ads, check out Chapter 19.

Looking at a Success Story: Chick-fil-A's Billboard Campaign

Sometimes a product just cries out for a billboard campaign. It lends itself beautifully to this advertising genre and, with a fairly heavy dose of creativity, it can make all the difference. For example, Chick-fil-A's signature product is the chicken sandwich, served primarily during the lunchtime hours — which means the restaurant chain competes in one of the fiercest battlegrounds: the fast-food restaurant market. When compared to giants such as McDonald's, Burger King, and Wendy's, Chick-fil-A is outnumbered in store count nearly four to one and outspent in media tenfold. Moreover, each of these competing chains has already etched distinct images in the minds of consumers.

Faced with these David-versus-Goliath odds, Chick-fil-A gave its advertising agency, The Richards Group, a tough assignment: Develop an integrated advertising campaign that clearly positions Chick-fil-A as a preferred alternative in the burger-dominated fast food marketplace. In the following sections, I outline how Chick-fil-A used outdoor advertising with great success.

Aiming for the target audience

The Chick-fil-A target audience differs from the average fast-food clientele, which includes many teens and children. The market for chicken is comprised of more adults, more females, and people with a higher level of education and income than the hamburger market. Customers have a more active lifestyle and are likely to be in white-collar jobs. Mindful of these demographics, Chick-fil-A avoided the usual fast-food locations to build their restaurants. Instead, they chose to operate in suburban malls and neighborhoods with a high concentration of their potential customers.

Setting up the marketing strategy

In order to efficiently reach the adult, professional, and mobile target audience, the media strategy emphasized outdoor and radio. The budget was allocated: 70 percent outdoor, 25 percent radio, and 5 percent print.

Capitalizing on the creative strategy

The Eat Mor Chikin campaign was launched. And it cleverly spotlighted a little known fact: the poor spelling ability of your average cow! On billboards everywhere, one three-dimensional cow statue stood on the back of another cow statue and, with paint brush in hand (or hoof) and black paint dripping down the stark white billboard background, the cow had scrawled the words "EAT MOR CHIKIN."

Reaping the results

During the Eat Mor Chikin campaign, same-store sales were up four times over the industry average. It was a thoughtful and clever way to differentiate the Chick-fil-A stores from their burger-dominated competition. Using cows to deliver the self-serving message (I mean self-serving for the cows, who do, of course, prefer you eat chicken rather than beef), Eat Mor Chikin was a brilliantly conceived and executed campaign.

It proves that clever copy and a great creative concept can cut through the advertising clutter like a hot knife through butter . . . or is that chicken?

Part III
Buying the Different Media

In this part . . .

The chapters in this part give you a real-world look at negotiating with sales reps and buying advertising schedules on the various media for your retail business. The advice I give here is done under the assumption that you want to save a few dollars wherever possible. I also show you a few tricks of the trade and give you a good understanding of the buzzwords you may encounter along the way. And if you find you can't do it yourself (or just don't want to), you can find information on when it's time to consider hiring an ad agency to do all this for you.

Chapter 12

Investing in Internet Advertising

. . . .

. . . .

*O*nline advertising is the newest ad medium, and even though it may seem like it's been around forever and you can't remember a time when you didn't check the Web for something, it's still fairly uncharted territory for many businesses — not just small businesses but even the big guys. In fact, an entire trade association, the Internet Advertising Bureau (www.iab.net), is devoted to increasing companies' knowledge and use of the Internet as a viable advertising vehicle.

Online advertising is definitely something that every small business needs to consider doing, because of the ubiquity of the Internet. For many people, especially younger people, searching the Web is the first place they go to find information, learn about new products and services, and buy stuff.

To help you navigate your efforts on the Web, this chapter guides you through how best to allocate this part of your advertising budget. If you've decided you need a Web site but you don't want to create it yourself, I guide you to a professional to do it for you. And if you're ready to go further and advertise on other companies' Web sites or start doing e-mail blitzes, I provide information on those options, too.

Hiring Someone to Create Your Business Web Site

If you've decided that you don't want the responsibility or don't have the skills or time to design your own Web site (I discuss design in Chapter 6: "Creating Your Own Web Site"), you should hire a Web designer to do this for you. In other words, you can always pay someone else to do this for you when you realize you can't do it all on your own. To get started, check out the following sites for lists of Web designers in your area who may be able to help you:

> ✔ **AAADesignList.com:** www.aaadesignlist.com
>
> ✔ **The List:** www.webdesign.thelist.com

You can also ask your Internet Service Provider (ISP) if it can recommend a Web designer (see "Finding an ISP to Run Your Site" later in the chapter). And believe it or not, even though you're developing something for the Internet, you can even find "Web page and site design" in your Yellow Pages — which is about as low-tech as you can get when searching for information!

Whether you're a do-it-yourselfer or contracting for services, particularly where Web advertising is concerned, it's a good idea to research your intellectual property rights, which will help ensure that they remain protected and won't be misused or abused by anyone else, particularly the copyrights and trademarks associated with your ads and with your business in general. Have a lawyer specializing in intellectual property rights go over your business and advertising plan with you if you aren't sure what to look for.

Choosing a Web designer worthy of your hard-earned dollars

Wait, you say! Finding a Web designer is one thing, but how do I know whether the developer is any good? Not all Web designers are created equal. If you choose to hire a designer, you want her expertise, yes, but you also want your own ideas steering the boat. Keep in mind, you're paying this person to translate your ideas into information that will be useful to your customers on the Internet, so make sure you get what you pay for!

Here's what you should expect from a good Web designer:

> ✔ **Several sterling references.** Be sure to call the references and ask how well the designer worked with the customer. Did the designer meet expectations? Was the schedule met? Were there unexpected costs at the end?

✔ **A trail of good Web sites.** Examine the work of the designer by visiting several Web sites developed by that person. Are the pages attractive? Are the sites easy to navigate? Do the sites have a look and feel appropriate to the Web site? Do any sites take an inappropriate time to load?

✔ **A clear list of what is and isn't provided in the Web design project.** Will the designer put your site on the Internet for you? Will the designer notify search engines that your site is available? Will the designer create a logo for you, or do you have one already? How many pages will your finished site contain? Will the graphics be custom-designed or taken from a graphics package?

✔ **The ability to optimize your site for search engines.** Find a Web designer who understands how to perfect your site so that customers can find you.

✔ **A delivery schedule.** The designer needs deadlines in order to know when you need the site up and running.

✔ **Milestones.** Will the designer give you a chance to approve or disapprove of the site at each step along the way?

✔ **A clear estimate of the costs —** *all* the costs.

✔ **A professional product.** The various pages on your site should all have a unified look and feel. Graphics should be tasteful and not too large. No single page should be so long that a visitor has to scroll way down to get to important information.

Before you hire anyone, examine the work of the designer by visiting several Web sites developed by that person. Consider the following factors:

✔ Are the pages attractive?

✔ Are the sites easy to navigate?

✔ Do the sites have a look and feel appropriate to the Web site?

✔ Do any sites take too long to load?

Your designer should expect professionalism from you, too. Here is what your designer can expect from you. Be sure you're providing the following:

✔ **A clear sense of purpose.** You should communicate the way you want your site to look and feel. Flashy? Understated? Jam-packed with information?

✔ **The content for your site.** You can't expect a Web designer to know your business as well as you do. You must provide logos, information, or whatever you've promised to the designer in a timely manner.

✔ **A list of a few sites that you particularly like.** The sites don't have to be in your same line of work, though.

✔ **A mind that's made up.** If you change your mind a little bit, that's to be expected. But no one can work with a person whose mind isn't made up.

✔ **Prompt payment.** Enough said.

Contracting with and paying a Web designer

When you find a designer you like, you (or your lawyer, if you're skittish about doing this yourself) should draw up a contract so you both know what work you're paying for — and what you're not going to pay for. This contract can be as simple as a letter of agreement, but what's important is that both you and your Web designer sign it so that it's binding.

You have several types of contracts from which to choose:

✔ **Hourly:** If you choose an hourly contract, make the reporting schedule frequent so you know exactly how far along the designer is at any moment. You don't want to be caught by surprise. Be sure to reserve the right to cancel the project if your expectations aren't being met.

✔ **Not to exceed:** Under this type of contract, the developer estimates the cost for you and probably charges by the hour, but the designer agrees not to go *over* a certain cost. If the developer has misjudged the estimate, he absorbs the cost.

✔ **Fixed price:** This contract is a flat rate. You and the designer agree to a single price for the entire job. Know exactly what you'll receive on a fixed-price contract. The number of hours your designer takes to complete the project is of no concern to you. Whether the designer finishes your site in a single day or a month, you pay the same rate.

✔ **Cost plus:** In this type of arrangement, the designer bills you for all costs, plus you pay a fixed fee or a fixed percentage on top of the costs. Some developers subcontract part of the work to other people, and you are required to pay the fee.

✔ **Design to fee:** Under this kind of contract, you tell the designer how much you're willing to pay. In return, you receive the best Web page possible for that price.

These various financial arrangements are the same for any design job — Web sites, print, collateral, whatever. You can mix and match or create other types of agreements as you and the designer see fit. Most designers require a payment before the project begins. Keep that initial payment as low as possible.

Make sure you include a payment schedule in your contract, no matter which type of contract you use. If speed is important to you, add a schedule incentive. For every week the project is late, deduct a percentage (about 5 percent). If the project is delivered early, add a bonus to the fee. Never ever make the final payment before the work is fully completed and you're satisfied. Also include a *cancellation clause* in the contract. You want to be able to cancel at your discretion at any time. (You have to pay for anything completed up to the point of cancellation, of course.) The developer wants a cancellation clause, too. That's only fair.

Finding an ISP to Run Your Site

Internet Service Providers (ISPs) are everywhere, and you have many options to choose from. Here are some questions to ask of ISPs when you're shopping for one that works for you:

- ✔ **Do you offer Web hosting?** The World Wide Web (the Internet) is, of course, a massive collection of Web sites, all hosted on computers (called *Web servers*) all over the world. The Web server where your Web site's HTML files, graphics, and so on reside is known as the *Web host*. Web hosting clients simply upload their Web sites to a shared (or dedicated) Web server, which the ISP maintains to ensure a constant, fast connection to the Internet. If your ISP doesn't offer Web hosting, you need to find another ISP.

- ✔ **What kind of technical support do you offer?** You want someone available to help you 24/7/365. Do they have a toll-free number? Is technical help available via e-mail? *Remember:* Technical support never seems that important when you're signing up, but it becomes the most important thing in the world when your Web site crashes.

- ✔ **How many e-mail accounts can I have?** You may need multiple e-mail addresses if you have several employees. Take stock of what you think you need — now and in the future.

- ✔ **Do you have traffic limitations?** Some ISPs have restrictions on the number of visitors you may have to your site. Popular sites may be zinged with unexpected costs. Find out what additional costs you can incur if you go over the limit. The goal is to attract lots of people to your Web site, so an ISP that charges you for doing precisely what you're striving to do may be one you want to avoid.

- ✔ **How much disk space will my site be allowed?** Tell the ISP whether you think your site will have numerous pages or just a few. Be sure to mention whether your site will have lots of graphics as well. This information helps the ISP choose the correct package for you. Most hosting packages offer at least 25MB of disk space, which should be plenty. That amount works out to about 500 Web pages — give or take a few.

✔ **Do you keep backups?** System crashes can kill your business. If the ISP says its system never crashes, don't believe it. What you want them to say is that, on those rare occasions when their system crashes, they keep backups on another machine. Along the same lines, ask whether the ISP has a backup power supply onsite.

✔ **Do you offer site statistics and log files?** This information is helpful if you want to keep track of how many visitors you have and which are the most (and least) popular pages on your site. You can find out how long each person stays on your site and where they came from — all very handy information.

✔ **Do you offer high-speed Internet access?** Ask your ISP whether it supports digital subscriber lines (DSL), integrated services digital network (ISDN), cable modem, and T1 and T3 connections. Does the connection work at all times? Are there peak hours? Can you get a refund for downtime?

✔ **How many users per modem does it have?** You don't want busy signals all day. The more access numbers, the better.

✔ **Do you have templates available to help me build my site?** Some ISPs offer simple boilerplates to fill out (called templates). You provide information pertinent to your site, and the template creates the correct HTML for you. (For more on templates, see Chapter 6.)

✔ **Can you help me find a Web designer/developer?** Many ISPs keep a list of Web designers because they realize that most people don't want to bother with learning HTML. These Web designers can create a Web site tailored to your individual requirements. Hiring a pro is a good way to go unless you're determined to master mounds of technical information. (If you want a go at designing your own site, consider checking out *Creating Web Pages For Dummies,* 8th Edition, by Bud E. Smith and Arthur Bebak [Wiley].)

✔ **Will you buy and register a domain name for me**? As ISPs discover more about what their customers want, they offer more services. In days gone by, you used to have to find an available domain name and then buy and register it. For a small fee, ISPs can take care of this little headache for you.

✔ **Do you offer shopping carts?** A *shopping cart* is what enables a buyer to select more than one item and pay for them all at the same time. If you're certain you *never* want to sell online, you can ignore this question. But the answer could prove important if you think you may want an online store later.

✔ **What e-commerce software do you have that can help me build an online store?** Does the ISP offer secure services for the customer? The current standard is called Secure Sockets Layer (SSL), which protects your customer's private information, including his credit card number. You don't want to operate an online store without it.

Ranking Your Site: Purchasing Key Words on Search Engines

You can also advertise your business on various search engines. For example, if you want to advertise on Google.com, check out "Get me on Google" (www.getmeongoogle.com). This site does exactly that: It advertises your business on Google, so that when people are searching for information on a particular topic, if your business has anything to do with that subject, your Web site appears on the right-hand side of the screen. "Get me on Google" also analyzes your Web site and finds appropriate keywords that you should match up to, and then it can run your ads for a monthly fee.

Buying Banner Ads on Other Web Sites

In addition to developing your own Web site (see Chapter 6), you may also want to advertise on other business's Web sites. Chapter 6 gives you the basic information you need for how to create those ads; the following sections provide information on how to get those ads up and running. You can get your banners and buttons on a Web site in several ways.

Using ad networks

A number of sites can place your banner ad for you. One of the leading sites used by many big advertising agencies is DoubleClick.com (www.double click.com). If you have a large company and a budget to match, DoubleClick. com is a great option.

You can also check out other sites known as *banner exchange networks*. With these sites, you have to display banner ads for other companies on your company's Web site, in exchange for them putting *your* banner ad on *their* sites. The cost is lower and makes this option worth considering. Microsoft has a useful exchange program. (Go to www.microsoft.com/small business. Then click on "Attracting Customers," in the Online Services section — attracting customers is what your advertising should do, right?) You can also find a banner exchange program at www.bpath.com: Just click on "Banner Exchange."

If you click on Bpath.com's "QuickBanner," you can also create various types of banners, for not a lot of money — for example, at the time of this writing, check out these prices:

✔ An animated flash banner maker costs only $19.95.

✔ An advanced (static) banner costs only $14.95.

✔ A GIF button costs $9.95.

✔ A GIF banner is free (heck — you can't deny your attraction to that word!).

You can also search the Web for "ad networks" to come up with a huge list of sites that can carry your ads for free.

Placing your online ads yourself

If your customer base is well-defined, you can find appropriate sites and approach them yourself. A simple way to do this method is to search the Internet by using a few keywords of interest to your customers. (You're looking for sites that share interests or content similar to your own.) You can get a list of sites that may be appropriate for placing your ad. Check them out and ask whether you can place your banner on their site for a fee or whether you can simply exchange banners at no cost to either party (called a *reciprocal link*).

For example, suppose you sell baseball cards. Go to a search engine and type in "baseball" or "sporting goods." The list that comes up under either search may have a site perfect for you. Don't type in "baseball cards" as your search term because the sites that appear there are your *competitors*. They won't want your banner on their sites, and you don't want their banners on your site.

Although this approach can be effective, it takes time and an ability to negotiate a fair price.

Online advertising via affiliate programs

You can also advertise your business via *affiliate programs* (also known as *partnership programs* or *associate programs*). You contract to place ads on your site, and you are paid when a visitor to your site clicks through or purchases something from another site.

Affiliate programs are carefully targeted to the interests of your visitor. For example, if you have a Web site dealing with antique furniture, you *don't* want to become an affiliate of a sporting good site, for example. Affiliate programs are good for sites that are narrowly focused — and zillions of topic-specific sites are out there. Amazon.com was the very first affiliate — it offers a percentage of the sale if one of your visitors buys from Amazon.com after clicking on its link from your site.

Pay schedules

Online ads have three major pricing structures:

✔ **Cost per thousand (CPM):** This cost of an ad is for every 1,000 times the ad is displayed. Most of the time, when you buy a CPM, your banner appears on big, highly trafficked Web sites. Sometimes this type of pricing structure is called *pay per face,* but it's the same thing — the cost of 1,000 impressions. (An *impression* is the number of times an ad appears on a Web page.)

✔ **Cost per click (CPC):** You only pay for this if someone clicks on your banner ad and is taken to your site. Be a little careful before plunging in to this type of ad. Your audience *is* better targeted, but the cost is higher, and you'd better be able to convert these visits to sales if you want to make money. Sites like www.valueclick.com buy unused ad space on prime locations. Some companies don't sell by CPC because the quality of a banner is a determining factor in how much they earn, and it's a factor those sites can't control.

✔ **Cost per transaction (CPT):** You pay when you make a sale. This choice offers great accountability, but you do pay a significant percentage for this type of fee structure. This structure is also known as *cost per action* (CPA).

One drawback, if you're considering becoming an affiliate, is that frequently a visitor who clicks through to another site doesn't return to yours. However, you have a few ways to ensure that a visitor actually remains on your site even though he has clicked on an ad. If you're not an HTML expert, hire a Web designer to help you accomplish this.

Find out more about affiliate programs by visiting www.associateprograms.com or www.clickquick.com.

Finding out whether your banner is working

After you run your banner ads, find out how effective they are. You can do this by using several kinds of statistics:

✔ **Impressions:** The number of times an ad appears on a Web page.

✔ **Click-through:** The number of times people select/click on your banner or button.

✔ **Click-through rate (CTR):** The number of times the ad is clicked on divided by the total number of times people see your ad.

✔ **Conversion:** The rate at which some goal is achieved (sales or orders or traffic building, for example).

✔ **Hit:** Every component of a Web site viewed by a visitor. If you have one Web page with 20 graphics and a visitor looks at all of them, you have 21 hits.

In general, the conversion rate is the most important statistic. Number of hits is largely meaningless, but I include it on this list because you probably hear the term everywhere. Don't be fooled. You're interested in click-through rates and conversion rates rather than just the number of impressions.

You can get these statistics in several different ways. If you join a program, you can either buy *banner placements* (a fixed number of impressions) or you can trade ad space on your page for ad space on someone else's Web site. When you join a program, you get access to individualized statistics that you can view any time you want. You can find out how many times people have seen your ad and also how many times people clicked over to your page. To get the conversion rate, you have to work with your Web host (the supplier of your e-commerce software).

You can also buy log-analysis software or even hire a company to track your data and provide you with customized reports. You can find companies that provide log analysis by typing the keyword "log analysis" in any Internet search engine.

Assessing the Cost-Effectiveness of E-Mail Advertising

Today the return on investment is high for e-mail advertising. One reason is that you have few upfront costs — an enormous advantage. You can, of course, simply do it yourself, by writing a message to customers just as you would to a friend, and then bcc'ing your customers' e-mail addresses. The only real "cost" of doing this is your time. This approach isn't very sophisticated; however, you may find it useful if your business is just starting out. (For tips on how to create a successful e-mail advertising campaign, see Chapter 6.)

If you think about the e-mail you receive from businesses, most of it has a Web site link attached to it, where you can buy goods. For example, I get frequent e-mails from Lands' End, The Container Store, and J. Crew because I've shopped there in the past, and they notify me when they're having a sale or when new merchandise is available. These huge companies clearly have an e-mail advertising team to handle their campaigns.

You can also hire a company to handle your e-mail ad campaigns: Simply type "e-mail advertising" into a search engine, and you can find companies that have software to handle mass e-mail (and other direct-response mass-marketing communication vehicles) and that provide their own servers that can handle huge bandwidth. They can also provide you with reporting feedback on how effective your campaign is: How many people have viewed your message, how many clicked-through from your message to your Web site, and how many people opted out of your advertising campaign. For example, www. emarketingblitz.com is just one site that offers this service.

Keep in mind that your e-mail is competing with hundreds of other e-mails jamming someone's inbox. And people grow less tolerant as time goes by. Most ISPs and other e-mail service providers have *spam blocking* programs, to allow clients the choice of filtering their mail. Advertisers may eventually have to pay for the chance to slip past the guards. That's not necessarily a bad thing. Sometimes paying a little more decreases the competition.

As Internet advertising continues to proliferate, marketing professionals develop new ways to measure its effectiveness. One company (Marketing Sherpa) conducted research in 2004 to find out how seasonality affected the best day of the week to send e-mail. It evaluated the open and click rates from more than 60 million e-mail messages sent by 7,000 marketers — and found that the best day of the week is a moving target. (If you're interested in the details, check out www.marketingsherpa.com.)

E-mail advertising effectiveness varies among industries. An August 2006 study that Harte-Hanks, Inc., a direct-marketing company, conducted looked at 4,300 business and consumer e-mail campaigns. Here are the best and worst results:

- ✔ Restaurants had the best result, with a 167.7 percent open rate (an open rate of more than 100 percent occurs when people pass along and/or reopen the e-mail); restaurants also had the best click-through rate, of 57.5 percent.

- ✔ Retail had the lowest open rate, of only 35.3 percent.

- ✔ The automotive industry had the lowest click-through rate, of only 5.7 percent.

In case you're curious, here are the click-through results for all 13 industry categories that Harte-Hanks, Inc. studied, from best to worst:

1. Restaurants: 57.5 percent

2. Publishing: 55.6 percent

3. Pharmaceuticals: 23.8 percent

4. Travel and hospitality: 23.4 percent

5. Conference events: 14.2 percent

6. Financial services: 11 percent

7. Technology: 10.9 percent

8. Government: 9.5 percent

9. Insurance: 9.5 percent

10. Consumer packaged goods: 8.6 percent

11. Entertainment: 8.1 percent

12. Retail: 6 percent

13. Automotive: 5.7 percent

These results don't mean that you shouldn't consider doing e-mail marketing for your business if it's ranked lower on this list. But it helps to know which industries have been most successful getting through to people.

Your best results come from past and prospective customers who've given you their e-mail addresses, because they want information from you on an ongoing basis.

Chapter 13

Buying Ad Space in Print Media

· ·

· ·

*P*rint advertising includes everything from daily and Sunday newspapers to consumer magazines, business-to-business publications (including trade journals, newsletters, and professional magazines), and even the Yellow Pages or other directories. According to *Advertising Age*'s 2005 "Fact Pack," the advertising pie included the following print media slices for the 100 leading national advertisers' spending in 2004:

✔ **Newspapers:** 17.4 percent (advertisers spent $46.6 billion)

✔ **Yellow Pages:** 5.3 percent (ad costs totaling $14 billion)

✔ **Consumer magazines:** 4.6 percent (a $12.25 billion price tag)

✔ **Business publications:** 1.5 percent (amounting to $4 billion)

By comparison, advertising on broadcast TV was 17.5 percent (comparable with newspapers), and direct mail advertising was the largest piece of the pie, with 19.8 percent. Keep in mind, though, that these leading national advertisers are the big guns who are spending big budgets. (Must be nice!) Still, these figures give you some idea of how companies allocate their advertising dollars, so you can determine the print advertising needs of your own business.

In this chapter, I show you how to select the right print publications for your particular business and how to negotiate with those publications after you have narrowed down the list. Pay close attention, because newspapers and other print publications have more discount rates than the stars in the heavens — and you don't want to pay one dime more than you have to.

Choosing the Right Publication for Your Print Ad

When you're ready to get your print ad out there for the world to see, the first thing you need to do is choose a venue. This task may seem like an easy one, and sometimes it is. You can choose among major daily newspapers, weekly papers, entertainment-oriented newspapers, trade publications (business-to-business publications), consumer magazines, mailing inserts, and on and on. Your mission is to choose the media that your potential customers are reading. How do you accomplish that?

Although you may be tempted to put your ads in the publications that *you* read (after all, they're the ones you know), your ads will be a bigger success if you put them where your *customers* can see them. Talk to people in your target audience — your customers. Ask your current customers the following questions:

✔ Why they choose your store or business

✔ How they decide to buy your product or service

✔ What publications they read — both at work and at home

✔ Which section of the newspaper they turn to first

✔ Which media they're likely to respond to when shopping around for what you're selling

With a little hip-pocket market research — where you ask a lot of relevant questions of people who already know your store or business — you can pin down the publications into which you should insert your ads.

Almost every consumer magazine and business publication offers a *media kit* that provides information on the demographics of its subscribers — typically in terms of gender, age, income level, and even marital status and the number of children, depending on the publication. Some publications provide this subscriber information online, but be careful when checking Web sites so that you're not just getting demographics for the online version of the publication, which may differ from the print version of the publication.

Media kits also give general guidelines to how much it costs to advertise in the publication's pages. Most kits have an annual schedule of theme topics the publication plans to cover, which can help you develop your advertising plans if your product or service is particularly tied to any of those topics. For example, if your business is wrought-iron patio and lawn furniture and you know that *Better Homes and Gardens* magazine is doing an article about buying outdoor furniture in the next May magazine, you may want to advertise in that month's issue.

Calculating Your Print Ad's Cost

I have good news and bad news about print media ad costs. The good news is that most print media actually have easy-to-read (albeit somewhat difficult-to-understand) rate cards that list the various costs for assorted ad sizes — a welcome relief from the way radio advertising is negotiated, as I describe in Chapter 14.

The bad news is that the rate card is nothing more than a starting point in the media-negotiation and buying process, because newspapers, especially, have created so many permutations of their basic (or *open*) rates that even a professional media buyer has trouble deciphering them in order to come up with the most frugal media buy. And after you discover the nuances of one publication's rates and myriad discounts, you can then call the next publication and start all over again — no two publications' rates and discounts are alike. (I think they do this just to totally confuse you and to give their salespeople a reason for being.)

After deciding where you're going to put your ad, you need the help of a sales rep (see the section "Finding a Good Sales Rep" later in this chapter) to figure out what the ad's going to cost you. But before you go into a meeting with a rep, you need to know a few things about how print ads are priced.

For example, somewhere in the mists of time, all newspapers made the diabolical decision that no two advertising pricing schemes would ever be the same. Newspapers and other publications generally price print ads by multiplying the number of columns wide, by the number of inches high, by a dollar amount for each column inch. For example, a quarter-page ad in most newspapers is 3 columns wide by 11 inches high, which makes it a 33-column-inch ad. So if the open rate for your local paper is $50 per column inch, you have an ad that can cost you $1,650 for one insertion.

Unfortunately, it's not always that simple. Here are just a few of the seemingly infinite variations possible to that simple pricing structure:

- ✔ The initial $50 per-column-inch rate can change for numerous reasons, because it's the *open rate* (the rate paid by a new advertiser who runs an ad only one time).

- ✔ If you're willing to commit to running your ad multiple times over a certain time period, you can reduce the open rate by as much as 50 percent.

- ✔ Newspapers and other publications often give discounts for new businesses, minority-owned businesses, first-time advertisers, political advertisers, nonprofit groups, and so on.

- ✔ If you're willing to commit to three ads per week, and if you're also willing to make a substantial dollar commitment over an extended time period, you can dramatically reduce your rate per ad.

- ✔ You may qualify for more than one of these discounts — for example, if you're willing to commit to a long-term buy and you're also a nonprofit.

Usually, newspapers offer what they call *pickup rates*. A pickup rate is a discounted rate newspapers give in return for running the same ad two or more times in the same week. For instance, if your first ad runs in the Sunday paper, your newspaper rep may quote you a pickup rate as follows: "Our pickup rates are 20, 30, 40, then 50, 50, and 50." That's her way of saying that if you run your ad a second time in the same week, you receive a 20-percent discount; a third insertion in that week gets you a 30-percent discount; a fourth insertion gets you a 40-percent discount; and for every time you run the ad in that same week after that point, you receive a 50-percent discount. And the discounts apply to all ads you run.

TIP

Cost per thousand

The cost of reaching the consumer via print is often expressed in *cost per thousand* (CPM), your cost if you want to reach 1,000 consumers with your advertisement. For instance, coupon booklets are usually target-mailed to groups of 10,000 households. To have your ad included in a one-time mailing of a coupon booklet to a particular group of homes may cost you $275, resulting in a CPM of $27.50 ($275 divided by 10). In that same market, you may find that running an ad in a daily newspaper may give you a much different CPM. For example, running a print ad that includes that same coupon may require a 3-column-by-2-inch ad (6 column inches). That ad, priced at an open rate of $80 per column inch, costs you $480. If the newspaper boasts a circulation of about 300,000, your CPM is only $1.60.

But hold on there! You have much to consider, much to factor in. First, depending on which section of the paper your ad runs in, count on about only 20 percent of the paper's total circulation actually *seeing* your ads. Second, a small coupon ad positioned on a full page of newsprint is dramatically different (read, *dramatically less effective*) than a color coupon printed and mailed to consumers in a coupon booklet.

What's the moral of this story? CPM is an important consideration when evaluating the cost of print advertising. However, you need to consider other factors if you want to compare apples to apples. My suggestion is to always factor in the variables, stir in some gut feel, and do the math so you're aware of the CPM. Then use all these aspects to make more sense of a sometimes-confusing media choice.

Clearly, the discounts definitely have a way of adding up! The ad in my example earlier in this section, which I priced at $1,650 for a single insertion, ends up costing $594 at the end of one week if you run it multiple times — which gives you a discount of 64 percent!

Ad pricing is complicated, confusing, convoluted, and intimidating. The only way you can be sure you're getting the best rate possible is to tell your rep, in no uncertain terms, "Give me *all* available rates."

Finding a Good Sales Rep

If you're buying print media, you deal, for better or worse, with sales reps from the various publications — newspapers, magazines, Sunday supplements, coupon books — into which you're inserting your ads. Sales reps come in many shapes, sizes, and abilities ranging from nearly comatose to able to leap tall buildings in a single bound. So, unless you own a portable defibrillator and can strap it on quickly, you want to look for a rep who is a high achiever.

In some cases, you may not be able to choose a rep: Many national publications assign accounts to sales reps based on region of the country, so if your business is in Detroit, you need to deal with a Michigan sales rep. Find this info out early on. Call the publication directly, or many publications list this information as well as the names, phone numbers, and e-mail addresses of their ad sales reps under the "Contact Us" or "Advertising" sections of their Web sites.

In the following sections, I describe a variety of ways you can find a good sales rep who will help you run your print ad, hopefully in the best format and at the best time.

Cold-calling a publication: Don't do it!

When you're interested in buying an ad with a particular print media, you don't have to take the sales rep that the receptionist transfers you to when you call the front desk. In fact, I've always believed that the really good reps are busy taking orders, or they're out in the field generating new orders, or they're visiting their many clients and taking care of business. So who answers your call? Yep, the rep who's lazy, or a rookie without a clue, or the guy who's waiting around the office hoping the phone will ring.

If you're *not* locked in by region or some other factor, don't give your advertising account to just anyone. Do everything you can, regardless of the size of your budget, to work with the best sales rep in the department. When you want a job done right, as the saying goes, give it to a busy person. Picking the right sales rep can mean the difference between a successful, mutually profitable relationship with an advertising partner and a frustrating and possibly expensive disaster.

Going straight to the top: Call the sales manager

To find the right rep, a great place to start is to call the publication's sales manager. Explain your needs and the kind of person you want to work with — tell the sales manager that you have been disappointed by some other media reps and want to work with the manager's best, someone who's sharp and motivated (and hungry); someone who actually returns your phone calls on the same day; someone who carries a cell phone; someone who's available to help you solve last-minute problems; someone who can be your advertising partner; someone the sales manager is proud and confident to have you work with.

Although asking the sales manager for his or her best rep has no guarantees, you're much more likely to get someone who works hard for you than if you just called and told the sales manager to send someone out to see you. The person the sales manager assigns to you after you give her some parameters (which implies that you're no rookie to this media-buying game) is probably given some very specific instructions about what your expectations are, instead of being handed a yellow sticky note saying, "Call/follow up."

Asking for referrals

Another method for finding a good sales rep is simply to ask for referrals. You can save yourself a lot of wheel-spinning and grief by taking advantage of insider knowledge. The two best sources for referrals are

> ✔ **Competing publications' sales reps:** Even though they're competing for the same advertising dollars, sales reps tend to know each other, hang out together, and belong to the same clubs. High achievers are going to be friends with people similar to themselves. Birds of a feather, and all that.

✔ **Friendly business competitors:** Your business competitors, at least those with whom you're on speaking terms, can be another great source of insider information. Some of them are undoubtedly placing advertising with the same publications you're looking to employ, and they can steer you toward sales reps you can enjoy working with, as well as warn you of sales reps you should avoid.

TIP

A simple way to find a sales rep worth your while is to call the publication and ask for the rep who handles your competitor's ads — or any ad you think is well done and well placed.

Becoming a Formidable Ad Buyer

Buying ad space in the many print mediums requires patience and tact — and a bit of conniving — if you want to get a good deal. In this section, I provide some helpful hints on getting the most for your money when it comes to print ads.

Acting as though you're reluctant

If you're thinking about placing a print ad, you've probably decided to use a particular newspaper (for example), and you may already know that you want to run a quarter-page ad every Saturday for the next six months. If you walk into a meeting with a sales rep and tell him what you're looking for, he will probably pull out a rate card, listing all the standard rates for ads of various sizes. But if you pay the rate-card cost for an ad, that's essentially the same as paying full sticker price for a car at your local dealership. And, if you're like me, you ain't gonna do that!

Buying reluctantly is all about not revealing all your cards to your sales rep. So when you meet with the rep, convey something like the following:

> I've been considering several different types of advertising, including advertising in your newspaper. I have a great deal with the Yellow Pages, I plan to buy some local radio, and I'm sending out a monthly coupon with a direct-mail house as well. I just wanted to find out from you whether your newspaper may be able to round out my media buy and complement what I already have in the works.

Emptying a sales rep's bag of tricks

Like most people, you probably have had the experience of someone trying to sell you something that you didn't really want to buy. Whether it was a time-share condominium in Mexico or a new car at the dealer down the street, the common (and happy) denominator of this excruciating experience was that the longer you *resisted* the initial offer, the better the deal got. Believe me when I say that all media sales reps carry with them a bag filled to the top with tricks to be used to close deals when the need arises. If you do your job, you eventually get a much better deal than you were offered originally, and in turn, you stretch your ad budget.

This language sends out a strong message to the rep — a message that states that you aren't just a pushover and that the rep has some work to do in order to get your business. The rep doesn't need to give you a big, fat sales pitch. You have shown, in your speech, that you know what you're doing, that you expect to be treated differently than other new advertisers, that you're not about to pay full sticker price, and that, bottom line, you want a deal. That's a powerful message!

Don't just stop with good opening remarks. If you're meeting in your office, leave a few business cards from this rep's competitors lying around your desk along with pages torn from the Yellow Pages on which you've scribbled notes with a red marker. Reps have a notorious talent for reading upside down, so he will read anything you leave on your desk. Ask the newspaper rep whether he thinks radio advertising is still a good value in your area. Prearrange to receive a phone call in the middle of your meeting and say things like, "No way! I'm not paying that rate. That's ridiculous!"

You've now set the stage for the sales rep to come back to you with a convincing pitch that his publication is not only the right media for you, but also one of the most affordable. Now is the time to sit back and listen. Let the rep go to work, and never give him the slightest hint as to which way you're leaning. And when he has quoted you the best rate he can personally offer, refuse it and send him back to his sales manager for an even better one.

During my decades in the advertising business, I've worked with hundreds of clients, big and small, and I can tell you that owners of small businesses, whose ad budgets are comprised of their own, hard-earned money, are instinctively reluctant buyers. As a matter of fact, in my experience, the smaller the account, the more client service is involved. These people correctly perceive their ad budgets as real dollars subtracted off the bottom line (that's their take-home pay), and they want to know how every nickel is spent.

Unlike small business owners, employees of large companies, who are spending corporate advertising budgets, tend to view those dollars as an abstraction, are often lazy with their buying, and are, therefore, much easier to sell and service. If you're spending your own money for print ads, I probably don't need to tell you to be a reluctant and careful buyer, but I'm reminding you to do so just in case.

Making your sales rep think she's got competition

If you don't create at least the appearance of a competitive situation, you won't receive the best price available. In other words, even if you're *not* talking with other sales reps from other media or other publications, you need to make your sales rep *think* you are. You need to introduce the possibility of competition (and reality) into the lives of your sales reps. You can accomplish this feat in countless ways, a few of which I outline in the following sections.

Asking for more perks

The mere mention of competition is usually enough to send your sales rep running for her pencil sharpener. The simplest method is to study the rep's first offer and then, casually, but with confidence, simply ask for more. If she offers you four ads for $1,000, tell her you need six ads for the same price — or she's forcing you to get quotes from other sources. You may not get exactly what you ask for, but I guarantee that you'll get *something*.

Wheeling and dealing

Call all the competitors, get quotes and bids, and then let them tear each other apart. Show reps their competitor's proposals and let the various reps analyze their competitors' bids. Then, sit back and watch the backstabbing games begin. This contest is despicable, but it works to your own advantage. It may get a little bloody, but I guarantee you can get the best rates and combo deals available from each and every publication.

Making an arbitrary change

If you've been using a particular newspaper for an extended period of time, make a surprise and very arbitrary change. Then when your sales rep drops into your office to get your monthly order, tell her you've decided to place your ads in another paper or switch your budget to radio this month because her competitor has offered you a deal that you simply can't refuse. Naturally, your rep may be shocked and dismayed, and she may lay a huge guilt trip on you by whining something like, "Gee, I thought we were working so well together." But don't even bat an eyelash.

The rep can then do one of two things: Go out to her BMW (all reps drive very tired BMWs), drive to the nearest grocery store, fill up on comfort food, and head home to spend the rest of her life watching daytime television and eating ice cream. Or return to her cubicle where she has to tell her sales manager that she lost your business this month. Her manager will then instruct her to go back to your office and do whatever it takes (offer lower rates, more insertions, better page position, whatever) to win back your business. What you hope is that your sales rep chooses the second option — not only does she go on to lead a long and happy life (with a lot less calories), but you get a good deal on the next month's ads at the same time.

Complaining when the time is right

If one of your customers bought a brand new whatchamacallit from you at a premium price, then took it home, used it once, and it broke, I guarantee that you would quickly see that customer back in your store, whatchamacallit in hand, ranting and raving for either an exchange or a refund. Or if you yourself order something from a catalog that turns out to be less than advertised, you get onto the customer service line in a heartbeat and complain loud and clear until you are either sent another item or given assurances of a full and immediate credit to your account. Complaining is sometimes the only way to get what you want (more so everyday, it seems), and you should use this tried-and-true technique to ensure that your print budget is always maximized. Newspapers and other print media don't go out of their way to make mistakes; it's simply a fact of life.

If anything is wrong with the placement of your print ad, don't be shy. Get on the phone and chew out anyone who listens to you. Start with your rep and move right up the chain of command until you find satisfaction. If your ad falls on a page that was printed a bit light because the roller was running out of ink, complain. If the newspaper buries your ad in some obscure section that you didn't contract for and would never select if given a choice, complain. If your ad was scheduled to run on Friday but didn't run until Saturday, complain. If the publication sandwiches your ad between two of your competitor's ads, complain.

Most publications have a fairly liberal policy when it comes to giving their customers *make-good ads* (ads that try to make good on the publication's promise to you). Instead of making a good customer angry about some fairly common mistake, the publication usually gives you another free ad to make up for anything you're unhappy about.

If you don't complain, whatever it is you *didn't* complain about is bound to happen again. In any publication, you can unearth good, great, and just plain lousy ad placements (or positions). However, most newspapers place ads in a section and on the page in a random and somewhat arbitrary fashion. The people who do the actual layout of the finished paper start with a stack of ads and a pile of pictures and stories and assemble the newspaper. Your well-timed complaint can cause your rep to hand-carry your ad back to that department and ask the nice folks for a favor. To further my point, if you and your competitor *both* get lousy ad placements and the other guys complain but you don't, then your competition gets the make-good ad, your competition gets better placement next time, and, because of all this, your competition has an advantage over you.

You can significantly stretch your print advertising budget by not pretending you have lockjaw every time a publication screws things up. Loud and vociferous complaints get you two things — make-good ads and better ad placement. The value of free make-good ads is fairly easy to determine, and a well-placed ad can be worth twice that of a poorly placed ad. In short, your ad does a heck of a lot better if it's positioned where someone can actually see it!

Most newspapers do, sadly, give you a legitimate reason to complain at least once every ten ads you run. Newspapers especially have a talent for getting it wrong, perhaps because of the sheer volume of ads they run each day. It is logical, therefore, that you can stretch your ad budget by 10 percent simply by not being shy. So stick up for yourself, and get the placement you deserve that will advertise your business well!

Chapter 14

Purchasing Ad Time on the Radio

In This Chapter

▶ Knowing which stations are best for you

▶ Mastering some radio advertising lingo

▶ Weeding through the data you hear from sales reps and getting to what counts

▶ Capitalizing on seasonal incentives

*R*adio stations target their programming to attract very specific audiences. You can find stations formatted for everyone from teenyboppers to Baby Boomers, from cowboys to classical music aficionados. Some stations feature hits of the '50s, '60s, or '70s; stations that broadcast only news; Spanish language, country, jazz, or good old rock 'n' roll stations. Radio has something for everyone.

However, radio advertising comprises only a small piece of the advertising pie — at least for those "leading national advertisers" I mention in Chapter 13. According to *Advertising Age,* radio ads made up only 7.4 percent of total media expenditures in 2004 — compared to 19.8 percent direct mail ads, 17.7 percent newspaper ads, and 17.5 percent commercials on broadcast TV (which together makes up more than half of all media placements). Remember that these percentages are for big companies like Procter & Gamble, General Motors, Dell Computer Corporation, Time Warner, and other giants; on the other hand, you may find that radio advertising works great for your business.

Radio audiences tend to be very loyal to their favorite stations, sticking with their favorites not only out of choice, but also out of habit. They're also loyal to many of the advertisers on their favorite stations, so finding the stations that can deliver the best audience for your commercial messages is definitely worth the effort.

In this chapter, I help you figure out which stations to advertise on, guiding you through the terminology you may hear from the people selling you the ads. I also let you know how to read a broadcast media invoice to figure out whether you're really getting the ads you paid for. And I let you know how you can stretch your advertising budget — and get something for yourself at the same time. (In Chapter 8, I provide information and suggestions on how to create memorable radio ads for your business.)

Determining the Best Radio Station for Your Ads

Before you get down to the nitty-gritty of negotiating and buying a schedule for your radio ads, you need to do a little homework to ensure that your schedule runs on the station best suited to attract customers to your business, customers who want to buy what you're selling. For instance, if you're selling pickup trucks, you're probably better off advertising on a country music station than on one that plays only classical. If, on the other hand, you own an art gallery or jewelry store, the classical station may be just the place for your ad bucks.

You probably have your favorite radio stations — ones you've programmed into your home and car radios. And you probably know of other radio stations that you specifically avoid, because what they play just isn't what you like. If you use these personal likes and dislikes as a starting point, you're well on your way to selecting the stations that are right for your advertising dollars. Without even knowing it, you've already done much of your research.

Knowing what you like and don't like helps you find the station that's right for your ads because you're aware that each station appeals to a certain audience. But the stations you listen to may *not* be the ones that your customers listen to. So don't limit your advertising to just the stations *you* like. If you do, you can miss out on a huge section of your target market.

In the following sections, I show you how to start researching which stations may be best for your business and what demographic group(s) you're really targeting, and then I go into more detail about how to research radio stations. In addition to all this info, I describe how to buy time for your ads on the radio stations you've chosen.

Specifying which demographic you're after

Who are your customers? Men between 18 and 35? Women between 35 and 54? Teenagers? Whatever demo you're after, you can most likely find a radio station in your market programmed specifically to reach that narrow audience segment.

Radio stations break down the various demographics into seven different age groups for both sexes, as you can see in Table 14-1. Ask the stations you're interviewing to show you a demographic profile of its listeners; this profile gives you a clear picture of whether a particular station is a good fit for your business.

Table 14-1	Demographic Groups
Men	*Women*
12–17	12–17
18–24	18–24
25–34	25–34
35–44	35–44
45–54	45–54
55–64	55–64
65 and older	65 and older

When presenting this information to you, most stations use ratings for a category called *Total Adults, 25–54.* This group is an extrapolation of the totals for three separate age groups of both sexes.

The problem with focusing on your demographic is this: The station that's programmed to appeal to your prime demo may not enjoy the best ratings in the market and, therefore, may not be your best buy. On the other hand, that station may be your best buy because of the fact that it's delivering your targeted demographic, in spite of its low ratings. Confused? No wonder: The challenge is calculating the *cost per targeted listener,* which is typically expressed in terms of *cost per gross rating point,* or GRPs. GRPs, of course, vary from market to market, because the size of the market enters into the calculation. To find out how to compare station ratings, check out the section "Evaluating station ratings." (You may also want to read the sidebar "When you *don't* need to buy the very best" for additional info.)

Doing your homework

Before you commit to advertising on one station, check out your options. You may be surprised to find out how many valuable resources are out there to help you make your decision. In this section, I give you a few valuable tools to research before you settle down with a station.

Don't panic! If you find this discussion of analyzing data too overwhelming, take a deep breath. Maybe it's time to hire someone to help you, so check out Chapter 16 for details on exactly that: Bringing in the professionals. Full-service ad agencies and media-buying houses are available, and they have analytical tools, ratings databases, and optimization software — along with the knowledge and prowess to negotiate the best deals for your business.

Utilizing the Internet

If you're interested in checking out *all* your options, researching various stations is easier than ever due to the Internet. For example, simply type "radio stations" into an Internet search engine like Google, and you can find Web sites that provide you station information, sites like www.radio-locator. com. This specific Web site allows you to indicate what region you're looking for — and then provides, for example, 74 radio stations in New York City (if that is the region you requested). This list gives the call letters of each station (like WBGO), the frequency (such as 88.9 FM), and a very brief format identifier (jazz, adult contemporary, hip-hop, talk, Spanish, religious, business news, top 40, and so on). Then you can simply click on the call letters and go directly to the Web site of the station that interests you, to find out more about its programming and determine whether it matches the target market of your ideal customer.

Evaluating station ratings

Picking the right stations is a complicated process, and, more often than not, you ultimately need to take a giant leap of faith when finally placing your buy. But a good place to start is with the most current ratings of all stations — information you can get from any and all the sales people who call on you. If, on the other hand, you're located in a small market with but a couple of stations, you don't need to sweat this stuff.

Getting ratings data from radio stations is very tricky. Data is very selectively presented and can be misleading (such as rankers, which I define in a later section). Often, a station shows you its ratings based on total persons 12 and older. You're most likely to find this information in a sales piece in the media kit. Be aware of what you're looking at as you sift through this information. You don't want to base your media buy on such a broad audience composition; you want to see the various age groups separated into the demographic categories (see Table 14-1) so you can be assured that your prime demo is well represented in a station's listenership. And, besides, how much spending power do 12-year-olds really have? (In truth, a lot more than their parents would care to admit, but still not as much as adults.)

The most current station ratings are published every quarter in what is known in the ad biz simply as a *book*. Companies like Arbitron, which is the largest and most-recognized ratings service, do the research and publish the books. Smaller markets have their own ratings services, which are less expensive and therefore more attractive to small market stations. The ratings services use different methods to rate the stations, including radio listening diaries, which are maintained by individual listeners, and random telephone calls within the survey area. Personally, I don't think the research is always accurate. (How can the listening habits of a few hundred accurately represent the listening habits of millions?) But it's all we have, and so we live with it. Just don't accept one ratings book as the gospel, because it isn't.

My agency's media director doesn't usually buy any station based on a single rating book, regardless of how well the station ranks overall. She tries to use a four-book average as a starting point, but with all the day-to-day changes in most markets, you often have to look at the most-current information. Otherwise, you're looking at irrelevant data. Getting a four-book average isn't always possible, because small markets may only have two books per year (and some only have one).

If you can get a four-book average (described in previous paragraph), you can see how a particular station has fared throughout an entire year (and believe me, station ratings can change dramatically from book to book, from month to month). And here's the best part: When you ask the sales rep for this information, you can totally intimidate him with your insider knowledge. Most station clients don't know these books exist.

When you *don't* need to buy the very best

Just to confuse you (and to contradict myself), I can tell you now that it's not always necessary to buy the top-rated stations. Why? Because the top-rated stations are so darned expensive that you can blow your whole budget without coming close to achieving your frequency goals. And the leading stations may not deliver the prime demo you're after anyway.

For example, the top-rated station may cost $1,000 a spot for the morning drive (and in some markets, it's a lot more than that). But the second- and third-place stations may each cost half or even a third of that price. So, you can buy the silver and bronze winners of the ratings Olympics and get twice to three times the number of spots and listeners. You achieve frequency, and you're not forced into bankruptcy. It's a beautiful thing.

Gathering information from your customers

One of your best sources to help you determine which radio station to choose is your current customers. These people already believe in your business, and you want to draw in more patrons like them. So find out what your customers are listening to.

Many car dealers use a very clever — and simple — method of market research to determine which radio stations to advertise on: They check the preset stations on the radios in the cars brought in for service. This tactic is a very shrewd way for them to find out the listening habits of their customers.

But you don't have to be in the car business to find out the radio habits of your customers. Do an informal survey. Ask your customers this question (and word it just this way): "What is your favorite radio station?" The answer to *that* question is the one you want to take to the bank. After you've surveyed a few dozen people, a pattern begins to emerge, and you can have a good idea about which stations to consider for your advertising. If a station is appealing to your existing customers, it's likely a good bet to attract new ones.

Buying the station

Narrow your list of possibilities to three or four stations, call each one, and ask to speak with someone in the sales department, preferably the Sales Manager (refer to Chapter 13 for why it's a good idea to start with the head of the sales department). Tell each salesperson that you're considering placing an advertising schedule on his station, and set some appointments. Yes, it's unavoidable: You need to invest some time and listen to sales pitches from several stations, but it's time well spent. The stations you call assign the sales call to one of its sales reps, probably a new hire who is trying to build an account list (the station's top people are too busy servicing their existing accounts).

Ask a lot of questions of the reps you meet with, both about the strengths of their station and about their competition. Clarify who their target audience is, and decide whether it meshes with your target (see the section "Specifying which demographic you're after" for more information). Talk about how you define the success of your campaign and what your expectations are. At the end of the day, one of the stations will stand out in your mind because that station's sales representative did the best job of finding your comfort level. *Buy the stations* (that's ad speak for "buy an ad on the stations") that have convinced you they can deliver your prime demo, tell them you'll be watching the results very carefully, and then put your commercials on the air.

Putting station events to work for you

Radio stations love to throw parties. Its personnel create special events at the drop of a hat. Most of the larger stations even employ a Promotions Director, who you may find to be a vivacious, enthusiastic person who could just as easily become a Cruise Director. They do promotions, like a remote broadcast at your store or place of business, in which the station's on-air personalities broadcast from your lobby or parking lot inviting listeners to "Hurry to XYZ Company and get your free station T-shirt and bumper sticker." These special events can be a great traffic builder, occasionally attracting real customers in addition to the ones just wanting the free stuff.

Ask your station rep what kind of promotions the station can put together to benefit your business. If you're spending a fairly sizeable budget, you can probably get this type of promotion for free.

Radio stations also participate in community events such as street fairs, outdoor concerts, and college campus events. The stations' crews set up their booths or park their electronics-packed vans and then broadcast and hand out free stuff. Many times they sell sponsorships of these events, as in, "The big downtown chili cook-off is sponsored by [Your Business Name Here]. Come down and meet the nice folks and pick up your free t-shirt, coffee mug, and key chain." If you can benefit from one of these sponsorships, and if the event is relevant to your business somehow, then go for it. These events are usually priced quite reasonably and include multiple on-air mentions (in the form of 10- or 15-second announcements, or *minicommercials*), which enhance your advertising schedule.

If you make a mistake — if the stations you choose don't do the job you expected — chalk it up to experience and take solace in the fact that soon, very soon, you will be contacted by every other station in your market. Yes, as sure as death and taxes, after you've placed an ad on one station, you will be contacted by all the others. Station reps spend most of their time listening to competing stations in order to hear which advertisers are buying which stations. If they hear a commercial for your business, and you're not already buying their station (ad time), you *will* be contacted.

Talking the Talk of Radio Advertising

Before you march out into the world of radio advertising, you need to arm yourself with the talk of the trade. These sections deal with some of the common terms you may hear bandied about by radio reps (which some may use just to confuse you, while also attempting to convince you that their station is the perfect match for your business).

Cume

Cumulative audience (or *cume* for short) is the total net unduplicated audience accumulated over a specific period of time, as in the total audience of a station during morning drive time. You don't really need to know how many people are listening to a station, but you do need to know how many people *in your target demographic* are listening.

For instance, suppose you want to reach men 25 to 34. If a particular station has a cume of 250,000, but most listeners are women and only a very few are within your target demo, then this 250,000 figure doesn't help you.

Be wary of station reps who proudly sell cume. In many cases, cume doesn't mean anything — it's too broad a measurement.

While cume is often unhelpful by itself, stations can certainly give advertisers *cume by demo,* which is the total unduplicated audience, measured within a certain timeframe, of members of a particular age group of either men or women or both — a much more relevant measurement.

For instance, a station can give you its cume for men 25 to 34, if that is the primary demographic group you're after. The cume measurement can be compared with newspaper circulation: It's comparable to the number of people who receive the paper, but it doesn't tell you how long they spend reading it.

Cume is a valuable measurement; it just doesn't tell the whole story. Because this is radio and you're going for *frequency* (the number of times an audience member hears *your* commercial), you need to know the amount of time people spend listening to a station (*time spent listening* is shortened to *TSL*). A station with really long TSL and a smaller cume (that is, fewer people tuned in but who stay with the station for a long period of time) is likely to have better *average quarter hour* (AQH) ratings than a station with a large cume and a small TSL (such as an all-news format where many people tune in but get only the news, weather, or traffic report they're after and quickly switch stations).

Ranker

A *ranker* is a computer-generated report showing a selected demographic audience of each radio station in a given market, ranked from highest to lowest (for example, how many women 18 to 35 listen to each station in a market). A ranker can be based on cume ratings, AQH ratings, share, or whatever.

By using qualitative data to create a ranker, nearly every station in a market can show you that it's number one — each station simply manipulates the data to highlight its own strengths, as in "We're number one with women 35 and older who have purchased perfume within the past year." Of course, if you're actually looking for women over 35 who have purchased perfume recently, buy that station in a heartbeat!

Beware of rankers, because each station puts its best foot forward and brings you a ranker based on parameters that make it look its best.

Dayparts

Radio stations sell advertising time in various chunks referred to as *dayparts*. Naturally, morning drive time (6:00 a.m. to 10:00 a.m.) costs a lot more than midnight to 6:00 a.m. because you're reaching more people during the former.

When you buy a schedule, you can either pick only prime time or make the more frugal choice and buy a schedule that includes spots in various dayparts, plus *rotators,* which are spots run in the best times available throughout the 12- to 24-hour period. A rotator may run at midnight, but sometimes you get lucky, and it runs in the middle of the day, or possibly in drive time. It all adds to your frequency, so regardless of what times your ads run, you can reach *some* listeners.

Reading the Fine Print

When you've made your decision to buy a radio schedule to advertise your business, the station sales rep presents you with a proposal and a contract for your signature. The proposal comes after the initial meeting, but before you agree to the buy.

Study the proposal carefully, but stop right there! Don't sign anything until you sit down with the rep and try to grind out a better deal. In the following sections, I show you how to evaluate and negotiate your contract as well as how to hold the radio stations accountable to it.

Hammering out the details

Radio can be made much more affordable if you just do a little horse-trading. Don't be afraid to ask for some free stuff. The rep expects it and likely has something in his pocket (something that the sales manager has preapproved just in case you ask) that sweetens the pot.

My agency buys millions of dollars' worth of radio time every year, and I don't think we've ever bought a schedule "as is." Instead, here's our approach:

- ✔ We negotiate by first asking the station for additional spots at no additional cost.

- ✔ If that doesn't fly, we ask for better spot positions in more desirable dayparts (we prefer that our spots run in the morning drive daypart than from midnight to 6:00 a.m.).

- ✔ If we're turned down on that request, we ask for free *billboards* (10- or 15-second announcements that are like minicommercials).

Our media buyer is continually looking for something extra from the stations — and you can benefit from doing the same. Getting extras from a station is often easier if you're willing to sign a long-term advertising contract, such as an annual one.

The contract is delivered or sent to you after both you and the station management have agreed upon the terms (and free stuff) that have been hammered out between you and the sales rep in the proposal. The contract describes the following information:

- ✔ The number of spots you get
- ✔ The dayparts in which your spots run
- ✔ Your total cost to run these spots

The contract is broken down to show the cost of each commercial message you're buying. Some dayparts are cheaper than others, so the spots may have different costs.

If you want to know how much a newspaper ad may cost you, the newspaper sales rep can show you a *rate card,* a printed sheet on which you can see the precise costs of each and every column inch (although newspapers also offer so many discounts that the rate card is simply a starting point — see Chapter 13 for more info). But when you're trying to find out how much a radio schedule may cost you, the sales rep doesn't show you a rate card because, on most stations, no such thing exists — *buying radio time is always negotiable.* And for that reason, when buying radio time, you shouldn't accept the first proposal as presented to you; you should always shoot for something better, for something extra. Nine times out of ten, the station adds something in order to get your name on the dotted line.

Holding 'em to it

Your contract promises that you can have a certain number of spots — some in morning drive, some in midday, some rotating in the best times available throughout the day, and some from midnight to 6:00 a.m., for example. When you receive your invoice from the station, do what is known as *post analysis:* Check the times your spots ran (all of which are listed on the invoice) and compare the *actual* run times to the *promised* run times. If you find any discrepancies, the radio station owes you *make goods,* which are free spots given to you in order to fulfill all contractual promises.

Many advertisers don't go to the trouble of doing post analysis. I do, however, and I continually find errors and always obtain make goods on behalf of my clients. Honest mistakes are made. Even though I'm sure the stations don't do anything to cheat you, you should still examine the invoices carefully and hold the station responsible for any errors and omissions.

Reading a station invoice can be a challenge — they're sometimes quite confusing. But *do* go over them carefully to assure yourself that you got what you paid for. The invoice you get from the station is divided into columns. All the spots in your schedule are broken down into the following categories:

- ✔ Day of the week (for example, Monday)
- ✔ Date (November 6)
- ✔ Length (60 seconds)
- ✔ Actual time/title of ad (6:56 a.m., Inventory Closeout)
- ✔ Rate ($450)

If a supplier on a co-op advertising program is paying for your spots, you also want to check your invoices very carefully to ensure that the stations have supplied you with all the requirements for co-op reimbursement. You won't get paid your co-op funds if you don't send all the paperwork! You have provided the stations with copies of your radio script(s), and now you want to make sure the stations have notarized your scripts and certified your invoice as proof of performance. (For more on co-op guidelines, see Chapter 3.)

Many of my agency's clients are co-op based. So around the tenth of each month, when the broadcast invoices begin to arrive in the mail, frustration and disappointment arrive with them. Even though we've been dealing with multiple radio stations for years on behalf of these co-op based clients, and even though the stations know that our accounts require notarized, certified

---

Don't get bored with your commercial

Because you're probably going to buy a 13-week radio schedule, you may be tempted to ask the station for *run times,* wherein the station calls or faxes you every day with a list of the actual times it scheduled your spots to run (within a few minutes). Most new advertisers ask for run times because hearing their commercials on the air is kind of fun. But if you tune in several times a day to hear your own spot, you can soon get very bored with it. Keep in mind, however, that the other listeners, the people who may actually become your customers, are *not* getting bored with your spot, because they're not hearing it every single time it runs.

So don't get all twitchy about changing copy every week. You can run the same copy for the full 13 weeks without boring anyone except yourself. Besides, the average listener won't actually "hear" your spot until she's listened to it at least four times (that's why you need to buy frequency).

Of course, a 13-week schedule is also a good opportunity to rotate two or three different commercial messages, broadening your sales pitch. So, if you have the time and the inclination, knock yourself out and write several spots.

---

scripts and invoices, they still occasionally send us incomplete invoices. Inevitably, we receive invoices from some stations that don't include notarized scripts. I then have to call the offending stations to get the problem resolved, cajoling them in order to get the corrected paperwork. Be diligent in studying your invoices from broadcast media.

Waiting Patiently for the Results

People are bombarded by radio advertisements on a daily basis. Customers need time to let your ad sink, which requires a good amount of patience on your part. In the following sections, I offer some guidelines for how much time you should give your targeted audience to truly "hear" your ad message and when you should review your ads to see whether they need a-changin'.

Giving your audience time to respond

Radio is a *frequency medium,* which means that every listener must hear your commercial message at least four times before remembering it. The newest research shows that due to the increasing amount of advertising clutter, advertisers in most markets need to shoot for what's referred to as a *four frequency.* Yes, regardless of how creative you've been and how brilliantly you've written your message, your commercial may have no effect whatsoever until the average listener has heard it four times.

When any given listener hears your spot at least four times, your message slowly begins to sink in. If what you're selling is appealing to that listener, she may then respond to it and become one of your customers. The station can show you how many spots you need to buy and how much money you need to spend, in order to achieve a four frequency. The more your audience hears your message, the more you entice them to become your customers. Don't freak out if they aren't knocking down your door within the first hours of airing your ad. Give 'em time!

Buying radio time: Too little, too much?

On radio, you're better off buying a minimum 13-week schedule to accomplish the frequency you need and to ensure that your commercial message reaches enough listeners to make your cash outlay worth your while. That's three months to make an impact. You don't absolutely *have* to buy a 13-week schedule, of course. You can step up to the plate with a heavy one-month budget and still accomplish the desired frequency. But, if you can afford it, I recommend the tried-and-true 13 weeks.

Hearing your commercials over a longer period of time ultimately gives you a presence with the listeners. Your name and message begin to sink in, which is precisely why you're advertising in the first place.

Evaluating your radio ads from time to time

No matter how many weeks of radio advertising you can afford, you need to give your ads time to work. But, a point in time comes when you need to step back and evaluate the effectiveness of your ad schedule. One way to tell whether they're working or not is whether you have more business. And as I mention earlier in the chapter, it's always a good idea to simply ask your clients or customers how they found out about you. Another option you may want to try is committing to, say, two weeks per month on a station, and then evaluating your results after three months.

If your store is still empty or your phone hasn't rung in a while, it's definitely time to revamp your ad campaign or the media you're using (or both!).

Convincing customers within the 72-hour window

Why do you suppose so many car dealer ads are on the radio (or any other advertising medium, for that matter)? It's because car dealers understand and endorse the concept of frequency, because of what they call the *72-hour window*. What is a 72-hour window? Car dealers know that when a person, any person, finally decides to buy a new car, he buys that new car within 72 hours of making the decision to do so. Remember how hard it was as a child (or maybe still) to wait for your birthday? Well, we're all still kids at heart, and we want instant gratification. It's because of the 72-hour window that car dealers need a continual radio presence.

For example, Bob finally decides to buy a new car. Prior to making that buying decision, every dime that every car dealer spent on advertising was wasted on Bob, because Bob wasn't in the market for a new car, and he ignored all those car ads. And after Bob has purchased his new car, every dime that every dealer spends on advertising once again is wasted on Bob. But, while Bob's 72-hour buying window is open, every dealer needs to be on the air in case Bob tunes in and happens to hear one of their commercials. That's why you hear so much car advertising on the radio. All those car dealers are waiting for Bob to make up his mind.

Remember: Consistency is the key. You can run ads one week a month, if that's what you can afford — as long as you stick with it.

In addition to frequency, you want to analyze your ad's effectiveness in terms of *reach,* the number of people who are exposed to your messages over the course of your radio schedule. Reach, when revealed to you by a station, is usually shown as a percentage, not a number. For example, if your schedule shows a reach of 5 percent men between 25 and 34 years of age, then that value is the percentage of all the men ages 25 to 34 within your market whom you are reaching with your schedule.

Taking Advantage of Seasonal Incentives to Reduce Your Costs

From October through December of each year, radio stations enjoy multi-millions of dollars in additional revenue from political, automotive, and retail holiday season advertising. Between politicians attempting to get elected, car dealers trying to clear inventory, and every retail store in the known universe hoping to get a piece of the holiday shopping pie, broadcast sales reps can just sit in their cubicles and answer the phone. As a matter of fact, most stations become so saturated with advertising that they're literally sold out — meaning you can't get a new commercial on the air even if you want to. This feeding frenzy also results in sky-high advertising rates for the final quarter of each year.

But, at the stroke of midnight on New Year's Eve, the worm turns. And that's the time when smart advertisers negotiate some very attractive deals with stations. Broadcasters know that first-quarter ad dollars are harder to come by. The competition gets fierce, and stations have to work harder for their money. It's first-quarter incentive time — the mother lode for businesses looking to save money on ads.

Nearly all radio and TV stations offer first-quarter incentive packages. These packages take many forms, but usually involve the following:

- **Free commercials.** (Buy one spot, get two spots free!)

- **Promotions.** (Buy a January schedule at full price, get February and March schedules for half price!)

- **All-expense-paid trips to destinations around the world.** (Spend a certain amount over the three-month period and fly off to Europe, Mexico, or Hawaii!)

The variations on the incentives are endless, but the bottom line is simple: During the first quarter, you can get a lot more bang for your buck. And people don't quit listening to radio on the first day of January, so taking advantage of what the stations have to offer makes sense.

Stretch your budget to the max during this new-year bonanza. If you're paying $150 per spot but getting another spot for free, you're actually paying only $75 per spot — which means you're getting twice the impressions for half the usual price. And, don't forget: *Radio is a frequency medium.* It takes three or four of your commercials heard by the same person to make an impression, so the more spots you can run the better.

If, after your first quarter ad schedule has run and been paid for, you get to board a plane for a week or more of free rest and relaxation at some exotic resort or European capitol . . . well, you deserve it for being so darned smart! Advertising agencies as well as its clients can earn free trips via first-quarter incentives. My staff, our clients, and I have traveled all-expenses-paid (air, luxury hotels, and most meals) to London, Paris, Hong Kong, Africa, Hawaii, Mexico, and New Zealand. We've even cruised down the Danube River through Germany, Austria, Slovakia, and Hungary — all in return for buying first-quarter radio or television-broadcast packages. Hey, you're probably going to spend the money anyway. Why not get something extra in return?

If a client incentive package is offered to you, and if you can afford to commit to an extended contract, grab it. Stretch your budget while taking advantage of some great deals and wonderful trips. You deserve it.

Chapter 15

Getting Your Ads on Television

. . . .

In This Chapter

▶ Paying attention to the programs you advertise in and the audience you reach

▶ Using stations' media kits to evaluate your TV advertising options

▶ Negotiating 101: Knowing your TV marketing terms

▶ Working out the details with the sales rep to get a contract you can both agree on

▶ Figuring out whether cable advertising is worth your time and money

. . . .

TV advertising still takes the lion's share of advertising. According to *Advertising Age*'s survey of U.S. ad spending in 2004, companies spent about 25 percent of their budgets on TV. Keep in mind, though, that number breaks down into 17.5 percent for broadcast (network and local) TV and 8.2 percent for cable TV. And the largest companies in the United States typically spent much of this money, because they're trying to reach the largest possible market. Nevertheless, many small businesses are also interested in advertising on TV: You just need to find the best network to advertise on!

And that's not as easy as it sounds: Buying an advertising schedule on television is an increasingly confusing proposition. Where can you find the most viewers? Where should you spend your money? The television audience has fragmented because of the hundreds of choices available with broadcast, cable, and satellite-dish technologies. The major networks' share of total viewing audience has been shrinking for a long time, and few see any reason to expect the erosion to reverse. No single network, station, or program seems to dominate anymore — people simply have too many viewing choices. Viewers can choose among the big four networks (ABC, CBS, NBC, and FOX), independent stations, and the numerous channels offered by cable and satellite systems. The Internet, DVDs, VCRs, and on-demand systems like TiVo are also vying for viewers' attention and siphoning them away from TV.

Consumers now have such a mind-boggling variety of choices that reaching audiences in large numbers is nearly impossible (unless you have unlimited funds, and even then you have no guarantee). As a matter of fact, it's not only difficult to *reach* viewers in large numbers, it's getting more challenging to *find* them in large numbers. The uncertainty of where to locate substantial numbers of television viewers has even professional media buyers confused.

Fortunately, millions and millions of people watch TV every day and every night — even if they're not all watching the same programs! In fact, according to A.C. Neilsen Co. (which tracks TV viewing patterns), the average American still spends at least 4 hours a day watching TV, and the TV is on for an average of 6 hours and 47 minutes each day in a U.S. household. And even though some viewers tune out the commercials (either literally or electronically), TV advertising *can* still offer you opportunities to reach consumers like no other ad medium. You just have to find the right place for your commercial, where you're most likely to reach the customers you want to attract.

If you think that advertising on TV can benefit your business (and if your ad bucks are burning a hole in your pocket), you need to find a reasonable share of the total television-viewing audience (especially in the demographic group you're after), combined with affordable advertising rates somewhere in your local television market. In this chapter, I help you do exactly that.

Buying the Programming, Not the Station

Virtually every TV station offers at least a few programs that deliver to your target audience. Unlike radio, in which each station delivers pretty much the same type of listener throughout the day (see Chapter 8), television demographics vary widely from program to program. Think about your own TV-viewing habits, and you can see what I mean. The same station that airs college football all day on weekends also airs a three-hour block of soap operas during the day on weekdays — and those who watch the former probably don't watch the latter.

Don't get locked into thinking of television in terms of stations. Think instead in terms of *programs* and *types of audience*. If you have several stations in your market, you may find that the best way to reach your target audience is to buy one or two programs on each station.

Depending on the size of your media market, you may likely find that if a show won a Golden Globe or Emmy Award, you probably can't afford it. Commercials on the top-rated sitcoms and dramas can be very expensive, even on a local level. But don't despair: You can find some affordable time slots in and around well-watched programming — affordable enough to give you a presence in your local market even though your ad budget may not be quite as large as that of General Motors or Anheuser-Busch, Inc.

If, on the other hand, you're situated in a smaller advertising market, you may indeed find that prime-time programming fits neatly within your budget parameters. The smaller the market, the cheaper the spots.

By doing just a bit of research, you may also find that cable stations and *independent stations* (those stations not affiliated with major networks), offer a good variety of programming with both loyal audiences and reasonable spot costs. For example:

- ✔ Your local network-affiliate TV stations have affordable early-morning talk shows and morning news programs with good ratings and loyal viewers.

- ✔ Daytime soaps and talk shows, especially if your target demographic is women, are a great buy.

- ✔ The early-evening local news and early fringe can bring you a good return on a modest investment. For example, my agency runs commercials on *Jeopardy!* and *Wheel of Fortune* on the San Francisco ABC-TV affiliate for very reasonable prices as part of a larger buy.

You're buying the programs and the audience, not the stations. So, be sure your target market is clearly defined before you contact the TV stations in your market.

Comparing TV Stations: Request Media Kits

Contact the TV stations in your area and request a *media kit*. This kit is basically a brochure package with general information on the station, such as the following:

- ✔ Coverage area
- ✔ Programming strengths

✔ Special programming they're known for

✔ History in the market

✔ Other sales-type information

Be sure the media kit includes a program listing, usually called a *program grid*. This listing can give you an idea what types of programs the station airs throughout the day. When you've reviewed this information, and given yourself a brief overview of the station and its programming, you're better prepared to have a serious meeting with the station sales rep.

When you're thinking about buying ads on TV, talk to more than one station, if you have that option. Not only will you have a basis for comparison, but you're also more likely to encounter a sales rep you really like. And working with a sales rep you like is important, because station sales reps can be your greatest source of information. (Be sure to check out the section in this chapter, "Working with a Sales Rep.")

When you're evaluating TV stations, don't assume you're comparing apples to apples. Television stations have a wide variety of ways to present their audience figures. The two most-common numbers you may see are:

✔ **Household ratings:** How many individual households with TV sets are tuned into a particular station

✔ **Demographic ratings:** How many people within certain demographic groups are tuned into the station

Stations sometimes use household ratings because they look so much larger — households usually consist of multiple individuals in a variety of different demographic groups all lumped together. However, if your target demographic is women between the ages of 25 and 54, what difference does it make to you how many *households* you're reaching? You just want to be sure you're reaching the women in *your target demographic*. Whenever possible, be sure you're looking at the ratings for your target demographic, and if the proposal isn't clear, *ask*.

Ready to Negotiate? Better Know Your TV Marketing Terms First!

When you're considering buying or are already buying TV advertising, you should know that TV stations and their reps use a lot of technical jargon (yes — you can go ahead and roll your eyes). And if you're working with more than one station, and the stations become more competitive with one another, they begin bombarding you with more and more detailed ratings information. This research data they share with you is designed to show their stations in the best possible light, while making the competing stations look inferior. So you need to have a basic understanding of what stations are presenting to you and where these numbers come from.

In the following sections, you can master the ad lingo — from sweeps to shares — to get the TV advertising your business really needs.

Understanding timing and sweeps

Unlike radio, which is measured almost continuously, TV audiences are measured primarily four times per year. The four ratings periods are February, May, July, and November. These periods of measurement are called *sweeps,* with May and November being the most important.

The top-ten national markets (New York City; Los Angeles; Chicago; Philadelphia; San Francisco/Oakland/San Jose area; Boston; Dallas/Fort Worth area; Washington, D.C.; Detroit; and Atlanta, in that order) are also measured in January and October as well. Selected top markets are also *metered,* which means that audiences are measured on a daily basis via reports called *overnights.* (The overnights let you know whether the latest reality show beat out that high-rated sitcom last night.)

However, in most markets, television has to live and die by the basic four measurement periods (the sweeps), during which networks air their best programming and local stations promote themselves most heavily. That's why you rarely see reruns during the sweeps periods. Sweeps months are when the TV stations pull out all the stops, bringing you all-new episodes of your favorite shows.

Measuring ratings and market shares

A.C. Nielsen is the company responsible for collecting TV-ratings data in nearly every market across the country. It does so through *diaries* — books that members of randomly selected households complete, listing which shows they watched and when.

Nielsen also uses *meters,* which are electronic devices attached to a randomly selected number of televisions across the country. Meters measure whether the TV is on or off and keep track of which stations people in the home view. Meters are only capable of providing household information on what programs the occupants watch, because the meters have no way to determine which household member is actually watching. Nielsen collects the specific demographic information through the diaries (still, believe it or not!). Some televisions are even equipped with *people meters,* electronic gadgets activated by individuals in the household when they're watching television and deactivated when they turn the darn thing off.

In any given market, the total number of persons or households with access to television is referred to as the *universe.* Nielsen describes the viewing levels as HUT (short for *homes using television*) and PUT (short for *persons using television*). So, if someone were to say, "Television rates drop in the summer because of the decrease in HUT," it would mean that, in the summer, fewer homes are using TV, and people are watching TV for fewer hours each day.

When stations present their numbers to you, the data is most likely in one of two forms: ratings or shares. In the following sections, I describe both of these terms.

Shares

A *share* is a station's percentage of the television audience at a specific time. For example, if a station shows you an 8 share for men 25 to 54, for its 11:00 p.m. newscast, you know that of all the men between the ages 25 and 54 who are watching television at 11:00 p.m., 8 percent of them are watching *that* particular station's news.

Ratings

Rating is a station's percentage of the overall universe, whether they're watching TV at that precise time or not. For example, if a station says its 11:00 p.m. news program delivers a 2 rating for men 25 to 54, then of all the men between the ages of 25 and 54 in the survey universe, 2 percent watch the 11:00 p.m. news on that station.

Ratings for individual stations can be expressed either as a percentage (2 percent of all men ages 25 to 54) or as a real number (7,500 men ages 25 to 54), but share is *always* a percentage. Because rating relates to the entire TV-viewing universe, and because share relates to the HUTs or PUTs, the share percentage is always larger. So if you compare one station's share to another station's ratings, you're comparing apples to rutabagas, and can't get an accurate picture. As much as possible, you want to be sure you're comparing the same measurement on each station.

Sourcing: Taking shares and ratings one step further

To get even more technical, stations *source* (or survey) their audience information in one of three ways. Here is a brief outline of each:

- ✔ **Actual:** This number is exactly as Nielsen research reports it. If a station gives you a February Actual, then the number came from the most-recent February rating book.

- ✔ **Projection:** This number is adjusted based on a standard mathematical formula, which is the same at every station. A *projection* is the HUT or PUT level from the time of year you're planning to advertise multiplied by the share percentage from the most recent book. Professional media buyers and stations often use this number, called a PJ (short for *projection*), and they consider PJ a good measurement because it utilizes the most-recent information but adjusts the data to the time of the year to account for seasonal variances in the viewing audience.

- ✔ **Estimates:** Estimates can literally be anything. If a station has a new program, moves a program to a different time, is running a special, or just feels it was shortchanged in the rating book, it uses an estimate. A station presents an estimate as a number, footnoted with a lengthy rationale for why the station thinks the program will deliver that rating number.

Unless estimates are all that's available, I don't recommend using these numbers in your research of stations. If an estimate is all you have, let the station know that you will hold it to that estimated number. If the program falls short in the next rating book, the station will need to air additional commercials for you to make up the difference.

You may be wondering, "What would be a good rating? Can't you give me a guideline?" Unfortunately, because ratings and shares are percentages tied to population and market competition, no guidelines work across the board. In a market with lots of competition and a large population, ratings are smaller than in a smaller market with fewer viewing choices. As you get more comfortable comparing stations and programs using the information provided in this chapter, you can soon get a feel for what constitutes good ratings in your market.

Working with a Sales Rep

After you've looked through the media kits the stations in your area provided, and after you have some idea of the kinds of programs you want to advertise on, arrange to meet with a sales rep from each station. This meeting is a fact-finding mission for both of you. When you meet with the sales rep, be very clear about your objectives, your target demographic, your business trading area, and anything else you feel is relevant in helping her put together a potentially successful schedule for you. Be sure she understands your expectations, as well as how you plan to measure your results.

Be sure to ask lots of questions. Any sales rep who isn't willing to help you understand her station and the television market as a whole isn't someone you want to work with.

The sales rep should be motivated to help you develop something that works for your business within your budget parameters, so that you continue to advertise. If you don't feel that the sales rep who comes to meet with you is the right fit, call the station's sales manager and request someone else. You don't want personality differences or a lack of trust to stand in your way when you're trying to make an objective decision about your advertising.

After you've met with the sales rep, she will go back to the station and work on a proposal, sometimes called an *avail*. Occasionally, a sales rep brings a proposal or avail to your initial meeting, but usually she wants to meet you and gather some information before making recommendations. A typical proposal includes the following information:

- ✔ The programs or *dayparts* (time periods) during which your ads will run (see the nearby sidebar, "Affordable dayparts," for more information on dayparts)
- ✔ The number of times per week your commercial will run in each program or daypart
- ✔ A rate for each program or daypart
- ✔ A weekly or total cost

Some stations have a special schedule already prepackaged for new advertisers or clients with smaller budgets. These types of schedules usually give you one cost for the whole schedule, as opposed to individual rates per daypart or program. They usually have names like *New Business Package* or *Retail Package*. These packages can be a great way to get started, but be sure you're aware of what they include, as well as any limitations or restrictions involved. If the schedule includes a limited number of commercials in the areas or programs you're interested in, you're probably better off paying a little more for fewer, but better targeted, commercials.

Affordable dayparts

You may be buying television by dayparts and not by specific programs. Buying by dayparts is a great way to save money because it gives the station some flexibility, which allows them to charge a lower rate. Just be sure that all or most of the programs that are included in the daypart you're buying make sense for your type of business. Some of the standard dayparts you can look at include:

✔ **Morning news:** 5:00 a.m.–9:00 a.m.

✔ **Morning:** 9:00 a.m.–12:00 p.m.

✔ **Daytime:** 12:00 p.m.–3:00 p.m.

✔ **Early fringe:** 3:00 p.m.–5:00 p.m.

✔ **Early news:** 5:00 p.m.–7:00 p.m.

✔ **Access:** 7:00 p.m.–8:00 p.m.

✔ **Prime:** 8:00 p.m.–11:00 p.m.

✔ **Late news:** 11:00 p.m.–11:30 p.m.

✔ **Late fringe:** 11:30 p.m.–1:00 a.m.

Keep in mind that these dayparts (including their time ranges and names) may vary slightly from station to station, so always be sure to clarify what the time period is. If your sales rep gives you a proposal by daypart, also be sure to clarify what the programming is during those blocks of time (or refer to the program grid that came in the station's media kit).

Talkin' the talk: Negotiating successfully

When you have the station's proposal in front of you, you may find some points that you want to negotiate. Negotiating doesn't have to be an adversarial process — and it's almost always more effective if it's not. In the following sections, I fill you in on a few of the rules I've developed for myself over the years as I've negotiated with television stations.

Telling the sales rep you want to do business

Let the sales rep know right up front that you want to do business with her and her station. Being forthright makes the deal hers to lose (which is something she doesn't want to do), and it gets her on your side right away. If she knows she's close to getting your name on a contract, you can get a lot more of her effort than if she believes you're just as likely to buy an ad on another station. So, be positive, and use phrases like, "Your news rate is just a little bit too high for me to buy the number of commercials I need, but I'd really like to use the station. What else can you do?"

Everything is negotiable!

If you think the rate is too high, ask whether the rate is flexible. If the sales rep can't go lower on the rate, ask whether she can add any bonus (free) commercials to the schedule. If she can't add any bonus commercials to the schedule, ask whether she can add any *billboards* to your schedule. Billboards are essentially your logo with a "brought to you by" mention (for example, "This news brief is brought you by XYZ Cleaners").

If you've offered some points of negotiation and haven't gotten anywhere, it's perfectly all right to say, "You know, I just don't feel comfortable with this schedule as it is. What else can you suggest?" You don't have to explain any further. The sales rep's job is to come up with something that makes you feel comfortable enough to move forward.

Letting the rep know that your advertising schedule must work

The sales rep needs to be aware that you'll be monitoring your results closely. After all, if this ad campaign works out well, you will be doing a lot more advertising with the station (and if it doesn't, you won't). Knowing that you're monitoring your results offers the sales rep further incentive to make sure your campaign is as effective as possible — and it also lets her know that you hold her accountable if it isn't.

Considering the time of year

As I mention in Chapter 14, the busiest time for TV (and radio) advertising is in the spring (leading up to summer) and fall (leading up to the winter holidays). Stations have considerably less demand for TV ads in the first quarter of the year (January, February, and March) and the third quarter (July, August, and September) than in the rest of the year. January, July, and August tend to be the lightest advertising months of all.

Therefore, stations have a lot more flexibility in the first and third quarters, and you can push a bit further for a better deal during those times. On the other hand, if you're trying to buy time in the busiest months, you may not be able to negotiate much at all (although it's always worth a shot).

Asking for promotions and other deals

TV stations have a variety of promotions going on all the time. In addition, they have the ability to design a traffic-building promotion specifically for your business. As you negotiate the advertising schedule, be sure to ask what else the station may be able to do, in addition to the advertising schedule, to help you achieve your objective. (These additional bonuses are sometimes referred to as *value-added* deals.)

Getting better rates with annual or long-term contracts

Often, stations can offer you better rates, or other incentives, for making long-term commitments. Some of these incentives may include a pool of bonus commercials to be added to your schedule throughout the year, as availability permits, or free trips in exchange for spending a certain dollar amount on advertising.

Stations may put your commercials into a bonus pool if you sign a long-term contract. The *bonus pool* consists of unsold commercial air time — a "pool" of time into which certain station clients will, as their commercials reach the front of the queue, enjoy free spots. Bonus-pool members even receive a monthly statement showing the exact times these free spots ran. Bonus pools can end up giving you a lot of extra impressions over the course of a year.

In addition to the bonus pool, many TV stations reward long-term commitments with yearly *client incentive trips* (just as radio stations do, as I discuss in Chapter 14). These trips are all-expenses-paid journeys to select destinations throughout the world and are usually done in a first-class manner (not too shabby, if you ask me). If you step up to the plate with a sizeable advertising commitment, you can often be wined and dined lavishly to make sure you stay with the station year after year.

Incentives and lower rates can be great opportunities, if the campaign already makes sense. Just be careful not to make commitments you wouldn't make otherwise just to get something for "free." (A temptation for anyone — including advertising gurus.)

Staying within your budget

One of the biggest mistakes new advertisers make is trying to buy too much. You may be faced with more programming that fits your demographic than you can afford to buy. Instead of trying to stretch your budget to cover as many of these options as possible, you're better off doing the opposite.

Choose one or two (maybe even three) options and buy those programs or dayparts as heavily as you can. Reaching *some* potential customers effectively is better than reaching a whole bunch of viewers ineffectively.

Of course, every rule has an exception! If you have the luxury of doing image advertising, where your goal is just to let people know you're out there, you can go ahead and sprinkle your commercials around. Some stations even allow you to buy *all-day rotators,* which air as time permits. These spots can be a very inexpensive way to go, but remember that you have no guarantees of when, or if, your commercials will air.

Don't forget that everything can be preempted

As you evaluate your options and negotiate with stations, keep in mind that nearly all television commercials can be preempted. *Preempted* means that if a certain program is a sellout (meaning more people want to advertise during the program than spaces are available), some advertisers may choose to pay a higher rate than you're paying just to get in. When this happens, in order to make room, the station starts dropping advertisers from the program based on their priority or *section code* (a ranking, usually 1 through 9, of the various rates paid by advertisers, which determines each advertiser's priority). If you've purchased your spots at level 5 — which is usually the cheapest rate for local advertisers — you will be told up front that your rate is preemptible, so you shouldn't have any surprises.

The *issue date* (when you, as an advertiser, bought a schedule) is also a factor. The last one in is the first one bumped. So if, for example, you're having a sale next weekend, you want to be sure that you don't negotiate rates so low that all your commercials can get preempted. Believe me, it has happened. On the other hand, if you have some flexibility, getting bumped may be less of a concern, and you should go for the cheaper rates.

Your station sales rep gets a preemption list daily for all her clients, and part of your negotiation is making sure she knows what you want done with your bumped spots. The options generally include the following:

✔ Run the commercial in the same program on a different day or week.

✔ Run the commercial in a comparable program.

✔ Credit the cost of the commercial back to you.

Before you sign your contract, be sure to discuss with your sales rep what happens when your commercials get bumped, so your invoice isn't full of surprises!

Is Cable Advertising Right for You?

In addition to broadcast or over-the-air television, almost all markets have the option of cable television. Unlike broadcast television, which is free to anyone with a TV and an adequate antenna, cable television is transmitted through a network of underground cables and is a subscription-based service. Cable subscribers have access to additional premium channels, which can't be received over the air (although some are available with satellite systems). Some examples of cable channels, or networks, include ESPN, CNN, HBO, A&E, HGTV, and MTV, to name just a few.

Keep in mind that not all cable channels are commercial channels that accept advertising, and not all are available to local advertisers. Check with your local cable company to find out which channels in your area are available for local retail advertising.

Cable offers the visual impact of television without the broad reach. Because so many cable networks are available to viewers, each one has become highly targeted and reaches a very specific audience. So, if you have a sporting goods store, you're probably going to focus on sports-related networks, like ESPN, Fox Sports, or ESPN 2. If, on the other hand, you own a day spa, you can focus on networks more appealing to women, such as HGTV (Home & Garden Television) or Lifetime. Not all situations are this clear-cut, of course, but the point is that cable networks have very specific target audiences, making it easy to eliminate those channels that aren't appropriate to you and to concentrate on the ones that better fit your target demographic.

In addition to targeting your customers by specific network, some of the larger markets offer cable advertising by *zone*. Zones are individual geographical areas within a cable system's total sphere of influence — small pieces of the cable pie. Zoning allows smaller advertisers to buy advertising only in the zones immediately surrounding their place of business. The San Francisco Bay Area, for example, has 11 regional cable zones as well as several subzones. So, if you have a clothing store in a particular San Jose suburb, you can buy cable advertising in the zone that covers just those households that are located nearby. On the other hand, if you have a chain of auto parts stores, with locations in various cities throughout the Bay Area, you can place your advertising in all zones, or *market-wide*.

A word of caution: The more complex your buy — the more networks and specific zones you choose — the more complex your invoices are. Talk with your sales rep about this issue up front so you have no surprises when your bill comes. You may find that you receive a separate invoice for each network included on your schedule, as well as for each zone, so be prepared! This amount of paperwork can be overwhelming and has been known to make even a professional advertising Accounts Payable Manager break down into uncontrollable sobbing.

Working effectively with a cable sales rep

So you're thinking that cable sounds pretty good and you want to explore it further. But you're frightened by a nagging thought: Do you have to meet sales reps from each network? Luckily, your local cable company has an advertising department, and a sales rep from that office will be happy to sell you commercials on any or all of their available networks, and in any or all of their zones. Depending on your local cable operator's agreement with the networks, it can insert your commercials on several networks, or on just a few. However, in all markets, the programming and the commercial inventory is controlled by the network, not the cable company.

Your first step is to contact the cable company and set up a meeting with an advertising sales rep. In general, this meeting will be a lot like meeting a network TV rep (check out "Working with a Sales Rep" earlier in this chapter), but you should know about a few nuances of cable. This meeting is an opportunity for your cable rep to get to know your business in order to prepare a proposal, but it's also an important opportunity for you to find out what options are available to you in your market. At the conclusion of this first meeting, you should know:

✔ What networks are available to you locally

✔ Whether your market is zoned

✔ The amount of local control on where your commercials can air

✔ Anything else unique to buying cable advertising in your neck of the woods

Your sales rep will want to come back with a proposal, and this part of the deal is where it could get tricky. Cable advertising has a reputation for sometimes being really cheap, and there is a reason for that: It's not uncommon for cable reps to sell very broad *rotators* (which are commercial spots run during available times, rather than prescheduled times, at the discretion of the station) over a single network or across several networks. They have so much commercial inventory that they may as well sell it for something! However, although just $2 or $3 per commercial (yes, cable time sometimes sells for a seemingly paltry amount) sounds too good to pass up, believe me it isn't. If you're advertising power drills and your $2 commercial runs in a 3:00 a.m. program on the Women's Network about getting in shape after you've had a baby, you just threw away three bucks. If your entire advertising schedule is made up of these cheap rotators, the likelihood of your commercial airing in prime time and on an appropriate network is slim. Cable companies don't give the good stuff away, and when you realize that fact, you can see that cable isn't always as "cheap" as it seems.

If you want to buy a spot during the Major League Baseball Championship Series or the Stanley Cup Finals on ESPN, you pay a premium. If you buy a rotator on ESPN, hoping to land in this well-watched programming, you will be disappointed. You definitely won't end up in the game. You may end up in the pre- or post-game, but then again, you may end up in the Introduction to Knitting or Celebrity Skeet Shooting hours. Don't risk it.

Hitting the bull's-eye with cable ads

Cable's biggest strength is its targetability, so use it. Buy programs or time periods on the appropriate networks, as specifically as you can. Then ask the sales rep to include some really cheap (or free) rotators in addition to your negotiated schedule. You can always check your invoices to see where and at what times the rotators ran and decide whether they're a worthwhile investment.

These cheapo rotator commercials can be a great way to enhance a schedule, but they should never be the meat of your campaign. *Remember:* If it seems too cheap to be true, it probably is. You get what you pay for.

Doing the math: Cable TV market penetration

One thing you should become educated on before you commit to any cable advertising is *market penetration,* the percentage of the total television households in your market that subscribe to cable. This topic is an important one to ask about before you evaluate the potential effectiveness of cable in your market. Your cable reps have this information (and so do your broadcast television reps, who use it to steer you *away* from cable).

Market penetration information, as it applies to cable, is important for a couple of reasons:

- **Penetration tells you the maximum number of households you can reach.** For example, if the cable penetration in your market is 50 percent, then the top-rated cable network in your market has the potential to reach only half of the total households in your area. That percentage also means you're eliminating half of your market right off the bat.

- **Demographics and location of cable subscribers can further limit your reach.** Looking at the remaining 50 percent who are cable subscribers, you need to narrow them down by demographics and geography, if applicable, in order to come up with the actual number of potential customers you can reach with your commercials.

By the time you slice and dice these numbers, they can end up fairly small. In fact, most cable networks (even the strongest, such as TNT, A&E, and TNN) don't deliver enough audience consistently enough to show up in the Nielsen rating book (for more info, see "Measuring ratings and market shares" in this chapter). And because they don't deliver enough audience to show up on Nielsen research, most cable companies use their *own* research, which is cable-specific.

ANECDOTE

You don't *always* get what you pay for

I once produced a TV spot for a Volkswagen dealer specifically targeted to women between 25 and 49. The 30-second spot featured an on-camera pitch by a well-dressed young woman who stood near the car in a lovely outdoor setting and outlined the many virtues of the new Jetta. She explained why it was perfect for the driving needs of busy professional women on the go. Our media department very carefully picked only cable programming for women — Lifetime, HGTV, and stations like them. We bought a fairly heavy schedule and anticipated good results.

A week or so later, whilst having lunch at a sports bar, I glanced up at the TV above the bar to watch a show called *The Lumberjack Olympics,* which was being televised on ESPN2.

Big, burly, sweaty guys in bib overalls and hob-nail boots were chopping trees to bits with incredibly sharp axes, climbing trees in ten seconds, doing log rolling, and performing all sorts of other macho feats of strength and dexterity. Guess which 30-second spot was the very first one I saw? Yep, our businesswoman selling VW Jettas.

The moral of this story is simply this: Read your cable invoices very carefully to make sure you get what you paid for. In fairness, I must report that the spot I saw on ESPN2 turned out to be a bonus spot and free of charge. However, free or not, it didn't do us one bit of good, because you could bet that not one female viewer was within a thousand miles of that programming.

TECHNICAL STUFF

Cable-specific research is fine, as long as they don't try to compare their research numbers to "over-the-air" television. Broadcast television ratings are based on a market population of total television households. Cable ratings, on the other hand, are based on a market population of *cable* households. This number can be *much* smaller than the total universe for television, depending on the cable penetration. Obviously, if cable doesn't penetrate 100 percent of the television households in the market, they would be at quite a disadvantage if they used the larger universe as the basis for determining their ratings. So, they use the smaller universe of cable households. And for this reason, you can't directly compare broadcast television ratings and cable ratings. If you do, you're comparing apples to rutabagas again.

TIP

Before you sign a contract, do the math to see whether advertising on cable makes sense for your business. Let's say your market consists of 100,000 television households. The cable penetration is 60 percent, which means 60,000 households have cable. The morning news on your local NBC affiliate, a broadcast television station, does a 2 household rating. The cable network, CNBC, has a morning news program, which also does a 2 rating, but with *cable* households. The 2 rating on the local NBC affiliate represents 2,000 households (2 percent of 100,000 households), while the 2 rating for CNBC represents just 1,200 households (2 percent of 60,000). So if you advertise on the broadcast station, you reach 800 more households than if you advertise on the cable station, even though both of them have a 2 household rating.

Although cable television delivers a smaller audience than over-the-air television, this doesn't have to be a disadvantage for you as an advertiser. After all, cable is usually less expensive, which means you can buy more commercials. In addition, cable can offer excellent targeting opportunities, both geographically and demographically.

You may decide you don't want to handle all these details on your own after all. That is, you still want to advertise on TV, but you just don't want to have to become an expert in TV production and scheduling. The good news is that you don't have to do all this work yourself: Instead, you can work with a media buyer. Luckily, Chapter 16 tells you all about how to avoid these headaches and turn them over to someone else — either a media buying service or a full-fledged ad agency.

Chapter 16

Deciding Whether to Hire an Ad Agency

In This Chapter

▶ Figuring out when to give your account to an agency — and how to choose one

▶ Understanding what an ad agency can do for you and who's involved in the process

▶ Knowing how an agency gets compensated for its work

▶ Communicating with your agency so that your ads — and your business — succeed

*W*hen you hire an ad agency, you're taking a giant leap of faith that these professionals can do a better job of promoting your business than you can do yourself. One sure way to make this a self-fulfilling prophecy is to give them a loose rein. Here are a few suggestions on how to do that:

✔ Let their creative department shine.

✔ Allow their media buyers to use their hard-earned experience to spend your media money wisely and effectively.

✔ Don't hire an agency and then dictate what it must do or what media it must buy.

✔ Don't turn down creative advertising ideas simply because they're not something you would have thought of yourself.

An agency can be only as good as its clients, and the best clients are those who recognize that, although advertising professionals can never know as much about your business as you do, they absolutely know more about creating and placing effective advertising. Your account will be important to your agency, and if your agency is truly dedicated to being your marketing partner, it will do everything it can to assure your business success and its long-range future with you.

In this chapter, I help you decide when to stop trying to do everything yourself and turn your advertising over to an ad agency — and how to find the right agency for your ad needs. I also clue you in on how agencies get paid so you can decide what's the best financial arrangement for you. Finally, I offer some advice on how best to work with your agency so your advertising accomplishes your goals: to get more business!

Determining When You May Need to Hire an Agency

Deciding when you need to hire an agency to help with your ads can be difficult. Here are some situations when hiring an agency makes sense:

- ✔ When phone calls from media sales reps are taking up too much of your time (see the nearby sidebar for more about this problem)
- ✔ When you're simply overwhelmed by the myriad details inherent in producing and placing your advertising
- ✔ When you no longer have the time, or the energy, to write and produce your advertising yourself
- ✔ When creating and placing your advertising on a regular basis has become a job instead of fun
- ✔ When your own creative efforts aren't yielding the results you desire
- ✔ When your advertising budget has grown so much that you're no longer certain you're spending it as wisely as you could be
- ✔ When the bookkeeping process of sorting through multiple media invoices each month has become too complicated and time-consuming
- ✔ When you finally admit that media invoices are written in a secret code that you'll never decipher, and you want to be assured that you're getting everything you're paying for
- ✔ When you're eager to have creative professionals generate fresh, new ideas for your advertising
- ✔ When you want to put a team of highly trained specialists to work, with the common goal of growing your business
- ✔ When you would welcome the professional creative, account service, and media buying expertise that an agency can provide
- ✔ When you'd like to do co-op advertising but don't want to hassle with the administrative details of finding co-op opportunities (that's a mouthful!) and following up on the funds

In addition, one of the first issues you should determine is whether you need a PR firm with design capabilities, an ad agency with some PR experience, or a true converged firm that can recommend and deliver PR and advertising.

Check out Chapter 18 for more info on PR and publicity. One of the major trends in marketing is an increase in PR over advertising; in advertising itself, the trend is an increase in promotion and interactive ads.

You don't need an advertising budget in the millions to seek out the services of an ad agency. Many local agencies provide you with all the services offered by the major agencies, but they're scaled down to fit within your budget and your advertising requirements. These agencies are the one-person shops and the smaller agencies that handle retail, direct-response advertising for all kinds of local and regional accounts.

When it comes to advertising agencies, one size doesn't fit every business. All full-service *shops* (that's advertising slang for agencies) perform the same duties; provide the same services; have the same access to research and media opportunities; employ the very best, most-talented people they can afford; offer the finest creative product they can possibly conjure up; and earn essentially the same remuneration, with one major difference — the size of their clients' businesses and their clients' budgets, as you can see in the following:

- ✔ The giants of the advertising industry handle the major national and international accounts — such as General Motors, which spends billions of dollars each year on advertising (yes, that's billions with a *b*).

- ✔ The not-so-giant agencies typically handle regional, not-so-giant accounts, though they may also handle some national (and even international) clients, especially business-to-business accounts. Also, many of the regional offices of the giant agencies compete for and serve relatively small accounts: For example, Publicis in Indianapolis served the Indiana State Museum with a very modest budget.

- ✔ Small local ad agencies, for the most part, specialize in retail accounts, such as local furniture stores, clothing boutiques, wedding or party locations, and caterers.

- ✔ Some agencies specialize in the design and development of collateral materials, Web site and Internet advertising design, the production of corporate videos, and other niches.

Agencies like mine have billings of several million dollars a year but nothing close to the astronomical billings of the major shops. The services we perform for our accounts are many and varied, and each account requires different services. But essentially, we, like all agencies, handle for our accounts everything from writing and designing ads, to negotiating with and buying the various media, and all the many details in between.

The best advice I have regarding the size of an agency is to select one where your account will be important. Talk frankly about your budget and ask — and check — references of at least three other clients with similar budgets.

These smaller agencies also know your local market intimately and may even specialize in a particular business segment such as health care, financial, telecommunications, or automotive. They know the local media; they know which radio stations are hot and which ones are not; they know rate cards and demographics and all the important research data relevant to your local market that they can put to good use when handling your business. They're friends with station owners and managers, newspaper editors and retail advertising managers, account executives and creative talent. They're a wealth of local knowledge.

Advertising is an extremely important part of your overall marketing plan. Hiring a team of professionals to handle it for you is something you should think about. When you hire an advertising agency, you eliminate a lot of daily phone calls and drop-in visits from various reps so you can focus on running your business. You also, in all likelihood, receive a more-polished creative product from the agency than you've been producing, because a whole gang of professional writers, designers, and creative directors are working on your business. And, in the case of many local ad agencies, it very likely won't cost you as much as you think.

Finding the Right Agency for Your Business

If you do decide that you need to hire an ad agency, you need to spend some time finding a good one. You want to find an agency that lists its specialty as retail, local, or direct response — an agency that operates on a local or regional level. When you're looking for an ad agency, don't just let your fingers do the walking through your local Yellow Pages and expect to find the best one right off the bat. Any of the media reps or sales reps who call on your account can put you in touch with some good ones, possibly agencies that specialize in your business arena. Of course, the agencies they recommend are the agencies that they work with, but after all, fair is fair.

If media reps or sales reps aren't calling on you, you can find an agency in more creative ways. Have you seen or heard an ad for a local business that was particularly creative and really caught your attention? Call the newspaper or the station that ran the ad and ask about it. Talk with the paper's Retail Sales Department or the station's Traffic Department and ask which agency is responsible for the ad. Then give that agency a call. What could be simpler? Upon receiving your call, the agency will be immediately flattered and will dispatch an account executive or account supervisor to your business to chat you up and try to get your business.

Nowadays most agencies also have Web sites. You can research the agency's work and its client list before you even call. See what the agency is doing first, and find out if it's compatible with what you're looking for. Figure out who the agency's clients are and whether its client mix appears to match with your specialty.

Then, invite a few agencies to come to your office to make their pitches — this is called an *agency review*. When the word gets out that you're having an agency review (and the speed with which industry gossip spreads never ceases to amaze me), you'll get calls from many agencies that you haven't personally contacted. That's okay: You may want to give them an appointment, too. Get to know each one, listen to what each has to say, look at and listen to their creative work, and see whether it feels right. Be sure to think about which of the agency account executives you will be able to get along with over the long haul. Check each agency's references and then make your choice. (More about account execs in the next section of this chapter.)

Many extremely competent, enormously talented, small or local advertising agencies are out there. With just a bit of research, you can find the one you feel most comfortable with.

Getting to Know the People Handling Your Account

Advertising agencies are made up of people performing many different jobs. Smaller agencies may not employ people in all these positions (in that case, the agency's employees may take on the responsibilities of more than one position and may even have a network of freelancers available as needed), but you may end up working someday with an agency that does. So knowing who the players are and what they do is always a good idea:

- ✔ **Owners and senior management:** These top guns usually are the people who meet with you initially, with their creative and account service staff, to make their pitch for becoming your ad agency. Unless their agency is very small, they aren't usually involved in the day-to-day servicing of your account.

- ✔ **Account supervisor:** This person supervises the creative and account service team handling your account on a daily basis. (She probably also supervises other accounts in addition to yours.) This person makes sure things are running smoothly in the day-to-day servicing of your business and usually has the last word when it comes time to make creative, account service, and billing decisions.

- ✔ **Account executive:** This member of the ad team services your account on a daily basis. He may have been the person who originally called on you and solicited your business in the first place. Depending on the size of the ad agency, the account executive may handle more than one account. The number of accounts the account executive handles is usually predicated on total advertising budgets: The bigger the budget, the more work is involved and, ergo, the fewer accounts handled by one person.

- ✔ **Creative Director:** This person typically oversees and shapes all the creative product, for all media, that the agency develops and designs for your business — radio, TV, print, whatever. The creative director supervises the writers, designers, photographers, actors, voice talents, and anyone else who contributes to the final creative product.

- ✔ **Copywriter:** As the job title says, the copywriter takes the basic facts about your business and writes the copy for your ads — hopefully, with wit, humor, or drama, and, above all, *sell.*

- ✔ **Graphic Designer/Artist:** Your graphics guy or artist works with the copywriter to make print and collateral advertising sparkle with eye-catching, unusual graphic elements and typefaces.

- ✔ **Media buyer:** You need to spend your limited and very important time productively running your business, and the media buyer helps you do just that. She negotiates the deals for buying the media you need for the ads your agency has created, fields the phones calls, and takes the meetings with the dozens of media reps. A good media buyer is fair but firm with the media, insisting on the correct format, impressive ratings or circulation, and the right audience composition and demographic before committing your hard-earned dollars to any ad medium.

A media buyer also does the very important job of *post analysis,* in which she pores over the media invoices to make sure everything bought is accounted for. And if she's diligent and knowledgeable, she gives you the most bang for your buck and stretches your media budget, regardless of its size, as tightly as it can be stretched without breaking.

The biggest benefit of using a professional media buyer — who has software to analyze and optimize your media buy — is that you can gain significant additional exposure within your target market and get significant savings and added value from professional media negotiation and buying.

Compensating Your Agency

As much as I enjoy creating wonderful advertising, as much as I look forward to writing a new commercial that presents a client's message in a fresh, new way, and as much as I appreciate the talents of those who work around me and the faith and trust placed in my agency by our clients, I also really like the getting-paid part! Nothing says, "I love you" like a big, fat check at the end of each month.

Advertising legend David Ogilvy gave the best advice I could ever direct toward an account: "Make sure that your agency makes a profit. Your account competes with all the other accounts in your agency. If it is unprofitable, it is unlikely that the management of the agency will assign their best people to work on it. And sooner or later they will cast about for a profitable account to replace yours."

You wouldn't work for free, so why should your ad agency? I have handled a few accounts during my career that begrudged every nickel I earned from them. It put too much strain on the business relationship, and I replaced (or simply resigned) those accounts at my first opportunity.

Advertising professionals, like any professionals, have the right to be paid a professional's wage. But (and here's some news that should allay your fears) advertising agencies don't cost nearly as much as most people assume. In the following sections, I clue you in to how the media you choose gets paid, what creating and then producing your ads can cost you, and whether you want to pay your agency a markup on its work or a regular retainer.

Media commissions

Since the dawn of advertising history, and because of some obscure arrangement made between the early founders of the advertising agency business and the newspapers of the time, an agency used to earn a media commission of 15 percent. Recently, however, the commission system has greatly eroded. More common than commissions are hourly charges for media planning, buying, and tracking.

If commissions are used, they are routinely negotiated based on the size and complexity of the media buy and services required: They generally range from 5 to 15 percent. Small or complex media buys on an hourly basis may require 20 percent or more of the media budget.

You can find a lot of research on agency compensation with the small business owner in mind. One source for smaller agencies you may want to check out is Second Wind, which is a network of agencies and the like (www.secondwind network.com).

Procter & Gamble bucks the system — and reallocates how it spends its bucks

Procter & Gamble has changed the way it pays its ad agencies. According to *The Wall Street Journal* ("In a Shift, Marketers Beef Up Ad Spending Inside Stores," by Emily Nelson and Sarah Ellison, September 21, 2005), P&G worried that agencies that were paid commissions on media costs would naturally tend to develop ads that cost a lot — especially expensive TV commercials. So it now links compensation to its ad agencies to product-sales increases. This change may not make the agencies happy, but it certainly is a fair incentive.

And more changes may be afoot: P&G reduced its cable TV advertising by 25 percent in 2005 and its broadcast TV ads by 5 percent, even while increasing its overall ad budget for the year. Where did that money go? To a new type

of advertising: In-store ads, where P&G believes that consumers make most of their purchase decisions anyway. P&G calls it *first moment of truth* (FMOT) and has hired 50 Directors of FMOT (pronounced "Eff-mott").

Finally, if you think just one company is making changes, consider that P&G popularized the concept of mass-market advertising almost 100 years ago, and it's still considered the go-to place for marketers just starting out in their careers to figure out how to market and advertise effectively. Also, keep in mind that P&G is a consumer-goods powerhouse of brands, including Tide detergent, Crest toothpaste, and Pampers diapers, to name just a few. Where P&G leads, others may follow.

The traditional commission is paid to the agency by the media in the form of a discount. If *you* buy a newspaper ad with a space cost of $1,000 directly from the paper, you are charged $1,000. If your ad agency buys the same ad, it is charged $850, but the agency bills you for the full $1,000 and keeps the rest ($150, or 15 percent) as its commission. So, in effect, having an agency place your media buys doesn't cost you a dime, because you're paying the same amount to buy that ad whether you have an agency handle it for you or you do it yourself — it's just that if you buy it with the help of an agency, some of your money goes to the agency as well as to the newspaper.

Creative and production charges

Agencies also charge their clients for something they call *creative and production,* which is essentially the writing and designing of the ad. How much an agency charges varies from agency to agency. So before you commit to having an agency design an ad or produce a radio or TV spot for you, ask the agency how much it charges for creative and production.

Some agencies have truly astounding creative charges (especially those that don't earn additional monies from media commissions); other agencies have fairly modest charges. The bottom line is that the media commission *isn't* enough to cover the cost of running an agency, and the addition of creative and production charges to the clients' invoices is a necessary one, so be prepared to pay for it.

Markups

An agency also adds a markup to all the buyouts it makes on your behalf. *Buyouts* are charges incurred by the agency for voice talent, recording studios, photographers, models, actors, props, photography, printing, commercial recording, filming, film editing, and so on — basically, everything that outside vendors contribute to the cost of producing your advertising.

Because the agency went on the hook to order these vendors and the agency is ultimately responsible for payment, these charges are added to your monthly invoice along with an agency markup. The markup your agency charges is another item you may want explained to you before approving certain creative and production jobs. You don't want any surprises when it comes time to pay your bill.

Retainers

Sometimes an agency and a client work out a monthly *retainer,* which is a set monthly fee you pay the agency for its services. The retainer may be in addition to agency commissions, or it may be in place of them — it depends on how much you (as the client) are spending on advertising and on whether all the media options the agency is purchasing for you are commissionable.

For instance, if you're buying only newspaper advertising at a retail rate — a reduced rate to make the publication more affordable for local advertisers like you — your agency usually won't earn a commission on that space. Why? Because the retail rate is usually so low that newspapers refuse to subtract a 15 percent commission from it. Instead of having your agency add markups to each newspaper invoice, you and your agency may opt for a monthly retainer figure that comes close to the amount of commissions that the agency would have earned had the newspaper space been invoiced at a higher rate.

Newspapers have very complicated, sometimes arbitrary, rate cards that make agency retainers a necessary evil in some cases. Retail ad space for a furniture store, for example, *isn't* commissionable, but automotive advertising for a local car dealer — which is, most certainly, retail — *is* commissionable. If you can figure out why this difference exists, drop me a note, because I never have been able to.

I've also never liked the idea of charging a retainer. Inevitably, either the client or the agency feels it's getting the short end of the stick. But in some cases, retainers are unavoidable, even desirable. However, the monthly dollar amount is something that needs to be carefully worked out between the two parties. Retainer agreements can be beneficial to both clients and agencies. For you, the client, a retainer may guarantee you a certain amount of access to the agency and all of its personnel, regardless of the size of your media budget. For the agency, the retainer helps it plan for the number of people who are directly employed to handle your account.

Working with Your Agency to Get What You Need

You hire an ad agency because you want to put its expertise to work for you. The advertising gurus know advertising, but they don't know your business. So when you hire an agency, keep one thing in mind: You must have a continual dialogue with your agency contact person to be sure you're working toward the same goal. Tell your contact everything you can possibly think of that's relevant to the advertising that will be created for your account — regardless of how minuscule and unimportant this detailed information may seem. Your agency needs to know as much as it can about your products and services in order to sift through the information to find your *unique selling proposition* (what is it that separates you from the herd?) and to develop the *creative hook* (a fresh, new way to tell the world about you and your business) that it uses when creating your ads.

You expect from your agency the finest possible creative product for your account. But that product can never live up to your expectations if the agency has to guess about what you want to convey to the buying public. The more facts you can provide, the easier it is for the agency writers, designers, and media buyers to make quality decisions when producing your advertising and placing it on the various media.

Tell your agency as much about your product and business as possible, and keep updating this information as time passes. Here are some key types of information you need to share with your agency:

✔ What makes your product so great and why people should buy it

✔ Which demographic group is your prime market

✔ What is unique about what you're providing (for example, your service, location, convenient hours)

✔ Whether you compete with giant, impersonal chain stores

✔ Whether you offer free delivery, a lifetime guarantee, or something the consumer won't find elsewhere

In addition to the information about your business that you'll provide for your agency, any good agency will want to dig far deeper. Good agencies learn their client's business. They read the client's industry trade magazines, spend time in the store observing customers, or tag along on sales calls. They attend trade shows and interview your major customers. They cry for research on your market, customers, competitors, and more. Keep that in mind when interviewing agencies: They should want to know as much about your business as you do!

Your agency will likely want to set a regular meeting time with you (for example, weekly or monthly). These regular meetings are a great time for you to impart all your wisdom regarding your business. If anything relevant pops into your mind outside of this meeting, call your account executive. The more your agency knows about your business, the better the ads it can create for you.

If your agency seems disinterested in the details you're sharing or doesn't want to hear your ideas, or worse, doesn't ask you tons of questions, start looking for another agency. You want to find an ad agency that views itself as an advertising partner and that views you as an integral part of the success of the ad campaigns it creates for you.

Part IV
Beyond the Basics: Creating Buzz and Using Publicity

The 5th Wave   By Rich Tennant

In this part . . .

Don't be afraid to go outside the box, especially when it comes to telling the world about your business. Buzz and word of mouth are free (or at least low-budget) ways to get your message out. And publicity — sending a press release to a publication in the hopes of getting some free ink — is most certainly a form of advertising.

In addition, premium items — the giveaway refrigerator magnets, key chains, mouse pads, and coffee mugs you know and love — as well as promotions and events (whether radio station invented or created by you) are unique modes of advertising. As part of an overall ad campaign, each of these ad models can increase your exposure in the marketplace. And in this part, I show you how to make them work for you.

Chapter 17

Creating Buzz and Word-of-Mouth Advertising

In This Chapter

▶ Understanding what buzz and word of mouth really are

▶ Recognizing the value of word-of-mouth marketing

▶ Choosing among various ways to generate buzz

*A*dvertising today not only includes the *paid* placement of marketing messages but also some free methods of getting your message out. *Buzz* and *word-of-mouth marketing* fit into this category — though you can also spend money to create buzz or great word of mouth. In this chapter, I explain what you need to know about these tactics and show you examples of how they work in the real world so you can put them to work for your own business.

Getting the Terminology Straight

Just in case you're still thinking that word-of-mouth marketing isn't a legitimate, controllable, manageable approach to promoting your product or service, think again. An entire professional association is devoted to word-of-mouth marketing, called (natch) the Word of Mouth Marketing Association, or WOMMA — a hilariously memorable acronym. (If you want to know more, its Web site is www.womma.org, and it's based in Chicago.)

More important, though, is the fact that WOMMA consists of corporate members only (not individuals), which means that big companies are just as interested in word-of-mouth marketing as small businesses and solo entrepreneurs. For example, just look at a few of the companies that are, at the time of this writing, members of WOMMA — the A&E TV network, Coca-Cola, Dell computers, General Motors, Yahoo!, and Zondervan religious publishing.

Moreover, *Adweek* magazine published a feature article on the topic of word-of-mouth marketing in October 24, 2005 ("Psst! How Do You Measure Buzz?"). The article described the rise of buzz and word of mouth, and it clarified, by way of WOMMA definitions, the subtle yet important differences between these recent marketing terms, which I share with you here:

- **Word of mouth:** The act of consumers providing information to other consumers.

- **Word-of-mouth marketing:** Giving people a reason to talk about your products and services and making it easier for that conversation to take place.

- **Buzz marketing:** Using high-profile entertainment or news to get people to talk about your brand.

- **Viral marketing:** Creating entertaining or informative messages that are designed to be passed along in an exponential fashion, often electronically or by e-mail.

Now that you know what's what, keep reading to see how word-of-mouth marketing really works.

Seeing the Power of Word of Mouth

Many advertising, publicity, and marketing experts believe that word-of-mouth marketing is the most powerful type of exposure that you can get for your product, service, business, or store. After all, who are you most likely to believe? A paid advertisement, featuring an actor who earns his fee by reciting a script written by a salaried copywriter working for a hired ad agency? Or the unsolicited suggestion by one of your friends that "you should see this movie; you'll love it!" or "buy that car; it's really reliable," or "try this restaurant, or gift shop, or dry cleaner, or face cream, or sneaker, or computer, or cell phone"?

Obviously, you're more likely to listen to your friend. After all, she hasn't been paid to recommend that product or business. She gains nothing if you do or don't try it. She's simply telling you what she loves or appreciates — and that's a powerful endorsement for any business. Now all you have to do is get those powerful endorsements!

In the following sections, I offer up a few examples of how word of mouth has worked effectively, for positive business results — and I show you how to prevent the opposite: negative buzz. For celebrities, it may be true that "there's no such thing as bad publicity," but the same isn't true of businesses!

Examining word-of-mouth marketing success stories

You can find plenty of real-world examples showing how successful word-of-mouth promotion can be. You probably have even experienced it as a consumer. In order to launch your own word-of-mouth campaign, you can glean some valuable tips by first looking at the success stories of others.

Emanuel Rosen describes a broad spectrum of these successes in his book *The Anatomy of Buzz* (Currency). Rosen describes how buzz was completely and absolutely responsible for consumer awareness of a software product he was involved with (called Endnote, a program to help academics footnote their sources more easily, to meet different guidelines without having to re-type each source). He was able to track consumer awareness to buzz (something he considers synonymous with word of mouth) because the company hadn't done any marketing or advertising or publicity when people started to call and ask about it. In fact, the product wasn't even available when the company received its first order! But the company had done a sneak preview locally, and word spread about it nationally. That first order came in from 3,000 miles away.

Word of mouth has been responsible for the success of other high-tech products as well. But it's not only the geeks in the world of computer technology who buzz about a product; it happens in the larger world, too. When was the first time you considered getting an MP3 player or a PDA? For most people, these gadgets became enticing only after hearing a friend or coworker rave about his new toy.

How many people make travel and vacation plans based on what people they know recommend or buy cars because of buzz about a particular style? How many times have you gone to the movies based on what your friends are talking about or recommend — often, even when you had no interest in a particular movie until people we know start buzzing about it? For example, remember *The Crying Game? The Sixth Sense?* And *The Blair Witch Project?* All of those movies benefited from buzz and word-of-mouth marketing.

People tend to buzz about certain types of products. Rosen did a great job narrowing down six categories of product that can generate buzz: products that are exciting, innovative, complex, expensive, observable (you can see others using them), or that involve personal experience. If any aspect of your business, product, or service fits into any of those categories, you should focus on that aspect when trying to generate buzz.

Books are another typical product that benefit from great word of mouth. In fact, book publicists typically send a copy of a new book to a targeted list of "big mouths" whom they know will talk up a book that they enjoyed. To book publishers, being a big mouth isn't a bad thing at all. Those people know a lot of people, they talk to many people regularly, they're free with their opinions, and people listen to what they say and what they recommend. Big mouths spread the word about a new book, and they can help it get noticed and sell — which is increasingly tough to do given the enormous number of new books that are published every year.

You may be surprised at the success stories of many titles you're familiar with. Rosen talks about how buzz contributed to the success of one such book: *Cold Mountain* by Charles Frazier (Grove Press). And Malcolm Gladwell, in his book *The Tipping Point* (Back Bay Books), writes about another book that caused a sensation: *Divine Secrets of the Ya-Ya Sisterhood* by Rebecca Wells (HarperCollins). Interestingly, word of mouth was responsible for the enormous success of each book, but the buzz on the two books happened in very different ways: One was top-down, and the other was bottom-up.

In the case of *Cold Mountain,* the buzz was driven from the top-down. The book started to sell as soon as it was published, but it became a bestseller because the publisher wrote personal letters to key booksellers and sent copies to people he thought would be key readers (and therefore had big mouths).

In the case of *Divine Secrets of the Ya-Ya Sisterhood,* the book didn't sell particularly well at first. It got a few good reviews and sold a modestly successful number of copies in the original hardcover edition. When the book came out in paperback, though, the author noticed that groups of women would come to bookstores to have her sign their copies, and they were buying several copies of the book for their friends. What had happened was that readers had identified with the theme of the book and were reading it in bookclubs and other communities, and those communities started to buzz. That word-of-mouth groundswell caused the book to sell 2.5 million copies.

Beware of negative buzz!

A product can also be affected adversely by *negative buzz.* Remember the problem with Intel's Pentium chip, back in the early 1990s? Someone found a small error in the chip, and news about it spread furiously fast on the Internet — so fast that Intel couldn't contain it and didn't remedy it fast enough. That negative buzz cost the company $475 million in write-offs — but it offered a great lesson in what to do and what not to do when someone discovers a weakness in your product or service.

Keep in mind the old adage that a happy customer may recommend your product or service or store to someone else, but an unhappy customer will definitely complain about you to at least three people. The power and speed of the Internet have increased that nightmare scenario exponentially. Do your best to keep your customers happy — no matter what.

Tips and Techniques on Generating Buzz

As I mention in previous sections, you don't have to just sit around and pray for good word of mouth or great buzz — you can actively work to promote it. Check out some suggestions I gleaned from Richard Laermer, author of *Full Frontal PR: Building Buzz About Your Business, Your Product, or You,* in the following sections.

Coining a great new phrase

One way to get people talking is to come up with a new expression associated with your business. People love to be in the know and ahead of the curve, and many people love things just because they're new — and that includes language. In fact, many great ad campaigns were successful because they (often unwittingly) created a new expression that people started using in everyday life and conversation. Think of the saying "Where's the beef?" This expression was first used in a Wendy's commercial, where a gruff little old lady was literally looking for the meat in her hamburger, but the expression came to be used in any situation where the substance of something was missing.

One way to coin a new phrase is to turn your business's or product's name into a verb. For example, Richard Laermer uses the example of Google.com, an Internet search engine you're probably familiar with. People now talk about "I googled it to find out more about it. . . ." So now, when someone needs to look something up on the Internet, Google.com is probably one of the first search engines to come to mind.

Companies used to hate this appropriation of their names. For example, Kleenex and Xerox fought to prevent their brand names from becoming synonymous with the product itself (in this case, face tissue and photocopying). Now, however, many companies are delighted to have that "problem," because it means that consumers view their names as the brand leaders. If your company or brand name becomes part of the popular lexicon, that's a great way to advertise your business!

Hiring beautiful people to promote your product

Another way to get people talking is to give them something interesting to talk about. If your product or business isn't already fabulous, try to attach it to something that is. And if your business is already exciting, associate it with something even more intriguing!

For example, Vespas are little known in the United States, though these little scooters are everywhere in Italy. Richard Laermer describes how Vespa helped make inroads (pun intended) into the U.S. market by hiring gorgeous models to ride around Los Angeles, stop in at various cafes and have a coffee while chatting with other customers about their cool mini-motorbikes. The models weren't famous, but they were beautiful, and they attracted attention to themselves first but then to the product they were promoting, and the whole stunt generated buzz — in a city where that's tough to do!

Taking advantage of celebrity endorsements

If you can get the attention of a celebrity — either purposely or serendipitously, you should leverage that attention as much as possible.

Okay, you can't solicit *spontaneous* celebrity mentions, but you can leverage them if they happen on their own. For example, Richard Laermer cites how Sandra Bullock became a one-woman marketing machine for Listerine PocketPaks (those little tab-sized breath strips that were introduced in 2005) when she talked about them nonstop at the Oscars in 2002.

Similarly, Rush Limbaugh created buzz for *The Millionaire Next Door,* a very interesting book that was little known until Limbaugh mentioned it on his radio show, which has an enormous listening audience. The book has since sold more than 2 million copies, and it was on the *New York Times* bestseller list for 3 years.

If I were working to promote either of the above products, you can bet your last dollar I would do everything possible to maximize that exposure. For example, I would have copies of the Oscar footage where Sandra Bullock talked about the Listerine PocketPaks, and I'd send that video and quote her in all future marketing for that product. And I'd get in touch with her to find out whether she'd be willing to go further and become a spokeswoman for the brand or whether I could use her endorsement in future ad campaigns. Regarding Mr. Limbaugh, if I had been the publisher of that book, I'd have immediately contacted him to get a written endorsement of the book, which I would then feature on every future copy and edition of the book and all subsequent marketing, advertising, and sales materials. You should look for the same opportunities.

So how do you maximize on celebrity exposure? Here are a few things that I would do:

✔ Get a copy of what the celebrity said about your product or business, or request a written endorsement.

✔ Obtain permission from that celebrity (in writing, of course) to use his comments in your future ad campaigns.

✔ Consider asking that celebrity to be your spokesperson.

Throwing a party

Generating buzz by throwing a big bash is considered a publicity party, and publicity isn't advertising, of course, but parties can generate word of mouth as well as publicity in newspapers, magazines, and other media. The party itself probably won't be free (unless you can get friends and fans to provide the space and the food and drink, and send out the invitations, which you quite possibly can!). But even if you do have to incur some costs to throw a party, it can be money very well spent because of the word of mouth it can generate.

You can throw a party to announce a grand opening of your store, to introduce a new product or invention, or to celebrate an anniversary, such as the tenth anniversary of your being in business for yourself — or anything else that's new with your business. Of course, you should invite newspeople, from all the local newspapers (your major city paper as well as smaller neighborhood papers, as well as freebies around town), local magazines, and local TV and radio personalities, but you also want to invite everyone you know who you think can talk about your product or business in an interesting, exciting way. If they have a great time at your party, they're more likely to tell all their friends, colleagues, neighbors, and acquaintances about it — especially if you've done something unique at the party or given away something fabulous.

For example, one publicity party I attended for a book about a very successful black entrepreneur generated lots of word of mouth. Why? Because the hostess invited Coretta Scott King — and she came, with one of her sons! That was exciting: She and her late husband, the Reverend Martin Luther King, are legends in the world of civil rights, and many people at the party welcomed this unique opportunity to meet her. Mrs. King's presence at the party got people talking, and it helped the book become a business bestseller and sell more than 100,000 copies, which is terrific for a business book.

Hitting the streets

Another way to promote buzz is to take your product or service literally to the streets: to pound pavements where people are out and about, walking and driving. This method isn't the same as outdoor advertising (covered in Chapter 11); instead, it's more about meeting and greeting potential customers.

For example, Richard Laermer recommends doing such simple and low-budget advertising as putting stickers on every lamppost to build awareness of your brand. Here's an example he offers in *Full Frontal PR:* When *The New York Times* started its online service, it hired a small ad agency that gave out paper spoons with the company's Web site (www.nytoday.com) on them, and when those people logged on, they could print out a coupon for a cheap but yummy meal at Daily Soup, a popular café in midtown New York City. That strategy generated buzz about the Web site.

Figuring out where to find your big mouths

In addition to finding the right type of big mouth (see the preceding section), you need to know where best to reach him. Finding your market maven requires creative thinking on your part, because you know best (or at least you should!) where your customers are most readily found.

For example, Malcolm Gladwell offers insight on this, too, by way of a great example. He writes how a nurse in San Diego wanted to make more black women aware of and knowledgeable about diabetes and breast cancer. She began in what she thought was the right place, by targeting black churches, but she found that the women who stayed after services were already knowledgeable, and the rest of the congregations just wanted to get home.

So she thought about finding a place where black women would have more time and be more relaxed and therefore be more open to receiving information, and she realized that the best place for her to generate word of mouth was at the beauty salon. So she taught hairdressers to be her mavens, her big mouths, and she generated the buzz she wanted in order to educate women about these diseases and to encourage them to get mammograms and find out even more about how they can protect themselves.

Creating a blog about your business

WOMMA (see the section "Getting the Terminology Straight" in this chapter) also offers a *Womnibus* (another great name) that posts useful information on the WOMMA Web site for people interested in word-of-mouth marketing trends. WOMMA touts the Womnibus as the primary resource for advertisers wanting to get involved with word-of-mouth strategies. One Womnibus described a study conducted by the Pew research organization about the prevalence of blogs (short for Web logs) as of mid-2006. Among the key findings:

- ✔ Eight percent of consumers (12 million U.S. adults) keep a blog, up from 7 percent in 2005.

- ✔ Thirty-nine percent of consumers (57 million U.S. adults) read blogs, an increase from 27 percent in 2005.

Pew concludes that blogs have become one of the key media for word of mouth. Maybe this strategy is something that could work for your business, if your target market spends a lot of time on the Internet.

As new technology comes along, so will new ways to communicate with an ever-widening circle of friends and acquaintances who can potentially be influenced by individual ideas, recommendations, and suggestions on products, services, businesses, and stores. So, keep current on the technology trends and jump at the chance of putting one to work for your business.

Chapter 18

Leveraging Your Advertising with Public Relations, Publicity, Specialty Items, and Events

In This Chapter

▶ Working public relations like a pro

▶ Mastering publicity by writing an effective public release

▶ Using specialty advertising items and promotions to get your name out

*I*n addition to the myriad ways you can advertise your business, you can find other marketing activities that are closely related to advertising. This chapter covers four of these options: public relations, publicity (especially via press releases), specialty item advertising, and promotional events. Before diving in, you should understand the difference between two of these terms, which people often confuse. Although closely related, public relations and publicity are two different things. *Public relations* (PR) is the ongoing process of promoting yourself and talking yourself up. *Publicity* is the occasional process of using a much bigger tool (usually in the form of media) to promote yourself.

Here's a simple analogy illustrating the difference between public relations and publicity: If your business sponsors a Little League team for kids who live near your store, *that* is public relations. You're endearing yourself to the kids' parents (the public to whom you're trying to relate), who may, as a result, become your customers. If, on the other hand, you send your local newspaper a written story bragging about your Little League sponsorship in the hopes of having it printed, *that* is publicity. You're now blatantly (some would argue, cleverly) trying to endear yourself to everyone who subscribes to the paper. A public relations campaign may cost you money — uniforms and equipment for your Little League team, for example — but publicity, for the most part, is free (the media doesn't charge you to publish or broadcast your story).

Of course, this chapter is only a quick primer into the ways and means of PR, publicity, specialty items, and promotional events. If you're really interested in knowing more about these types of marketing, check out the *Public Relations For Dummies,* 2nd Edition, by Eric Yaverbaum, Ilise Benun, and Richard Kirshenbaum (Wiley). To get the basics, though, read on!

Starting a Public Relations Campaign

From the sponsorship of a local Little League team to allowing local service clubs the use of your store or conference room for their meetings, PR can take many forms. Public relations is just that — relating to the public, which, in this case, means your current and future customers. Your PR effort doesn't have to be grandiose and expensive — it can be modest and still be highly effective. If you own a pet-supply store, you can offer free dog-training classes or low-priced vaccination clinics (these offers could also be defined as *promotions*). If you own a restaurant, you can offer your banquet room free of charge to the local Toastmasters or Rotary Club (of course, you charge them for the food and beverages). And regardless of your business, you can offer free goods for charity auctions or buy ad space in the high school yearbook, ticket books for worthwhile raffles, and so on.

One of my clients, a furniture store owner, donated a very expensive dining room set to a local fundraising auction and, as a result of his generosity and the ensuing publicity, he has been enjoying new cash customers from the sponsoring club ever since.

The trick to PR is to do good works for the community while gaining at least a subtle recognition for yourself and your business.

Unlike the immediacy of a press release, where you're looking to get a story published right away, PR is a continuing process just as your advertising campaign is (or should be) a continuing process. Your PR campaign is an integral part of your entire communications course of action and is no less important than a blockbuster TV or radio commercial or a full-page ad in the local daily. And, if yours is a small to mid-size retail or service business, a solid PR effort in your community is doubly important. A well-planned PR campaign keeps your name in front of your customers (and prospective customers) even when you're not actively advertising.

So how do you make friends and influence people; create understanding, acceptance, and awareness of your business or product; and gain a favorable response from your marketplace? As with all aspects of advertising, know what messages you want to communicate (see Chapter 4 for more details on forming your message). Think about what your various audiences need to know about your product or service. What is it that makes what you sell better than, or different from, anything else consumers can get elsewhere? Are there audiences who should know about your community involvement, your environmental record, your particular expertise that adds value to your sell? Should people know about the comprehensiveness of your offer, key endorsements you have received, the credibility of your investors, the partnerships you've formed, or the promotional tie-ins you provide with other organizations?

Your messages should directly answer the question: "Why should anyone care about what you offer?" When you know what you want to communicate through your PR, how do you go about delivering that message? You can use many different vehicles for communicating with the audiences you want to reach. Here's a list of potential communications vehicles:

- ✔ Publicity or press releases targeted to mass, trade, or community media (see the next section on publicity for more information)

- ✔ Article reprints of publicity you've received from various media, which you then mail to specific lists

- ✔ Professional-quality photography to accompany your press releases

- ✔ Volunteer participation in community and charitable organizations or foundations

- ✔ Scholarships you've awarded and that carry your name

- ✔ Seminars, speeches, and lectures you give to various groups

- ✔ Web site and Internet postings of publicity you've received

- ✔ Contests you sponsor that carry your name

- ✔ Newsletters you write and send out on a regular basis

- ✔ Donations of products or services to community causes, events, and clubs

Understanding How Publicity Can Bring Customers

Apart from the single article or broadcast segment you may notice and envy, what you may not realize are the many benefits that an organized and continuing publicity effort adds to your other advertising endeavors. If you're using paid advertising, articles in which you or your company appear help infuse your campaign with credibility and detail. Plus, publicity adds reach and frequency to your message that you may not otherwise be able to afford.

Most people understand the power of favorable news coverage, whether it's *The Wall Street Journal,* the local daily, *Time* magazine, local radio or TV, an industry trade journal, or a community weekly paper. Restaurants receiving positive media coverage are swamped with phone calls for reservations. Companies get a flood of orders for their well-reviewed widgets. Designers become "hot." New respect is derived from customers, competitors, family, and friends.

The Pet Rock: A publicity phenomenon

The Pet Rock was quickly transformed from a novelty gift with an uncertain future into an international retail phenomenon, thanks to the incredible power of publicity. I was unable to afford a huge advertising budget, so I wrote a publicity story and sent it, along with photos of its inventor (me), the product, and its packaging, to major weekly news magazines. On November 10, 1975, a half-page publicity story about the Pet Rock and a photo of me were featured in *Newsweek.*

Maybe it was a slow news day. Or perhaps the tongue-in-cheek qualities of both the product and the publicity story attracted the editors' attention. Whatever the reason, *Newsweek* printed my story and gave the item media credibility — in my opinion, the Pet Rock was more of a media event than a sales event. Although we sold (literally and figuratively) tons of them,

the media attention generated by the product far outweighed the sales produced. During its five-month retailing life span (yep, that's all it had), the Pet Rock was referenced in nearly every daily newspaper in the country, most major magazines, all network national news programs, *The Tonight Show* and other late-night talk shows, most radio talk shows, and international media, such as the BBC. I was personally interviewed hundreds of times.

The Pet Rock generated multimillions of dollars of free publicity that continues to this day. More than 25 years later, I am *still* contacted by major media to comment on new novelty items. The Pet Rock has become a part of the lexicon, a permanent piece of Americana. The moral of the story: Don't doubt the influence of publicity. Use it to your advantage, and you shall prosper.

The publicity blitz I conceived to put the Pet Rock on the tip of everyone's tongue (see the nearby sidebar) was accomplished at absolutely no cost. I never spent a dime to advertise the product, and the national and international publicity was free. I must admit that I had the advantage over other inventors: I had an advertising and public relations background and knew the various steps to take to obtain free publicity. But you're in luck! I'm sharing these insights with you in this section.

Writing an effective press release

The backbone of publicity is the *press release,* which is simply a news story written by someone other than the editors and reporters of the media to whom that person submits the release for publication. It is, when written properly, a valuable tool for businesspeople, because it can generate what amounts to free advertising. And when your local paper prints your press release, it becomes an endorsement of sorts by that publication.

Writing an effective release is harder than it looks, so in the sections that follow, I walk you through each step — from choosing an appropriate topic that news media may be interested in, to organizing the information you're providing in ensure that you cover everything the media will want to know and in a format they're familiar with and can use.

You may also consider writing a simpler *fact sheet,* which is a brief description of your business, what you do, where you're located, how to contact you, and other basic information. The fact sheet isn't a news story; instead, it simply answers the who, what, where, when, how, and why of what your business does.

Choosing a newsworthy topic

Press releases have one purpose: to get you free publicity (a form of advertising) by informing the media that your company has done, or will do, something newsworthy. Here are just a few of the subjects you could use as a basis for a press release:

- A purchase of a competitor's business or a merger
- A community project your company has sponsored
- An industry award won by you or one of your employees
- The introduction of a new product or service
- A new location or the addition of a branch office
- A highly successful year or quarter
- A change in business policy, a new affiliation, or a significant new hire

The bottom line is to send news that may be of interest to a broad audience. To get the best result, however, keep in mind that your press release should describe something that can really intrigue readers. In fact, some publicists say the guiding principle for publicity should be a story where "Man Bites Dog" — in other words, an unusual or unexpected twist. (And keep in mind the opposite — if your story is "Dog Bites Man," who cares?)

Reporters and editors all have the same problem: They must fill their pages or their broadcast news airtime with interesting stories each and every day. For this reason, they welcome the receipt of a well-written, attention-grabbing press release from time to time. It helps them do their jobs. They may not print the story verbatim — instead, they may use your press release as a basis for a story they write themselves, after interviewing you for more information. But newspapers always print stories they find worthwhile. Getting good ink isn't hard, as long as your subject matter is of interest.

Don't send out a press release unless you have something important to say. Make sure the story is interesting, relevant, possibly amusing, always newsworthy, and, above all, not frivolous or boring in its content. You can make an editor very crabby with a story about the roof of your store leaking during a recent rainstorm. If, on the other hand, the roof of your store caved in but you saved dozens of shoppers from injury, you're going to get all the free publicity you can possibly handle.

ANECDOTE

What editors and reporters look for in a press release

I asked a columnist for the *San Jose Mercury News* what he looks for in a press release — why he prints one story and discards another. His response was succinct: "What's a good press release? Brief, to the point, and promising information no one else has." He then said, "If I were to offer one suggestion to people sending out press releases, it would be to first read the publication the release is going to and to read the writings of the editor or reporter to whom the release is being sent. That, more than anything else, will increase your chances of being published."

Remember: Sending out a press release isn't a guarantee that you'll ever see it in print. You may think your story is newsworthy, but the editor may not. Editors only print news that can interest their readers. And they know what their readers want. Your story could also be killed because you had the unfortunate timing of sending it in just when a major news story erupted. Because space (whether print or broadcast) is finite, your story could get bumped in favor of more important news. Sometimes, it's the luck of the draw.

Organizing the information in your press release

When you have something interesting to say and you want to submit a press release, you need to write the release in the form that editors and reporters are used to seeing. The standard press release format is a fairly structured one, written in the *journalistic style* (a narrative style in which the most important facts come first) and contain the five *W*s: who, what, when, where, and why. The reader of a press release should be able to grasp all the necessary facts after reading only the first paragraph.

Your release should include the following information, in this order:

- ✔ The sending company's name, address, phone number, fax number, e-mail address, and contact person (that's you).

- ✔ The date of submission and the instructions as to when the story is to be released to the public — usually "For immediate release."

- ✔ The words "Press Release" — this way the editors know what this story is.

- ✔ A headline: a straightforward, one-line summary of the story. Although some people feel that including a headline on a press release is an insult to the editor of the publication (who may want to write his own headline), I usually add a headline anyway to attract the editor's attention and to make the story easily understood.

- ✔ An introductory paragraph: a slightly more-detailed summary of the story.

✔ The bulk of the story containing straightforward, pertinent information, written with the copious use of quotes. Using quotes allows you to impart information that then appears to have been gleaned by a reporter from an actual interview of the person "speaking."

✔ Fluff: information of some interest, but not directly relevant to the story.

✔ A photo, drawing, chart, or other graphic element directly related to the story, along with a suggested caption written by you.

✔ The end of the story should be clearly marked with # # #.

In addition to the press release, a full media kit could include some or all of the following information:

✔ **A Q&A simulated interview:** Providing an interview in this format would call attention to some of the key points you want to make about your business. Broadcast news media may then use this format as the basis for an actual interview with you, and print media may simply reprint it in their publications.

✔ **A detailed bio of you or other key people who founded or run your business:** This biography should be no more than one page, but that should be more than enough for you to highlight what you're most successful at or experienced in doing! It's okay to brag a little, as long as you can back it up!

✔ **Endorsements or testimonials from satisfied customers or clients:** You may have collected these over the years, if you've gotten them in writing, or you can contact some of your best customers and ask them to provide you with one now.

Make sure you have your clients' permission, though, to include these comments in your press materials — you don't want to surprise anyone who wouldn't expect to see his name in print or on the air!

✔ **Articles previously published by or about you in other publications:** If you or your business have already been profiled in some magazine or newspaper, include copies of those. Ideally, they should be glossy reproductions of the actual article, with the publication's masthead. If you don't have that, though, a simple black-and-white photocopy is fine, but try not to use printouts from the Web: They don't have the same note of authenticity — even though they're real — as a reprint does.

Getting the story to the right media

You can either deliver, mail, or e-mail your press release directly to your local publication. Or if you're eager to get the story published by multiple publications or broadcasters (if the story has national implications, for instance), you can use a professional service such as the Business Wire.

Business Wire (www.businesswire.com) is a service that electronically disseminates your story and photos to a wide variety of national and international media. You choose the list of recipients (specific editors for magazines, radio or television stations, daily newspapers, or all the above), and you pay for the service based on the scope of your media choices. You may also send your press release to PRWeb online (www.prweb.com), where many people post press releases these days.

You may also consider hiring your own PR firm or freelance publicist, if you decide that doing it yourself is too much for you to take on, in addition to all the other aspects of running your business. By doing a little research, you can find professional help that matches up with your business's publicity and financial needs.

The worst thing you can do with your press release is send it to a post office box or general street address or to the editor-in-chief. Your release will get lost in a huge pile of daily mail received by the publication, and it may never reach the proper editor or reporter. Unfortunately, the right person for the right story varies at each publication or broadcast station. It could be the news director, news editor, city editor, executive editor, or senior editor.

Take the time to call or write the publications and ask who should be addressed for a particular story. Get a name, title, and routing address for this person. Your release has a much better chance of seeing print if you invest this small amount of effort.

The secret to getting a reporter's attention for your story is salesmanship. You must pursue your target market, in this case the media, with a nicely packaged product (meaning a well-written story or provocative story outline). And your product must be something that the reporter needs or desires, meaning a story about a subject he covers that can be resold to the editor or producer. Like all sales efforts, you need to sell reporters on you, on your product, on your story, and on why they and their audience should care. Tell them how your story adds to any particular point of public discussion or marketplace need. The sell must be timely or must be cultivated over time (serving that reporter as a source of tips and information). The reporter must trust you and be interested in what you have to say.

Unless you see the story as having very broad implications and want to get as much news coverage as possible, limit the number of publications you send it to. If the information is highly technical and specific to your own trade, send it to journals and trade publications within your industry. If the release is more general (you're introducing a new product or you're involved in a community project, for example), send it to your trade journals, plus all area newspapers, magazines, broadcast stations, and publications.

Dealing with the news media

When you have a story, keep it simple, clear, brief, and to the point. Here are some tips for dealing with the news media:

✔ **Target media representatives covering your area of business.** Send notes complimenting them about stories they do. Call or write and let them know that you could be a good resource on specific topics. Alert them to things you may know about.

✔ **Provide good photography whenever possible.** Use the photography to help tell your story.

✔ **Develop a point of view.** To the extent possible, make your perspective colorful, entertaining, provocative, confident, and visionary.

Remember: If you know how to work with the news media effectively, you can get all kinds of free publicity for your business — and publicity is a great form of advertising.

Editors receive piles of press releases each week. They are all read and considered, but they are not all published. Every publication has its own ideas as to what constitutes news. Some releases may result in a phone call, an interview, and a full write-up; others may get only a line or two of copy. If you've sent along a photo, you may see the story but no picture, or vice versa. Or, sadly, none of the above may happen. Don't be too discouraged if your story never gets ink. Try again with another story at some future date.

If you don't see your story printed within a reasonable amount of time, you can call the editor to whom you sent the story to innocently ask whether she received it. Keep in mind, though, that your release probably arrived as part of a huge pile of mail, so don't get all bent out of shape because the editor doesn't know what you're talking about. Calling alerts the editor that your story is somewhere on her desk and will likely get her to at least look at it. Remember to be respectful, not confrontational. Don't nag or pester or stalk the media, but it's okay to follow up politely.

If a reporter does cover your business in response to your press release, be sure to follow up promptly with a thank-you note! Reporters depend on experts in a variety of businesses, and if they know they can count on you for useful information, that you're professional and easy to talk to, and that you'll get back to them quickly when they need information, they'll add you to their calling list, and you become one of their go-to sources — and you'll start to see your name in print or on air more often!

Advertising on Specialty Items

Despite all the critical things consumers often say about advertising, they're increasingly willing to be walking billboards for various brands as they don all sorts of promotional wearables and display everything from logo-covered coffee mugs to candy jars on their desks. In the world of advertising, these free gifts are called *specialty advertising* (which is stuff on which you print your company logo and slogan) and *premium items* (which are bonus gifts intended to entice you to buy the regularly priced item in order to get the "free" gift that comes with it, such as the toys and goodies your kids get when you buy a kid's meal at a fast-food emporium). Specialty advertising is often the only advertising many small businesses do.

For better or worse, specialty advertising items are everywhere. Here are just a few of the many specialty advertising and premium items you're probably very familiar with: baseball caps, t-shirts, golfing jackets, sweatshirts, umbrellas, letter openers, stadium blankets, bumper stickers, calculators, calendars, and coffee mugs, to name a few. Figure 18-1 shows examples of the various types of "freebies" often made available to customers. All of these items are adorned with company logos, graciously received, and passed along by us to friends, clients, or office neighbors who don't mind parading around wearing or displaying advertising.

In the following sections, I tell you why these items are good ways to advertise your business, how to select the right item for your business, and how best to include information about your business on a specialty item.

Figure 18-1: Examples of promotional and giveaway items. The company logo is prominently displayed on each item.

Recognizing the advantages of specialty advertising

If you plan carefully and select a truly useful specialty advertising item to include in a promotion, an item with intrinsic or decorative value that your customers are glad to receive and certain to use, this form of advertising is worth including in your overall campaign. In the following sections, I cover a few good reasons to add *quality* premiums to your media mix.

Specialty items are relatively inexpensive

If you're advertising on a budget, then specialty advertising items may be just the thing to get your name before the buying public. For the most part, specialty items can be very affordable. For example, you can print your logo onto a fairly good ballpoint pen for 50 cents apiece. A plastic clip that reseals opened potato chip bags, a rubber circle that helps open jars, a razor-blade letter opener — people may use all of these items every day, and none of them costs more than a dollar a piece. If you print your logo on them and give them out, the recipients will be continually reminded of your business.

You can pay thousands of dollars for a television package and hope that a few of your spots run in good viewing times — and that viewers are watching, instead of getting a snack when your spots run. But for just a few bucks apiece (or less), you can get a whole pile of specialty items printed with your logo, ready to advertise your company on a long-term basis (provided that you select an item people actually want).

A radio station once gave me a really nifty pocket calculator that folds away and takes up no room at all on my desk. I use this item each and every day. And when I touch the little button that unfolds it, I can't help but see the station's logo, and I am reminded of who gave it to me. This specialty advertising item — an item I actually use on a daily basis — has a purpose. You want to be sure to find a premium that people can enjoy and use for years to come — otherwise, you're just wasting your money.

Specialty items are stand-alone ads

Specialty advertising products are one of the few advertising vehicles that can stand alone. Most other types of advertising need to be supported with more advertising. For instance, you need to buy advertising on mass media in order to direct people to your Web site. But a promotional item, whether mailed to your customer list or handed out at your place of business, is pretty much self-sufficient in getting your advertising message across to your customers.

You can imprint anything

In addition to t-shirts, coffee mugs, and key chains, you can find companies that can laser-etch your logo onto the shells of live lobsters so you can send them to clients you *really* want to impress. You can have your logo engraved onto solid-gold putters for golfers you desperately want to do business with. A bakery in my area will inkjet (using edible inks) your logo, four-color photo, or whatever onto delicious cakes, which they will then deliver to your clients. And I used a local microbrewery to make a batch of beer with my own private label, packed the bottles in wooden cases that were laser-etched with my logo, and sent the brews to clients as holiday gifts. It was a big hit.

If you can look beyond the obvious promotional items, the ones everyone sends out, then you can truly make an impression.

Multiple impressions are a good thing

When I measure the effectiveness of radio or television buys, I do so in terms of *gross impressions* (the number of audience members delivered by a media schedule without regard to duplication) and *cost per thousand* (the cost per 1,000 people or households delivered by a media schedule). With specialty items, using these methods of measurement is impossible, because specialty items — at least the ones that are useful and have actual value to the recipient — have the advantage of scoring repeated impressions without repeated costs. You buy it once, and it sits on a customer's desk forever.

One Christmas, a radio station sent me beautiful note cards and envelopes with my name richly embossed on top-quality paper. Every time I send a note, I'm reminded of that station — which had the good taste to send me something I'm proud to use. Multiple impressions are a *very* good thing!

Premiums reinforce your other media efforts

Burger King, McDonald's, and other fast-food giants use premiums to reinforce their mass media efforts, so why shouldn't you? When Burger King gives away an item tied to a movie promotion (like *Open Season*, the animated film comedy where Boog the bear moves from his home in a suburban garage to the real world of the forest), it calls attention to its giveaway items in its TV and radio advertising, saying something like, "Eight toys for the taking: one toy in every kids meal while supplies last." Likewise, the premium items themselves call attention to BK's broadcast efforts — in this case, the toys were plastic replicas of characters in the movie: a spinning Boog the Bear, a bucking Elliot the deer, a hopping McSquizzy the squirrel, or a chopping Reilly the beaver. Every form of media reinforces every other form of media, thereby making the entire promotion just that much more effective.

If you're giving away a premium or a specialty item with your logo affixed, by all means tell people about it in your other advertising: "Come in today, browse our new selection of fine kitchen cabinets, and be sure to ask for your very own laser-etched lobster." This cross-referencing will go a long way in stretching your advertising dollars.

Premiums are user-friendly

Advertising, by its very nature, is designed to be intrusive. If it weren't intrusive, how would anyone notice it? Specialty advertising items, on the other hand, aren't so intrusive that they irritate people — especially items with a purpose. People actually want and appreciate advertising specialties that have utilitarian, intrinsic, or decorative value. What they *don't* want are commercials interrupting their favorite TV shows.

Selecting specialty items with a purpose

Coffee mugs, key chains, baseball caps, and t-shirts are the mainstays of specialty advertising, but literally thousands of items are out there, onto which your logo or ad slogan can be printed or etched. The trick is to select an item that has real appeal to the consumer; something unusual and interesting; something that will be gratefully accepted and actually used.

In general, it's a good idea to select specialty items that have relevance to your product, service, or business and your target audience. For example, a yardstick or tape measure is relevant to a lumberyard; an accountant may give clients a calculator just as a restaurant may give coffee mugs. I know of an auto service shop that gives each regular customer an air pressure gauge, which not only keeps the shop's name in the car owner's glove box but also sends a clear message that this shop wants to help its customers take care of their cars.

Also, one trend in specialty items is to give gifts that aren't imprinted or are discreetly imprinted. Clients are more likely to use a gift that doesn't advertise your name, and they will still be likely to remember who gave it to them.

Finally, consider gift-wrapping your items. For example, if you're giving out a pen, invest in a nice one (around $4.00), and go the extra step of buying the twenty-five-cent box. Clients greatly overestimate the value of something as simple as a pen: They appreciate it because it's useful. Similarly, pulling an ordinary golf shirt out of a big carton isn't nearly as impressive, exciting, or appreciated as receiving a gift-wrapped box with a shirt that ideally has your name embroidered on it and is the correct size. Bottom line: Going the extra mile can pay off.

Twenty years ago I received a candy jar with a wooden lid on which a radio station's call letters were etched. It's a tasteful item (in more ways than one), and it still sits, two decades later, on the coffee table in my office, continually filled with a fresh supply of M&M's. The candy jar was a specialty item with a purpose. Over the years, I have tossed out hundreds of caps, t-shirts, and bumper stickers, but I still keep the candy jar.

More than 250,000 premium items and specialty advertising items are on the market today, just waiting for your logo. Look for something that you would be proud to give away and your customers would be happy to receive. In just a quick glance around my office, I see specialty items of every size and shape. Here are my favorites:

- ✔ A very utilitarian folding calculator
- ✔ A candy jar
- ✔ Embossed personal stationery and note cards
- ✔ A desktop business card holder
- ✔ A clever, razor-blade letter opener

I use these items many times throughout the day. All the other stuff — mugs, golfing jackets, baseball caps, magnetic vinyl bumper stickers, key chains, ball-point pens, and other things — are still lying around the office only because no one has bothered to throw them out. The neat stuff gets used. The not-so-neat stuff just takes up space — and wastes your valuable advertising dollars.

If you thoughtfully select your specialty advertising items, you can measure their effectiveness in terms of frequency just as you would a radio or TV commercial. Why? Because if the item is used daily, perhaps multiple times every day, then each time the item is used you have made another impression with the same advertising message. That principle is called *frequency*.

However, to attain frequency, you must first select an item that has either a utilitarian or a decorative value and can, therefore, be used or displayed by the recipient. You're not going to get a lot of mileage out of some cheapo t-shirt that's relegated to the bottom of a dresser drawer (especially if it's a one-size-fits-all — it usually doesn't). But you can win friends and influence people with a gift item that solves a problem or fills a need. When my barber gave me a logo-imprinted rubber pad that aids in opening sticky jar lids, I thought he was nuts and had wasted his money. But that was only until I used it once and found out that this goofy item actually works! Hard-to-open jars are no longer a problem (especially important for a guy who loves pickles). It turned out to be a specialty item with legs — its effectiveness is, therefore, measurable on a frequency basis.

If you want to get an overview of the incredible array of specialty advertising items that are available, as well as some great promotional ideas and insights, visit the Advertising Specialty Institute Web site at www.promomart.com. You can also check your local Yellow Pages to find specialty advertising sales-people in your area.

Some specialty advertising items can be quite effective. However, choose your items as though you were picking out something for yourself. Ask yourself: "Would I actually use this thing? Would I be grateful to receive it?" If you answer *yes,* incorporate it into your overall advertising scheme.

Keep the copy simple on a specialty item

Keep in mind that a promotional product isn't an information source — it's an advertisement. Its job is to capture people's attention and help them remember you. If the product does its job, you often have no need to include additional information. The phone call or e-mail you'll likely receive provides that opportunity. Keep your copy brief and to the point, toss in some selling points or a slogan, and let it go at that. Don't try to include everything you do or a list of your entire store inventory. Stick to the main selling proposition. A logo, phone number, Web site address, and perhaps your company slogan are more than enough information to include on a specialty advertising item. For more information on how to write simple, effective copy, check out Chapter 5. In general, when you're delivering your message, just remember to KISS: Keep it simple, stupid!

Generating Traffic: Promotional Events

Sometimes, getting the world to beat a path to your door requires that you offer a little bribery — an incentive to get the world to even *consider* your door, let alone beat a path to it. *Promotions* are events designed to generate traffic, to get lots of people together in one place at one time in order to do a sales job on them. Promotions and events are a good way to call attention to yourself, your business, your current sale, your new inventory, or your expanded showrooms. They're also a great way to meet prospective customers face to face. But these advertising forms can add to your bottom line only if you're careful about what you participate in and objective as to whether the promotion or event is truly relevant to your business.

T-shirt hysteria

It never ceases to amaze me what people endure in order to get a free t-shirt. *The San Jose Mercury News,* my area's major daily newspaper, sponsors a charity-based 10K race promotion each year and gets 10,000 runners, walkers, strollers, saunterers, and staggerers — many of whom are only there to get the free t-shirt (which isn't really free because there is a $10 entry fee). The radio and TV stations in the Bay Area trot out a nearly infinite variety of promotions each year to attract new listeners and viewers for the stations and new customers for the advertisers, who are willing to pony up extra dollars to buy space at the event and the advertising to tell people about it. What do the folks who attend these promotions receive for their trouble? Yep, you guessed it. Free t-shirts — oh, maybe water bottles, almost certainly CDs specific to that station's formatting, and perhaps a flimsy painter's cap with a cheesy logo, but always a t-shirt!

Radio stations are famous for devising promotions to create value-added benefits for their advertisers and for selling sponsorships designed solely to get more income from their advertisers. Some are good, and some are simply awful. So what makes a good promotion, how do you know it's good, and should you participate? Should you do your own promotion, and will it actually bring customers through your door? I explore these questions and others in this section while trying to steer you into well-conceived promotions and events that stand a good chance of succeeding.

Radio: The promotions king

When you buy your radio advertising, you have two kinds of promotions that you can tie in with your radio buy: Station promos and sales-drive promos. In the following sections, I explain what these promos are and show you how to use them to your business's advantage.

Getting your goods out: Station promos

A *station promotion* is one invented by the station and is often produced on a regular basis. The station then solicits advertisers to provide goods and services to fold into the promotion.

For example, one of the radio stations in my area has a promotion called "The Coffee Break." This promotion is designed to encourage people to listen to the station while they're at work. Regular listeners are asked to fax to the radio station their names, the names of their companies, the number of employees, and so on. Then this information is put into a hopper and drawn at random each day or week. The winning company gets a visit from members of the station's promotions department and members of the on-air staff, who bring along gourmet coffee provided by a coffee shop that advertises on the station, donuts or bagels provided by a bakery that advertises on the station, flower arrangements contributed by a florist that advertises on the station, and so forth. In return, each of the station advertisers who donate goods to the coffee break (the coffee shop, the bakery, and the florist) get multiple free mentions throughout their paid broadcast schedules.

If you're an advertiser and have something radio stations need to produce a station promotion, chances are they'll come to you. In case they don't, a good time to get involved is when you buy your media schedule. Ask the sales rep what promotions are available to you as *value-added advertising* (extra stuff, generally free) to help boost your paid media buy. You can't find a radio station in the known universe that doesn't produce a multitude of promotions on a regular basis, and what you're selling can probably fit nicely into at least one of them. If you don't have a food or beverage operation, not to worry. The stations also need a variety of goods and services to use as prizes.

Radio station remotes: They still work

Many station promotions are tied to *live remotes,* which bring on-air personalities (disc jockeys) to your location. In addition to broadcasting their shows from the remote location, the DJs bring along all kinds of logo-emblazoned specialty items — t-shirts, bumper stickers, coffee mugs, movie tickets — to give away to the lucky people who show up for these events.

These live-remote promotions are usually offered to advertisers as part of their media buy. They're called *value-added,* and they're usually free. Because you're going to have to do a lot of advertising anyway to get people to your location, why not throw a remote into the mix and give listeners an added reason to visit your store? The only additional out-of-pocket expense is a modest talent fee for the on-air personality, which makes these promos an inexpensive way to stretch an ad budget and to

publicize a new location, new inventory, new restaurant, the latest model cars, or anything else you can think of. In addition to the 60-second spots you buy, you also receive a multitude of 10-second promotional announcements inviting listeners to your store on such and such a date where they can meet, live and in person, that wacky morning guy.

The beauty of a live remote is that you, the advertiser, don't have to do anything to make it happen (other than make some merchandise available as giveaways). The station does all the work. Your broadcast commercials will, of course, talk about what you're trying to sell during the promotion, but the 10-second announcements that the station throws into the pot drive the traffic to your store on the appointed day and time. And employees of the station's promotions department are there to make sure everything runs smoothly.

Getting the exclusive: Sales-driven promos

Sales-driven promotions are advertiser-specific — they're invented for the advertiser and are exclusive to that advertiser. Sales-driven promos are always sold in conjunction with a media buy. A surprising number of large-budget radio advertisers won't even buy a station unless the station develops and includes an exclusive promotion at no extra charge.

So how does a sales-driven promo work? Imagine that you own a kitchen store, and you want to build a promotion around a celebrity chef doing demonstration cooking in your store. You can simply give this information to the station sales rep, who conferences with his promotions department and comes back with multiple ideas. Your rep may ask you to provide some merchandise for prizes, make your store or business available on a certain day, contract for a noncancelable media buy, and pay a modest talent fee to any on-air personalities who may show up. The station may have on-air call-in contests in which its listeners can win a cookbook autographed by your featured chef, or dinner and wine for two at the chef's restaurant. And for your store, it puts forward everything from rolling-pin tossing to pancake races to pie-eating contests.

In addition to your paid media schedule, you get a large number of on-air mentions (10- or 15-second announcements specific to your promotion) for a couple weeks leading up to the event, and, hopefully, a bunch of traffic to your business at the appointed date and time. Your problem is to sift through all their suggestions to find the ones you can live with. Radio station promotions directors really get into this stuff — they're your best source for ideas.

Not every station promotion brings in hundreds of new customers, so don't set your expectations too high. One of my clients seems satisfied if a promotion brings out a few dozen new faces. **_Remember:_** The promotion needs to be relevant and interesting to the station's listeners. In other words, don't do a promotion for an antique furniture store on a station with a teenage audience. If a promotion fails miserably, you may tend to blame the station, not the fact that what you're selling isn't compatible with its listener's tastes — but there's more to it than that. If a promotion fails, you may want to reconsider your media buy on that particular station, because if its listeners won't even come out to your location for free stuff, how can you expect them to respond positively to the selling message in your 60-second spots?

A promotion so successful, it saved the business

I was once given a make-or-break advertising budget by an underperforming local micro-brewery and restaurant whose owners had decided to take one more shot at success before closing their doors forever. Accepting the challenge was both daunting and invigorating. The target market was young adults, and the brewery/restaurant had been wasting a lot of advertising dollars in newspapers, an advertising vehicle not famously efficient in reaching yuppies. I chose to spend every last dime of their budget on an all-or-nothing radio blitz, selecting stations that had good ratings in the adults 18 to 34 demographic.

One radio station came back to me with a "Beer and Burger" lunchtime promotion. The idea was that customers could come in on a certain day and have a great lunch (a giant cheeseburger, fries, and a brewsky) for just five bucks. The promotion was, of course, tied to a station live remote, which would feature its "morning man" and his sidekick — two guys who were very well known in the market — broadcasting live

from the brewpub. The promo would also feature the ubiquitous station specialty advertising items for the people who came and a drawing for a $500 bar and restaurant credit. The cost of the advertising schedule covered everything.

The big day came, the doors opened at 11:00 a.m., and we had to step quickly back to avoid getting trampled. It was a restaurant owner's dream come true. Hundreds of station listeners stampeded through the door until it was standing room only and a two-hour wait for $5 worth of burgers and beer. The promotion had everything going for it — discounted food, free prizes, cheap beer, a famous disc jockey, and a great place in which to eat and drink. The restaurant was "discovered" by hundreds of new customers (many of whom stayed all that day to sip more beers and became long-time regular customers), was able to remain open, eventually prospered, and, when it was back on its feet, fired me because it no longer needed my services! Go figure.

Other promotional opportunities

Radio station promotions aren't the only way you can go. You can come up with your own unique promotion as well. Many other media forms lend themselves to successful promos. Here are just a few promotional ideas:

- ✔ **In-store counter displays:** You can have your customers register to win a contest by having a drawing. Or set up a buy-one-get-one-free offer.

- ✔ **Direct mail:** Send your customers coupons as a way to get them into your store. Or mail them a card that they return to register to win a contest. Send out open-house invitations to get them into the store. (See Chapter 10 for more on direct mail.)

- ✔ **Newspaper:** As part of your newspaper ad, you can provide coupons as promotions to get people into your store. You can tell readers to present the ad for half off their purchase or offer coloring contests for kids, which is sure to get their parents into your store.

- ✔ **Printed flyers:** You can have flyers printed, and then place them on parked cars, telling people to bring the flyer in for a discount or advertising a one-day-only sale or a parking-lot sale. Chapter 10 gives you details on how to do this effectively.

- ✔ **Statement stuffers:** When you send out your monthly statement to your customers, you can put an ad in with the statement, offering loyal customer discounts, coupons, or buy-two-get-one-free offers.

When you're trying to decide which kind of promotional materials to use, think about items of which you've been on the receiving end. Have you ever received a promotional piece that not only caught your attention, but compelled you to respond? What was it about that piece that cut through all the advertising clutter and struck a nerve? Was it the design, the offer, an impossible-to-ignore deal, a clever attachment, or a promise of something free? Chances are, if something works well in grabbing *your* attention, it can grab your customers' attention as well. Promotional ideas are limited only by your own imagination. I'm sure you can come up with some great ones.

Participating in Sponsored Events

Sponsored events — events that are devised and produced with commercialism and financial gain foremost in mind — are available in many forms. A few examples of sponsored events include the following:

- ✔ **Tech fairs:** Recruiting fairs at which high-tech companies hope to meet future employees.

- ✔ **Home-improvement fairs:** Here, homeowners can find the very latest decorating ideas for their houses.

✔ **Campus fairs:** Colleges and universities use these fairs to show off their erudite wares to prospective students.

✔ **Trade shows:** A trade show is usually an annual event for a particular industry to show off new products to its customers. An infinite variety of trade shows are just waiting for your business's participation.

✔ **And many more:** You can find a plethora of chili cook-offs, jazz festivals, bluegrass festivals, arts and crafts fairs — you name it, it's out there.

The types of events you participate in are plentiful, but your involvement is what counts. You can participate in a sponsored event in two ways:

✔ **Sponsor an event.** You have a myriad of ways to sponsor an event — from contributing financially to an established event in your area to organizing an event on your own (and many in between). Sponsoring an event is a great way for you to get your business's name mentioned in various ad mediums and to boost your business's reputation.

If you're interested in being involved in an event at this level (and because I can't cover all the splendid details in one tiny section of this book), I suggest that you check out *Meeting & Event Planning For Dummies* by Susan Friedmann (Wiley).

✔ **Set up a booth.** You can pay for and provide staff for an on-site booth at the event and hope that all the expense and work involved result in some added exposure and new business.

While both of these options are worth considering, I focus on the second — setting up a booth — because you can transfer the information you find in the following sections to any type of event. So keep reading to determine whether this advertising method is right for your business and how you can pull it off.

Determining whether you can staff the event

Whether you can participate may come down to logistics — do you have (and can you spare) the manpower? Ask yourself the following questions before committing yourself or your staff to an event:

✔ Can you take time away from your business to staff your own booth, particularly if the event runs multiple days?

✔ Do you have trustworthy employees who can represent you at the event if you can't be there yourself?

✔ Do you have access to and help from enough employees to staff the booth?

If your answer to all these questions is *no,* you probably know that setting up a booth isn't the right option, at least right now.

You may also want to consider whether you can get volunteers (family members, employees who are willing to work without pay) or hire temps so you can have a presence at the event. While hiring extra help does cost you more initially, it can pay off if your business gets the exposure it needs.

Calculating the costs: A valuable investment?

When you participate in a trade show or street fair event, you pay for exhibitor space, and this varies widely depending on the venue, the duration of the event, and the city it's in. This booth (probably ten feet square) is made up of a metal frame holding flimsy cloth panels on three sides to create the illusion of privacy. You get nothing else for your money — no tables, chairs, banners, signs, display backgrounds, nothing. So on the day before the show opens, you have to arrange for all these important items to be delivered to the location and set them up yourself, or you can bring your own from home, but that's a pain in the neck.

The event sponsors can steer you to their prearranged source for the furniture and accoutrements you need. Don't be leery of asking for guidance.

You may also want a sign company to create a display banner and other signage for your space. And what about your giveaways? (You have to have some tchotchkes at these things.) All these extras cost you extra dough. So, before plunking down your hard-earned money for a booth, consider all the costs.

Deciding which events are worthwhile

When deciding whether to participate in a sponsored event, you need to ask yourself: "What's in it for me? Will I really get added exposure to qualified customers?" Be objective. Do a bunch of people looking for a bowl of free chili and a paper cup of beer fit the demographic profiles of your customers? If not, then regardless of the number of people the event promoters guarantee will attend, you want to avoid the Red Hot Chili Cook-Off.

But what if you're in the large appliance business and the big Home Improvement and Remodeling Expo is coming to town? I'd say, jump on it. Pay for the booth, haul your sample refrigerators and ranges to the convention center, and get it on. Choosing to participate in an event is all a matter of relevance.

Finding sponsored events that work for your business

So how do you find out about these industry events? Because you own a business, you should be on the mailing lists of the Chamber of Commerce, the local convention center, arenas, stadiums, or any other source of information as to what events are coming to your town. If you aren't being kept up to date on upcoming events and shows either by mail or through your manufacturer's reps, then find a way to do so. You can't participate if you don't know what's happening, and by the time you read about an event in a newspaper ad or hear about it on the radio, it's probably too late to get space.

If all you want is the booth space to demonstrate your wares, go directly to the event promoter. If you want to pre-announce that you'll be there and you can afford the added expense, or you were going to buy advertising anyway, buy the station's package deal. Pre-show advertising is an important consideration and is well worth the extra money.

For example, you're the owner of a plant nursery and want to participate in the gigantic, bombastic Annual Flower and Garden Show coming to an arena near you. The event promoters are more than happy to sell you booth space for, say, $1,500 for the three-day show. But what you're getting from the promoters is the booth to exhibit your stuff in — that's it. Believe it or not, you can also buy the same booth from your local radio station for $5,000. What you receive from the radio station is the booth, dozens of 10- to 15-second on-air mentions, a *run-of-station spot package* (a group of commercials scheduled throughout the day and night at the sole discretion of the station), and a link to the station's Web site.

You can use the 60-second spots to tell listeners what you're selling and why they should visit your booth. The promotional announcements that mention your store name for two or three weeks leading up to the show aren't going to hurt you a bit. And linking your Web site to theirs just may generate a few extra hits. The station has made an arrangement to sell sponsorships (and additional exhibitor space) in exchange for a large media buy from the promoters of the event. Out of your $5,000 package deal, the station still has to pay the promoters the $1,500 for your booth, but it keeps the additional advertising revenue for itself.

Dishing out a little extra money to your local radio station for pre-advertising an event can pay you back in droves. Let your customers (and potential customers) know where you're going to be, when you'll be there, and why they should visit your booth.

Part V
The Part of Tens

The 5th Wave   By Rich Tennant

"There you go Mr. Mellman. As agreed, every bird I sell over the next 12 months will be trained to say, 'Hello,' 'Pretty bird,' and 'Mellman's Carpet World.' Some of the birds have trouble with the word 'carpet.' It comes out 'crapet.' That gonna be a problem?"

In this part . . .

*I*t is a tradition in all *For Dummies* books to include the Part of Tens. You may not choose to read every page of this book, but I strongly urge you to read through the following two chapters. Here you find tips for writing effectively for all media. I also help you decide whether your business could use the services of an advertising agency. Plenty of valuable advice in just a few short pages — you can't find more bang for your buck anywhere.

Chapter 19

Ten Secrets for Writing Memorable Advertising

In This Chapter

▶ Making your creative hook work for you

▶ Keeping your message simple, clear, and effective

▶ Bearing in mind your budget

*W*hen you're creating ads, your primary goal is to come up with something that sticks in the minds of your target audience. In this chapter, I offer up ten great tips for doing exactly that.

Ignoring the Rules of Grammar

Advertising legend David Ogilvy admitted that he didn't know the rules of grammar. In spite of this revelation, he was, unquestionably, one of the greatest advertising copywriters ever to have strolled down Madison Avenue. He said, "If you're trying to persuade people to do something, or buy something, it seems to me you should use their language, the language they use every day, the language in which they think. I try to write in the vernacular." This is wonderful advice from the master — advice that I've always tried to remember when writing ads for my clients, and advice that can work equally well for you when you crank up your own creative machine and begin to write ads for yourself.

You can ignore the rules of grammar at times — even write incomplete sentences — and do whatever it takes to create a hard-hitting sales message. In radio, you have only 60 seconds; in TV, you have just 30 — and, increasingly, even less time! And in print or outdoor ads, you want your message to be quickly understood and acted on. Those requirements don't always lend themselves to correct sentence structure. In short: Write the way people think.

Nike knew what it was doing when it coined the slogan "Just do it." Grammatically, this phrase makes no sense. Your high-school English teacher would scold the copywriter for not being clear about the antecedent for "it." (That's grammar-speak for "what does 'it' refer to?" or, more likely, "to what does 'it' refer"?) But forget those teachers (don't worry — I won't tell!); Nike's slogan was great and memorable because it reflected the way people really talk.

Though ignoring grammatical rules can be effective in advertising, don't go overboard. Depending on how you phrase something, or depending on the products or services you're selling, it's all too easy for a grammatically incorrect ad to make you look like an idiot rather than clever. If you're advertising a used bookstore, for example, you definitely want to use good grammar in your advertising!

Making Your Ads Effective

Whether your advertising budget is a million a month or a thousand, you're wasting your money if your ads aren't effective. And what makes ads effective is a combination of content and creativity. Your ads must do the following:

✔ Give the consumer a good reason to act (content).

✔ Be unique enough in design and copy to attract the consumer's attention in the first place (creativity).

Consumers are exposed to so much advertising on a daily basis — some of it so subtle, they don't even know they're absorbing it — that you need to make sure your ads cut through all that clutter. For more on how to do just that, go to Chapter 5.

Knowing Why People Buy Your Products

Most retail businesses (and many manufacturers and other small businesses) don't know why people buy their products. They just know that people *do* buy their products, so they're somehow satisfied with their less than in-depth marketing knowledge. Before you begin the creative process of finding your inimitable message, ask yourself a few simple questions:

✔ What are you selling, and what makes it so unique?

✔ To whom do you want to sell it?

✔ Why should people buy it from you as opposed to your competition?

Some companies come right out and say in their advertising who they're targeting — witness Volkswagen's slogan for "Drivers wanted." But you don't have to create the next big advertising slogan to attract people to your store or business. You just have to use a bit more creativity than the other guys in devising a compelling message so people choose your business over your competition's. (To dig a little deeper on this topic, turn to Chapter 4.)

Finding a Creative Hook

Because you want your ads to stand head and shoulders above the crowded universe of advertising, you need to work hard at finding a *creative hook* — something that grabs potential customers (but not necessarily by the neck) and drags them to buy your products or services. A creative hook is an emotional trigger that attracts the buyer, something that appeals to the self-image of the buyer, an affirmation that you provide what the buyer is looking for. It may be a slogan, a phrase, a jingle, a single line of copy, or a unique look that appears in all your ads. But whatever it is, your creative hook must be yours and yours alone, because you use it, across all media, to differentiate your business from all the others.

Take a moment to glean from this example: DeBeers is the most well-known diamond dealer to most people, and it continually updates its advertising. It has been wildly successful in developing creative hooks for its ad campaigns. Check out the following DeBeers slogans and how the company adjusted its message to its target audience:

- ✔ **"A diamond is forever."** DeBeers created this now-famous slogan to ensure that people wouldn't sell their diamonds, which would create a secondary market.

- ✔ **"Tell her you'd marry her all over again."** To expand its market beyond just engagement rings, DeBeers targeted a new market of the husbands of older, married women, with the "eternity ring" for anniversaries and a creative ad campaign that pitched this slogan.

- ✔ **"Your left hand says you're taken. Your right hand says you can take over. Your left hand celebrates the day you were married. Your right hand celebrates the day you were born. Women of the world, raise your right hand."** To appeal to women directly, either single or married women who want to buy a ring for themselves, DeBeers crafted the creative hook of "the right-hand ring."

All of DeBeers's campaigns have strong creative hooks. They focus on the emotional trigger of buying a diamond and appeal to the self-image of the buyer — whether it's a man trying to impress his future wife with the size of the diamond in the engagement ring he's offering or whether it's a "right-hand ring" symbol of self-worth that a woman buys herself. The creative hook can mean the difference between a first-place ad and a dud that nobody notices.

Remembering That Creativity Is Hard Work

Advertising agencies, when designing new ad campaigns (or redesigning old ones) often hold what is called a *creative session* — a meeting where all the people who are working on a particular account gather together to come up with ideas. Owners, creative directors, copywriters, artists, and even the account service people contribute. These ideas then beget more and more ideas, which, eventually, result in the perfect creative answer to the problem at hand. The only rule of these meetings is that no idea is laughed at or discarded out of hand. No idea is too far-fetched or too stupid. Everything gets tossed onto the table.

Even if you're not a part of an agency, you can hold these kinds of brainstorming sessions with your coworkers, your partners, your family, and your friends to come up with ideas for your business's advertising campaign.

Ideas don't just jump up and bite you. You need to search for them very diligently.

Letting Your Creative Hook Dictate Your Media Buy

When your great new idea hits you right between the eyes, when the light bulb of creativity suddenly shines brightly, it's time to begin incorporating this message into a full-blown ad campaign — or, at least, as full-blown an ad campaign as you can afford. Assuming you've identified all the reasons you truly do have a unique product or service and have put your finger on a hard-to-resist reason that people should seek you out in order to buy it, you need to find ways to make this idea fit into various forms of advertising.

Often, your creative hook dictates what media you use — your creative hook literally drives your campaign. For example:

- ✔ If your hook is visual, then you can use print, collateral, TV, or the Web.

- ✔ If your concept is audio-driven, you want to use radio.

- ✔ If your clever new idea is a catchy slogan or a headline, you can consider using any variety of media, including billboards or other outdoor signage; you can also use online here.

For the ins and outs of these ad mediums, check out Parts II and IV in this book.

Considering Your Budget

Before you get carried away with all the great things you want to do in your ad campaign, you need to think about your budget. You can't buy a 50-pound ad campaign with a 10-pound budget. So you need to carefully pick and choose your media and adjust your message accordingly.

You don't need to buy every media in town to get your message across. You can accomplish your goals with not only a creative message, but also with a creative media buy. So, before you start writing your campaign and before you get too carried away with your creative hook, come to grips with how your message translates into various media and how much of this media you can afford. (For a more complete discussion, Chapter 2 is where you want to be.)

Striving for Continuity

Whatever your unique message turns out to be — whether it's a headline, a sentence, a slogan, a graphic, or another creative hook — use that message consistently in all forms of media. You need to apply the *same message* in all the forms of media in order to establish that message as yours and yours alone. Plus, continuity gives the consumer a better chance to remember it.

Don't say one thing in your radio advertising and another in print. Don't advertise one item in the newspaper and another on TV. Many businesses (large and small) make this mistake over and over again, and it only serves to confuse the consumer and to water down your overall advertising impact (and budget). If your radio commercials are talking about a half-price sale on a specific item, then your newspaper ads should be featuring the same price and sale terms for the same item.

Keeping It Simple

Here is the best rule you can use as you work toward creating memorable advertising for today's marketplace: KISS. That simple acronym is something to keep uppermost in your mind as you go through the process of writing and producing your ads. As you probably know, KISS stands for "Keep it simple, stupid."

Today, consumers are deluged with information at a rate unheard of in kinder, gentler times. The fact that people are even capable of absorbing a tiny percentage of the information available to them is remarkable. And into this cauldron of information, you now must inject quality advertising for your business, and hope that, at the very least, consumers notice, recall, and act on your ad. And the best way to accomplish that is to keep it simple.

Being Clear in Your Message

Whether you're writing advertising for print, radio, television, direct mail, or any of the myriad forms of media, deliver your message in clear, easy-to-understand terms. That way, consumers can see at a glance what it is you're selling and make a snap decision as to whether they want to read or listen further.

Place your most powerful selling message at the beginning of the radio or TV spot, or in the form of a headline for your printed advertising. Cut right to the chase! Don't get bogged down in details — the consumer doesn't care and won't take the time to decipher too much copy or superfluous information. Consumers need to read or hear your selling message immediately, and it must be compelling enough to get them to act. If you don't write your advertising in clear, concise terms that can be easily understood, you're wasting your money.

Chapter 20

(Almost) Ten Ways to Know It's Time to Hire an Agency

....

In This Chapter

▶ Knowing when the time is right to hire an agency

▶ Being honest with yourself about your limitations

▶ Discerning the advantages an agency brings

....

Y ou don't need a multimillion-dollar advertising budget to seek out the services of an ad agency. Many local agencies provide you with all the services offered by the major agencies, but scaled down to fit within your budget and your advertising requirements. If you're thinking about hiring an agency, take a look at the sections in this chapter. Chapter 16 gives you pointers on hiring an ad agency, but this chapter lets you know *when* you should hire one in the first place. If you see yourself in one or more of these reasons to hire an agency, give it some thought.

Advertising is an extremely important part of your overall marketing plan. Hiring a team of professionals to handle it for you is something you should think about. And, with many local ad agencies, it may not cost you as much as you think — and it may even *save* you quite a bit of time and money.

Your Ad Budget Has Become Substantial

If your advertising budget has grown to major proportions, ask yourself one question: "Am I spending my ad budget as wisely as I could be?"

Other clues that it may be time for you to make the call include the following:

- You think you aren't being as diligent as you could be in allocating your advertising funds.

- Your media selections no longer give you the amount of return that your business needs and must be expanded.

- You're ready to admit that you need the services of a team of professionals to advise you in this area.

You Need the Expertise of a Professional Media Buyer

If you need one good reason to hire an ad agency, here it is: the media buyer. If he is diligent and knowledgeable, he can stretch your media budget, regardless of its size, as tightly as it can be stretched. This person fields all phone calls from, takes all meetings with, and gently or firmly (as the case requires) says *no* to the dozens of media sales reps who want a piece of your business.

A good media buyer insists on the correct format, impressive ratings or circulation, and the right audience composition and demographic before committing your hard-earned dollars to a station, newspaper, or magazine. He also pores over media invoices to make sure you received everything he purchased on your behalf. A media buyer can save you time and money.

Your Creative Light Bulb Has Burned Out

If you're burned out with the creative process, no longer have the time to devote to it, would rather spend your days running your business, and want a team of creative professionals working to generate fresh, new ideas for your business, you can find no better place than in an ad agency.

From the agency creative director to the copywriters and artists, everyone gives you his best shot. The highly trained group of specialists employed by most agencies work on your account with a mutual goal — to grow your business, keep you happy, and retain your account.

You're Overwhelmed by the Demands of Production

If the myriad details of producing and placing your ads has you completely bogged down, you need to think about calling in the pros. Start reviewing agencies when:

- You simply don't have the time, energy, or desire to write and produce your own advertising.

- Creating and producing your ads has become more of a chore than a pleasure.

- You dread sitting down at the computer to create unforgettable prose.

You're Having Trouble Keeping Up with the Bookkeeping

If the bookkeeping process of reviewing multiple media invoices each month has become a major chore, you may want to hand off this responsibility to a professional who does this laborious task all day long. Make a call, hire an agency, and relax if:

- You've come to the conclusion that most media services (TV and radio stations, newspapers and magazines, or outdoor ad services) write their invoices in a secret code that you can never crack.

- You've reached a point of frustration with trying to determine whether you've received all the spots or column inches you've been billed for.

- You're avoiding the invoices until the media's collections department makes a nasty call.

You're Leaving Co-Op Funds on the Table

If you aren't receiving co-op reimbursements (see Chapter 3) because they're just too much trouble, hire an agency. Many businesses hire agencies to handle co-op funds, and, for the agency, managing these funds isn't a big deal. It's time to call an agency when:

- ✔ You're fed up with all the obligations, rules, and restrictions for collecting your co-op reimbursements.

- ✔ You're sick and tired of calling the various media to remind them that you need notarized scripts and the proper tear sheets in order to collect your money.

- ✔ You recognize that you have much more important things to do than compile invoices, scripts, tapes, tear sheets, and God-only-knows-what in order to receive a payment from your manufacturer.

Your Time Is Being Taken Up by Media Reps

Avoiding media reps (saving you time and headaches) may be one of the best reasons to hire an agency. Media reps aren't necessarily obnoxious or bothersome, but they have a mission: to get as large a share of your advertising budget as possible. They phone you, drop in on you, and send you faxes and e-mails to "simply stay in touch," and then they drop in on you again. They're extremely tenacious and rarely take *no* for answer. Their sales managers give them a quota and, if they know your business is buying local media, they target you. An advertising agency removes these pesky (albeit, well-meaning) people from your life.

You're Running Faster to Stay in the Same Place

You need to spend your limited and very important time productively running your business. Do you really have the time and energy to give full attention to your advertising? When you hire an advertising agency, you can do the following:

- ✔ Eliminate a lot of daily phone calls and drop-in visits from various reps.

- ✔ Remove mountains of monthly paperwork from your desk.

- ✔ Receive a more-polished creative product from the agency than you've been producing on your own, because you have a whole gang of professional writers, designers, and creative directors working for your business.

No one knows your business as well as you do (you become the best source of information for your agency), but unless you want to sell your business and become a full-time ad person, you do well to hire specialists who can take an objective view of your advertising needs.

You Want a Bunch of Free Stuff

You should rush right out to hire an agency if you want to get all sorts of free lunches; rounds of golf; lift tickets to ski resorts; tickets to rock concerts, sporting events, and movie premieres; and even vacation trips to world-class resorts and exotic, international cities.

Okay, maybe I'm exaggerating a bit, but your agency always has a good supply of some of these freebies (which it gets from the media it's buying from). And if the agency is honest about these giveaways, it passes most of the good stuff along to you and its other clients — the people whose advertising budgets earned these perks in the first place.

You're going to spend your budget anyway. You might as well get something extra for it.

Glossary

He re I provide definitions for a few common *ad-speak* terms — the insider words and acronyms used by advertising professionals to confound all of those who are not. If you are sanctioning and approving media plans and buys done by others (like your ad agency), knowing advertising jargon will give you a better understanding of what is being proposed. For any advertising terms not presented here, please visit the Online Advertising Glossary, at www.adglossary.com.

accrual: The amount of co-op advertising funds earned over a stated period.

ad/edit ratio: The ratio of advertising pages to editorial pages in a print medium. An ad/edit ration of 70/30 indicates that 70 percent of all pages are advertising and 30 percent are editorial.

add-on rate: A different rate, negotiated at the time the schedule is purchased, for any subsequent additions to the schedule.

addressable: The ability of media such as magazines or television to direct advertising to specific individuals.

advertorial: A print advertisement styled to look like editorial content. Most publishers require that advertorials be labeled "advertisement" so that readers are aware that they're reading an ad.

affidavit: A notarized statement from a broadcast station that confirms the actual run time of a commercial or commercials. In order to collect co-op advertising funds, you will be required to get an affidavit from the broadcast station.

alternate weeks: A method of scheduling advertising for a period of one week, then skipping a week, then running it again for a week, and so forth.

average hours of viewing: The number of hours (and minutes) a household (or demographic group) views television during a particular time frame (daily, weekly, and so on).

average net paid circulation: The average number of copies of a publication sold per issue, as opposed to copies given free of charge.

average quarter hour (AQH): The time segment in which an average rating is measured. It is the average minute of a 15-minute segment.

average time spent listening (TSL): The time spent listening to a radio station by the average listener.

bleed: In print media, to extend the illustration or copy to the edge of the page so there is no white border.

bonus circulation: The circulation of a publication that is above its average circulation. Advertisers are not charged for this extra circulation.

bridge: In print, an advertisement that runs across the center margin of two facing pages in a magazine or newspaper. Also called a *double truck*.

broad rotator: In broadcast, a commercial, usually sold at a discounted rate, that will run on an "as available" time and date at the sole discretion of the selling station.

bulldog edition: The morning edition of a newspaper, usually distributed the night before its issue date.

bump rates: The costs that must be paid by an advertiser to secure a commercial position previously sold to another advertiser. To bump the previous advertiser, the new advertiser must pay an inflated rate.

car card: An advertising unit within a transit vehicle, such as a bus or taxicab.

closing date: The deadline set by a publication for the receipt of material in order for an advertisement to appear in a forthcoming issue.

combination rate: A discounted rate given to an advertiser who advertises in both morning and evening editions of a newspaper.

cost-per-point (CPP): The cost of an advertising unit (for example, a 60-second radio spot) divided by the average rating of a specific demographic group (for example, women 18–49). A unit that costs $1,000 and delivers a 10 women 18–49 rating has a CPP of $100.

cost-per-thousand (CPM): The cost per 1,000 people (or homes) delivered by a medium or media schedule. A media vehicle that costs $10,000 and has an audience of 500,000 men 18–49 has a CPM of $20.

dailies: Newspapers that are published at least five times a week; the video or film footage from each day's shoot, which is viewed at the end of each day.

daypart: A broadcast time period or segment.

diary: A questionnaire that asks the respondent to record his television-viewing or radio-listening habits for a specific period of time.

earned rate: A rate given to an advertiser that reflects the frequency of ads running or the volume of advertising placed over a given period of time.

electronic tear sheet: Notarized documentation provided by broadcasters on the script itself to certify the number of times a particular script was broadcast and at what cost. Important in collecting co-op funds.

facing: In outdoor advertising, the direction a billboard faces (for example, a south facing can be seen by northbound traffic).

flighting: The scheduling of advertising for a period of time, followed by a hiatus and then another schedule of advertising.

frontload: A scheduling tactic where the bulk of the advertising is scheduled in the beginning days or weeks of a campaign.

gross rating points (GRPs): The sum of all ratings delivered by a given list of media vehicles.

gutter: The white space on the inside margin of a printed page within a newspaper; the inside edges of pages facing the bound, or stapled, side of a magazine.

impressions: The gross sum of all media exposures (number of people or homes), without regard to duplication.

insertion order: A form or document sent to a publication or station that contains information relating to an ad's placement or a broadcast schedule.

junior page: In print, an ad-size unit that is smaller than a full page and is surrounded by editorial content.

liner: A 10- to 20-second mention of an advertised product or service, usually tied to a promotion.

log: A chronological listing created by television or radio stations and networks of programs and commercials showing exact air times of each element.

masthead: The title of a newspaper or magazine displayed at the top of the front page.

mechanical: A camera-ready paste-up of artwork; includes type, photography, line art, and so on, all on one piece of art board or on computer disk. Also known as a *keyline* or *finished art.*

middle of the road (MOR): A radio programming format that appeals to an older demographic (big band, very soft hits, and so on).

offset: Printing on a surface (such as paper) by putting the surface in contact with another surface that has been freshly inked.

open rate: The maximum rate charged by a print media for one insertion.

per inquiry (PI): A figure used to evaluate the relative performance of inquiries received as a result of advertising.

pod: A group of commercials run back to back during a commercial break.

point-of-purchase (POP) display: An advertising display at the point where people purchase goods (for example, a counter card at a retail location).

post analysis: An analysis of a media schedule's success after it has run.

qualitative research: Research based on the quality, type, or components of a group and applied to advertising audience research in order to determine the quality of audience responses to advertising.

quantitative research: Research based on the measurement of quantity or amount, applied to advertising audience research to develop actual numbers of audience members in order to accurately measure market situations.

ranker: A computer-generated report showing a selected demographic audience of each radio station in a market, ranked from the highest to the lowest.

rotator: A broadcast commercial in rotation.

rotogravure: An impression (art, copy, photo) engraved or etched on a cylindrical printing surface (usually copper) whereby the ink is held within the etched crevices. Paper is run through a rotary press that prints both sides of the paper at the same time.

run of station (ROS): A tactic used in broadcast whereby commercials are scheduled throughout the day and night at the discretion of the station, as opposed to time periods designated by the advertiser.

short rate: In print media, the dollar penalty an advertiser pays for not fulfilling space requirements that were contracted for.

skew: A statistical deviation. A radio station that has proportionately more younger than older listeners is said to *skew* to a younger audience.

spot times: The specific times that a commercial airs.

station format: The type of programming carried by a radio station (for example, rock, news, or classical).

time spent listening (TSL): The time spent listening to a radio station by the average listener.

total audience plan (TAP): A radio term for a schedule of spots airing in multiple time periods meant to accumulate high levels of audience reach on a station.

under-delivery: A situation in which a media schedule or unit generated less audience than originally estimated by the media. Under-delivery usually results in make goods.

zone (or zoned) edition: An edition of a newspaper geared toward and distributed to a particular geographic zone (usually determined by zip codes). You can buy less than a newspaper's full circulation by targeting your advertising to particular zones of the paper's circulation.

Index

• D •

• S •

• *Y* •

Notes

Notes

USINESS, CAREERS & PERSONAL FINANCE

0-7645-9847-3   0-7645-2431-3

Also available:
- Business Plans Kit For Dummies
  0-7645-9794-9
- Economics For Dummies
  0-7645-5726-2
- Grant Writing For Dummies
  0-7645-8416-2
- Home Buying For Dummies
  0-7645-5331-3
- Managing For Dummies
  0-7645-1771-6
- Marketing For Dummies
  0-7645-5600-2

- Personal Finance For Dummies
  0-7645-2590-5*
- Resumes For Dummies
  0-7645-5471-9
- Selling For Dummies
  0-7645-5363-1
- Six Sigma For Dummies
  0-7645-6798-5
- Small Business Kit For Dummies
  0-7645-5984-2
- Starting an eBay Business For Dummies
  0-7645-6924-4
- Your Dream Career For Dummies
  0-7645-9795-7

OME & BUSINESS COMPUTER BASICS

0-470-05432-8   0-471-75421-8

Also available:
- Cleaning Windows Vista For Dummies
  0-471-78293-9
- Excel 2007 For Dummies
  0-470-03737-7
- Mac OS X Tiger For Dummies
  0-7645-7675-5
- MacBook For Dummies
  0-470-04859-X
- Macs For Dummies
  0-470-04849-2
- Office 2007 For Dummies
  0-470-00923-3

- Outlook 2007 For Dummies
  0-470-03830-6
- PCs For Dummies
  0-7645-8958-X
- Salesforce.com For Dummies
  0-470-04893-X
- Upgrading & Fixing Laptops For Dummies
  0-7645-8959-8
- Word 2007 For Dummies
  0-470-03658-3
- Quicken 2007 For Dummies
  0-470-04600-7

OOD, HOME, GARDEN, HOBBIES, MUSIC & PETS

0-7645-8404-9   0-7645-9904-6

Also available:
- Candy Making For Dummies
  0-7645-9734-5
- Card Games For Dummies
  0-7645-9910-0
- Crocheting For Dummies
  0-7645-4151-X
- Dog Training For Dummies
  0-7645-8418-9
- Healthy Carb Cookbook For Dummies
  0-7645-8476-6
- Home Maintenance For Dummies
  0-7645-5215-5

- Horses For Dummies
  0-7645-9797-3
- Jewelry Making & Beading For Dummies
  0-7645-2571-9
- Orchids For Dummies
  0-7645-6759-4
- Puppies For Dummies
  0-7645-5255-4
- Rock Guitar For Dummies
  0-7645-5356-9
- Sewing For Dummies
  0-7645-6847-7
- Singing For Dummies
  0-7645-2475-5

NTERNET & DIGITAL MEDIA

0-470-04529-9   0-470-04894-8

Also available:
- Blogging For Dummies
  0-471-77084-1
- Digital Photography For Dummies
  0-7645-9802-3
- Digital Photography All-in-One Desk Reference For Dummies
  0-470-03743-1
- Digital SLR Cameras and Photography For Dummies
  0-7645-9803-1
- eBay Business All-in-One Desk Reference For Dummies
  0-7645-8438-3
- HDTV For Dummies
  0-470-09673-X

- Home Entertainment PCs For Dummies
  0-470-05523-5
- MySpace For Dummies
  0-470-09529-6
- Search Engine Optimization For Dummies
  0-471-97998-8
- Skype For Dummies
  0-470-04891-3
- The Internet For Dummies
  0-7645-8996-2
- Wiring Your Digital Home For Dummies
  0-471-91830-X

eparate Canadian edition also available
eparate U.K. edition also available

ilable wherever books are sold. For more information or to order direct: U.S. customers visit www.dummies.com or call 1-877-762-2974.
customers visit www.wileyeurope.com or call 0800 243407. Canadian customers visit www.wiley.ca or call 1-800-567-4797.

SPORTS, FITNESS, PARENTING, RELIGION & SPIRITUALITY

0-471-76871-5

0-7645-7841-3

Also available:

- Catholicism For Dummies
  0-7645-5391-7
- Exercise Balls For Dummies
  0-7645-5623-1
- Fitness For Dummies
  0-7645-7851-0
- Football For Dummies
  0-7645-3936-1
- Judaism For Dummies
  0-7645-5299-6
- Potty Training For Dummies
  0-7645-5417-4
- Buddhism For Dummies
  0-7645-5359-3

- Pregnancy For Dummies
  0-7645-4483-7 †
- Ten Minute Tone-Ups For Dummies
  0-7645-7207-5
- NASCAR For Dummies
  0-7645-7681-X
- Religion For Dummies
  0-7645-5264-3
- Soccer For Dummies
  0-7645-5229-5
- Women in the Bible For Dummies
  0-7645-8475-8

TRAVEL

0-7645-7749-2

0-7645-6945-7

Also available:

- Alaska For Dummies
  0-7645-7746-8
- Cruise Vacations For Dummies
  0-7645-6941-4
- England For Dummies
  0-7645-4276-1
- Europe For Dummies
  0-7645-7529-5
- Germany For Dummies
  0-7645-7823-5
- Hawaii For Dummies
  0-7645-7402-7

- Italy For Dummies
  0-7645-7386-1
- Las Vegas For Dummies
  0-7645-7382-9
- London For Dummies
  0-7645-4277-X
- Paris For Dummies
  0-7645-7630-5
- RV Vacations For Dummies
  0-7645-4442-X
- Walt Disney World & Orlando
  For Dummies
  0-7645-9660-8

GRAPHICS, DESIGN & WEB DEVELOPMENT

0-7645-8815-X

0-7645-9571-7

Also available:

- 3D Game Animation For Dummies
  0-7645-8789-7
- AutoCAD 2006 For Dummies
  0-7645-8925-3
- Building a Web Site For Dummies
  0-7645-7144-3
- Creating Web Pages For Dummies
  0-470-08030-2
- Creating Web Pages All-in-One Desk
  Reference For Dummies
  0-7645-4345-8
- Dreamweaver 8 For Dummies
  0-7645-9649-7

- InDesign CS2 For Dummies
  0-7645-9572-5
- Macromedia Flash 8 For Dummies
  0-7645-9691-8
- Photoshop CS2 and Digital
  Photography For Dummies
  0-7645-9580-6
- Photoshop Elements 4 For Dummies
  0-471-77483-9
- Syndicating Web Sites with RSS Feed
  For Dummies
  0-7645-8848-6
- Yahoo! SiteBuilder For Dummies
  0-7645-9800-7

NETWORKING, SECURITY, PROGRAMMING & DATABASES

0-7645-7728-X

0-471-74940-0

Also available:

- Access 2007 For Dummies
  0-470-04612-0
- ASP.NET 2 For Dummies
  0-7645-7907-X
- C# 2005 For Dummies
  0-7645-9704-3
- Hacking For Dummies
  0-470-05235-X
- Hacking Wireless Networks
  For Dummies
  0-7645-9730-2
- Java For Dummies
  0-470-08716-1

- Microsoft SQL Server 2005 For Dummi
  0-7645-7755-7
- Networking All-in-One Desk Referen
  For Dummies
  0-7645-9939-9
- Preventing Identity Theft For Dummie
  0-7645-7336-5
- Telecom For Dummies
  0-471-77085-X
- Visual Studio 2005 All-in-One Desk
  Reference For Dummies
  0-7645-9775-2
- XML For Dummies
  0-7645-8845-1

HEALTH & SELF-HELP

0-7645-8450-2   0-7645-4149-8

Also available:

- Bipolar Disorder For Dummies
  0-7645-8451-0
- Chemotherapy and Radiation
  For Dummies
  0-7645-7832-4
- Controlling Cholesterol For Dummies
  0-7645-5440-9
- Diabetes For Dummies
  0-7645-6820-5* †
- Divorce For Dummies
  0-7645-8417-0 †

- Fibromyalgia For Dummies
  0-7645-5441-7
- Low-Calorie Dieting For Dummies
  0-7645-9905-4
- Meditation For Dummies
  0-471-77774-9
- Osteoporosis For Dummies
  0-7645-7621-6
- Overcoming Anxiety For Dummies
  0-7645-5447-6
- Reiki For Dummies
  0-7645-9907-0
- Stress Management For Dummies
  0-7645-5144-2

EDUCATION, HISTORY, REFERENCE & TEST PREPARATION

0-7645-8381-6   0-7645-9554-7

Also available:

- The ACT For Dummies
  0-7645-9652-7
- Algebra For Dummies
  0-7645-5325-9
- Algebra Workbook For Dummies
  0-7645-8467-7
- Astronomy For Dummies
  0-7645-8465-0
- Calculus For Dummies
  0-7645-2498-4
- Chemistry For Dummies
  0-7645-5430-1
- Forensics For Dummies
  0-7645-5580-4

- Freemasons For Dummies
  0-7645-9796-5
- French For Dummies
  0-7645-5193-0
- Geometry For Dummies
  0-7645-5324-0
- Organic Chemistry I For Dummies
  0-7645-6902-3
- The SAT I For Dummies
  0-7645-7193-1
- Spanish For Dummies
  0-7645-5194-9
- Statistics For Dummies
  0-7645-5423-9

Get smart @ dummies.com®

- **Find a full list of Dummies titles**
- **Look into loads of FREE on-site articles**
- **Sign up for FREE eTips e-mailed to you weekly**
- **See what other products carry the Dummies name**
- **Shop directly from the Dummies bookstore**
- **Enter to win new prizes every month!**

parate Canadian edition also available
parate U.K. edition also available

ilable wherever books are sold. For more information or to order direct: U.S. customers visit www.dummies.com or call 1-877-762-2974.
customers visit www.wileyeurope.com or call 0800 243407. Canadian customers visit www.wiley.ca or call 1-800-567-4797.